D1432133

ENGLAND, SLAVES AND FREEDOM, 1776–1838

ENGLAND, SLAVES AND FREEDOM, 1776–1838

James Walvin

University Press of Mississippi
Jackson and London

First published in the United States of America
in 1986 by the University Press of Mississippi.

Library of Congress Cataloging-in-Publication Data
Walvin, James.
England, slaves and freedom, 1776–1838.
Includes index.
1. Slavery in Great Britain – History – 19th century.
2. Slave-trade – Great Britain – History – 19th century.
3. Slavery in Great Britain – Emancipation – History –
19th century.   4. Blacks – Great Britain – Social
conditions.   I. Title.
HT1161.W35   1986   306'.362'0942   86–7766
ISBN 0–87805–299–2

For Mr George and Miss B.

Contents

Introduction

In the past decade there has been a remarkable output of work – of all kinds – on the history and sociology of the British black community. In large part this is a result of the desire among many Britons – black and white alike – to explore and understand the generally neglected field of the black historical experience. The impulse to learn more about black history – in Britain, the New World and Africa – is of course one of the key forces behind the renaissance of black studies over the past generation. In Britain itself, the 'coming of age' of the modern black community has created a series of demands for fuller exploration of British black history. It is true of course that other ethnic communities – notably those from the Indian subcontinent – have made similar demands. Cumulatively the result has been a widespread insistence that the ethnic communities and the 'host' society make conscious efforts to rethink and reappraise both the history of these communities and, inevitably, the history of the relationship between the British metropolis and those imperial possessions which provided the humanity for the ethnic communities. It is now widely appreciated that it is as important for the British to learn about their ethnic communities as it is for those communities to rediscover their own history.

The earliest demands for such a historical re-evaluation came, inevitably perhaps, from those schools serving the black communities. Much of the substance of basic school history makes even less sense for British blacks than it has, traditionally, for generations of indigenous school children. But to demand a history which is both relevant and valuable is to seek a complete reappraisal of the very substances of British history as traditionally taught in British schools. Such demands are often treated with suspicion or distrust by those people in educational authority (within the schools or from within the controlling authorities) as a change motivated more by political (and even

1

radical) intentions than educational ideals. Such suspicions, however, ignore the degree to which the insistence on the teaching of 'traditional' history is itself value-laden and replete with unconscious political overtones. Furthermore, it needs to be stressed that the history of the British black community is both as interesting and intellectually challenging as any other field of recent British history, a point which this book is partly designed to reinforce. Yet the fundamental issue remains that, of all the mutually reinforcing demands for black history over the past decades, the most persistent and influential has been not so much the academic tradition but the community-rooted search for personal and collective history and identity.

It is possible to see that more people than ever before, now learn about British black history primarily because of the efforts of schools, local self-help groups and community organisations. It would be wrong to claim that more academic contributions have failed to play a part, but those researches – often too complex, too detailed (and too costly) for use in schools and local projects – have needed to be reshaped into a more appropriate form. Moreover, the researches by schools and community-based groups have helped, in a number of areas, to make significant contributions to our wider knowledge of black history. Earlier writers, for instance, tended to stress the breaks and discontinuities in British black experience between the nineteenth century and the emergence of more recent black communities from the 1880s onwards. Recent community research however has revealed many more striking continuities. Notably in Liverpool, a black community appears to have existed, in recognisable form, throughout the nineteenth century.[1] Similarly it is now clear that peripatetic blacks – visitors, students and refugees – were much more in evidence in nineteenth-century Britain than was previously thought.[2] There were, too, a number of prominent black Britons in various walks of life – music, the theatre, medicine and politics[3] – throughout the nineteenth century. Thus at a simple but none the less important level it is now possible to argue that blacks were much more *visible* in the nineteenth century than historians had previously argued. There was, in effect, a much clearer continuity of black experience than was previously claimed. However patchy and imperfect it may seem, black society in Britain can claim to have a continuous and unbroken history which stretches back for the best part of four centuries. Moreover much of the evidence to substantiate this case has derived, primarily, not from professional or academic historians, but from within the black community itself. There are few other areas of modern British history where strictly (and self-proclaimed) amateur groups have succeeded so quickly in complementing and redressing the work of professional historians.

Parallel to this community-based rediscovery of black history has been an emergent interest in the wider field of black history on the part of the media. By careful use of existing printed sources, by turning to that (generally untapped) wealth of visual evidence about British black history and, again, by careful research in black communities, it has been possible to make television films which are true to the historical evidence, are entertaining, and educational.[4] It is doubtless true that historians as a group tend to be suspicious of history re-created by the media. But in this case (and others) television has been able to add substantially to the wider understanding of black history. Yet it would be wrong to imagine that this relates uniquely to the black community, for the media have been active in researching and recreating the history and sociology of the whole range of Britain's ethnic and immigrant communities.[5]

Indeed there is a strong case to be made that television has itself proved instrumental not merely in persuing the *facts* of black history but has been – inevitably perhaps – inordinately influential in bringing that evidence before an enormous audience. However transient the impression, many more people have come to know of the existence of British black history via television programmes than by reading scholarly books. This may ultimately tell us much more of course about the pre-eminence of television in modern Western society but, none the less, this medium is a force to be reckoned with. Nothing in the British experience can remotely compare to the seismic impact on the USA of the historical television series *Roots* (and its deeply flawed accompanying book). But it would be wrong to overlook the important role played by television in enhancing public awareness and consciousness of black history in both Britain and its global setting.[6] Many people will doubtless rue this influence; but it is quite impossible to ignore it.

It is also true that the academic and literary study of black society has been transformed since the late 1960s. When researching for *Black and White* the author was unaware of any other historians working in the same field (although others were in fact pursuing parallel work). In September 1981, however, a major international conference took place in London, devoted uniquely to the history of blacks in Britain. Over three days, hundreds of delegates – from Britain, the USA, Canada, Australia, Africa and Europe – discussed a series of eighteen papers spanning the whole range of the arts and social sciences. Papers ranged from blacks in pre-modern Britain, to blacks in Hogarth's works; from black showground artistes to the history of pan-Africanism. It was, in brief, a remarkable testimony to the maturity of a historical study which only a few years before had scarcely been in its infancy. It may seem at first glance that something dramatic had taken place in the course of the 1970s to bring this about, for it would, without doubt, have proved impossible to organise a similar conference in, say, 1971. In fact, the development of interest in British black studies emerged from the convergence of a series of distinct, but related, intellectual and social forces. The first – and ultimately most important – factor was the change in the black community in Britain. Since the Second World War there has grown up in Britain a remarkable mosaic of ethnic communities, consisting of immigrants and their British-born children from Britain's far-flung imperial possessions. In fact Britain was only one of a number of former imperial powers whose colonial policies (and laws), and the rapid collapse of imperial power led to substantial movements of people, migrating from the colonies to the metropolitan heartlands. France, Portugal and Holland also experienced the growth of sizeable ethnic communities in their major urban areas, with many of the problems and tensions between host and settlers which characterised the British experience. The migrations to Britain however were more sizeable and more varied – a reflection of course of the size and diversity of the former British empire. Although many of these more recent settlers had older historical links with Britain, the sheer size of modern immigration has rendered it a qualitatively different phenomenon from any other human settlement in Britain. Indeed the only remotely comparable settlement was that of the Irish in the 1840s.

By 1971 the total non-white population of Britain was

1.4 million (the largest single group originating from the West Indies). By 1977, it stood at 1.85 million – though we need to recall that in a total population of 55 millions this formed only 3.4 per cent of the total. By the year 2000 it is calculated that there will be some 3.3 million Britons of 'New Commonwealth' origin, less than 6 per cent of the overall population. Concentrated overwhelmingly in the country's half-dozen major conurbations, the ethnic communities have endured a series of deprivations and discriminations and have, inevitably perhaps, become the object of heated political argument. Since 1963 there has been a series of legislative changes which have severely curtailed the rights of entry to Britain. Indeed, so severe have some of the changes been that they have involved redefinitions of the very nature of British nationality. It is possible to exaggerate the all-pervasive impact of the growth of ethnic communities in post-war Britain, but it is indisputably clear that British society has, in many key regards, been changed substantially by dint of immigration; whole sections of British cities are black; British eating habits have been changed by the adoption of ethnic foods; British popular music has been revitalised by music from the ethnic communities; many British sports have been transformed by black players. Even the patterns of British worship have begun to change under the pressure of 'newer' (for Britain) religions, notably from the Indian subcontinent.[7] But the most fundamental change – the most abiding and inescapably influential change – is that the ethnic communities are becoming progressively more 'British'.

The patterns of settlement into Britain differed greatly between the various communities, but as West Indian and Indian families began gradually to reconstitute themselves in British cities, their offspring – born in Britain – quite naturally eschewed the terminology and labels previously attached by the host community to their parents. Men and women born in, say, Bradford, Brixton or Birmingham take a dim view of being described as 'immigrants'. They are, like their white neighbours, British in the broadest sense. Moreover they – and their settler parents – naturally expect (and have come to demand) the full range of social and political rights enjoyed by society at large. It is true that such rights – of work, housing, education and the like – have never been shared or enjoyed equally throughout British society. Since the emergence of an industrial society deeply fissured by the crevices of social class, the inequalities of birth, circumstances and opportunity have effectively ensured the continuation of absolute and relative deprivation among great swathes of the population towards the lower end of the social structure. Not even the foundation of a welfare state after 1945 has been able to eliminate fundamental inequalities and to guarantee a widely based and consistent social justice in Britain. The material rewards and social rights in modern Britain have never been equally enjoyed by Britons of all social classes. It ought not therefore to be surprising that more recent settlers have similarly failed to claim their rightful share of material and social well-being. Yet the problems of the ethnic communities – and of the black British – are not merely those of British working people.

The overwhelming majority of West Indians – and Indians – came to Britain to do manual labour of various kinds. Even skilled men and professional people found themselves obliged to accept labouring work; skills were consistently relegated or ignored. But this is only one of a series of inescapable discriminations which blacks have come to endure – and expect – of life in Britain. Moreover there are discriminations which are bequeathed, like family traits, from one generation to another; the British-born, no less than their settler parents, find themselves discriminated against at every turn. At school, in housing, in work and, more especially, at the hands of the police, blacks endure conditions, treatment and prejudice which are qualitatively different from the traditional deprivations endured by urban working people. It is however, perfectly clear that younger generations of blacks simply will not accept such treatment, nor will they accord to the varied – and generally insulting – stereotypes demanded of them by white society. Through local community-based action (groups, politics, the Press and more) black Britons are making concerted efforts to insist on their individual and collective rights. Their difficulties have been greatly accentuated by Britain's economic problems, which worsened throughout the 1970s. The land of opportunities and material well-being, which lured West Indians and Indians in the 1950s, has rapidly established itself as the economic sickman of Europe. Indeed so severe is black disillusionment with British life – both economically and socially – that many settlers have returned to their homelands. Between 1971 and 1973, for example, 9000 West Indians settled in Britain, but 14,000 returned to their islands.[8]

Black society – and all its ramifications for British life – has, then, become an inescapable feature of modern British society. Immigration, race, racial harmony (or disharmony) and the broader related fields of social policies, are political and social issues which are fiercely debated throughout the country. Even in remote communities – where a black face is not seen from one year to another – race and black society are topics of passionate argument. Although, demographically, black society is concentrated in certain parts of the country, it has generated an interest – and a passion – far beyond its geographic limits. This was, of course, equally true in the eighteenth and early nineteenth centuries. Now, however, the arguments about black society – both within the ethnic communities and in white society – will not go away (as was the case previously, with the ending of slavery and with the decline of the earlier black society) for the obvious reason that black society will not, this time, effectively disappear or become relatively insignificant.

In the 1970s black society had a much higher 'visibility' than even its demographic strength would suggest. This was, in large part, because black life and politics in Britain belonged not simply to the domestic politics of British life, but to a much wider political constituency. Those former West Indian colonies which sent so many settlers to Britain are now independent nations with an importance and voice in world affairs which no one could have predicted even a generation ago. Within the UN and the Commonwealth, Britain's former colonies have a parity with their former rulers. Indeed in many organisations dominated by representatives from Third World countries, the former imperial powers find themselves at a political disadvantage, and certainly in a minority. At a simple level this has meant that British policies towards ethnic communities – more especially shifts in immigration laws and British citizenship – are of direct and sometimes acute interest to a number of politically-influential former colonies. Indeed the British immigration policy (i.e. restrictions) can only be fully operated through the good offices and help of the governments of old colonies. Thus, at a simple though important level, the New Commonwealth countries involved have a legitimate interest – and rightly claim a voice – in British immigration policy. Furthermore the sizeable ethnic communities in Britain are important political constituencies in the politics of their various homelands. West Indian governments, for instance, make representations to the British Government about the interests of their nationals in Britain. Similarly, the independence of action of British authorities has been qualified, since entry to the EEC, by the legal and political safeguards of that Community. Indeed aggrieved immigrants and settlers have had recourse to European courts in disputes over British immigration policy; their legal victories have invariably proved to no practical effect in the teeth of official British determination to pursue an independent and 'tougher' policy on immigration.

Another crucial factor in the 'politicisation' of race and immigration in Britain has been the complex ebb and flow of black politics in the USA. Some of the more important changes in black American life have been projected into British society by television. The rise of the civil rights movement, black voter registration, the extraordinary impact of Martin Luther King Jr – and the devastating consequences of his murder – and more, all gave a finer focus to arguments about black rights and white discriminations. The rise of American black consciousness served, if only indirectly, to heighten the growing concern and anxiety in Britain about the wider problems of immigration and race. Indeed, throughout the past 20 years the Home Office has acted to prevent the more radical black US activists landing and speaking in Britain; so too have West Indian Governments. Men in authority in Britain and the Caribbean widely assume that the radical and often violent rhetoric of certain black American activists would prove too volatile for their own social stability.[9]

On matters of race – domestic or international – the British can no longer expect to act as a completely independent and unrestrained agent. Politically exposed to the critique of former colonies, sometimes found wanting in international courts, this once mighty imperial power has, understandably perhaps, sometimes seemed confused and contradictory about its responses to race and immigration. Both Labour and Conservative Governments have been, nominally, committed to racial equality (at home and abroad) but none the less, since 1963, both have enacted fundamentally discriminatory laws.

Moreover the claims of successive British Governments to pursue racial harmony are greeted with cynicism by those who point to the special economic relationship which persists – and thrives – between Britain and South Africa.

This account of the wider international debate about race serves merely to underline one simple point, namely that black society in Britain is no longer a 'domestic' issue. The progress or difficulties of Britain's ethnic communities are not simply a British concern. Similarly, the politics of race in Britain are, increasingly, shaped and determined, not merely by domestic British forces, but by international pressures which cannot be ignored. Of course this fact in itself is a source of deep resentment among many Britons. For older generations, who vividly remember Britain at its imperial prime, the thought that former colonies can 'dictate' to the 'mother country' on let us say, relations with South Africa is both perplexing and annoying. Indeed the re-emergence of extreme right-wing politics in Britain over the past 20 years is closely related to the growth of substantial ethnic communities. And while it is true that the most extreme fascist fringe are the best known of political groups to use race as a political weapon, it must not be assumed that racism is the unique preserve of the extreme right.

Throughout the 1960s and 1970s one social survey after another revealed the overwhelming opposition in Britain to 'coloured' immigration and settlement.[10] The evidence is clear enough; the very great majority of British people are much 'tougher' on matters of race than their various governments have been. Indeed there is strong evidence to show that the divergence between popular opinion and government policies on race and immigration is a key factor in the widening disillusionment with political life. The exception to the general, popular denunciation of politicians' approach to race has been Enoch Powell whose own political career was effectively destroyed by his outspoken criticism of immigration and race policies. However tortuous and subtle Powell's speeches on race, he has consequently established himself as the spokesman for the populist antipathy to people in the ethnic communities; he has in fact lent credibility and succour to the articulation of widespread and malevolent racism. While Powell may claim, with some justice, that he eschews all racist sentiment, he has become the political talisman for armies of people who are openly – and often viciously – racist.

Since the early 1960s, the politics of race has become an inescapable element in British life. And while this may seem, at first glance, to be a simple and natural consequence of the physical growth of ethnic communities, it is in fact a result of a much more complex mix. Furthermore the emergence of the politics of race has, in many respects made life for British blacks more difficult. Faced not merely by material and social deprivation at every turn, they have, increasingly, found themselves confronted by open political antipathy which has gained respectability in the host community. For this – and many other reasons – the ethnic communities have themselves been politicised, turning their political efforts towards existing parties, unions and new, specially created, self-help groupings. It may seem ironic, however, that their complaints and demands were given serious consideration (by national politicians at least) only after the major urban disturbances in the summer of 1981.[11]

Not since the extraordinary apogee of anti-slavery sentiment in the 1820s and 1830s, have issues of black society been so widely and vigorously debated in Britain. At that earlier period the issue was discussed at a distance, far removed from the human realities of slavery. It was, to put the case cynically, easier perhaps for the British to appear altruistic and concerned about black slavery, for it thrived 5000 miles from Britain itself. Black society in the 1960s, 1970s and 1980s was however an integral feature of British urban life. The problems of black and white could not be discussed at a distance, but were of immediate and inescapably close consequence. One by-product of the growing awareness of the far-reaching problems of black–white relations has been a proliferation of investigations into these problems. Research units have been established in a number of universities, the Home Office itself sponsors research and there has been a parallel multiplication of academic, journalistic and governmental investigations. It is only natural that the overwhelming bulk of such enquiries should focus on contemporary (or future) issues, but it is equally natural that more and more attention should be paid to the history of black migrations and of black–white relations. Indeed there is a strong case to be made that our understanding of the broader historical issues is necessary for a firmer grasp of contemporary relations between black and white. Thus, the 'Blacks in Britain' Conference of September 1981 provided an important and apposite illustration of the remarkably diverse investigations into black history in Britain.

Much of the impulse behind the initial development of the historiography of black society was a uniquely 'academic' concern. The earlier establishment of African historical studies, and the rapid flowering of slave and black studies in North America and the British West Indies had clearly pointed to the need for a reappraisal of Britain's relationship with black society in its wider setting. Furthermore the transformation in British social history in the 1960s, led most significantly by E. P. Thompson's *Making of the English Working Class*, effectively redirected the attention of historians (more especially a new generation who were fortunate enough to benefit from the expansion of higher education at the same time) to neglected areas of research. Black history no longer seemed to be quite the arcane field older historians had previously alleged. And to complete the process, there was a large and growing black community in Britain in the 1960s whose history seemed ill-known or ignored. Beginning with a number of tantalising historical leads which suggested the existence of a significant and revealing black community in earlier times, it was at this point that a number of scholars, unknown to each other, began to converge on the beckoning but relatively undefined field of British black history.[12]

What followed is now a matter of record; in little more than a decade the study of British black history rapidly established itself as a legitimate and important subculture. Moreover it is now possible, because of recent work, to detect future patterns of scholarly interest. Indeed the rapid growth of black historiography is likely to have an importance well beyond the limits of black history itself. It seems certain, for example, that the findings of historians of black society well encourage a reappraisal of the relationship between the British host society and other generations of immigrants. Although there has been a thriving study of particular immigrant communities (few more extensively studied than the Jews and Irish) what has not yet been fully explored is the longevity and durability of foreign settlement in mainland Britain. The English need to be reminded of the historical forces which have made them a much more polyglot nation than they imagine. Nor is this uniquely a post-1945 phenomenon for, over many centuries, 'outsiders' have left their imprint on the social and human composition of the English people. In the past quarter of a century however the most bitterly disputed feature of immigration into Britain has been the complex question of race and ethnicity. The arguments about immigration are, in fact, not so much about immigration *per se*, but about non-white immigration.

It is perfectly true that we now know a great deal about the development of black society in Britain over a period of four centuries. Yet even more striking are those areas of black history about which we know very little, few more perplexing than the history of black women and family life. It is reasonably certain that the study of black women – however fragmentary the evidence currently appears to be – will attract increasing scholarly attention. So too will those blacks in history who attained a contemporary prominence which history has, for whatever reason, denied them. Indeed it is only when we have a fuller appreciation of the achievements of such people – in a host of creative activities – that it will be possible to assess the broader history of black society. After all, not all blacks sank without a trace under the (undoubted) weight of oppression. It is important that we know more about the unusual (however bizarre or contingent) as well as the mundane and the commonplace, among people traditionally relegated to the margins of history. The black 'personalities' in past history may seem to some no more than ephemeral curiosities, but we need to study them to understand black history more fully. Similarly it is important to consider the impact (direct or indirect) of black society on the development of important literary traditions. Black writers – and white writers discussing black life – may, again, seem an arcane field to study but, like black history itself, they have an importance which transcends their own immediate achievements.[13]

Even more contentious, perhaps, is the study of racial attitudes between black and white. Since it appears clear that racism is a pervasive influence in British society (and other societies), it is important to seek the evolution of that phenomenon. Furthermore there is a powerful case to be made that racism in Britain is a creation of a particular set of historical circumstances. It is possible to argue that it is quite unrealistic to understand the changing nature of white responses to black society without confronting the distinctive historical forces which have bound black and white together, over many centuries, in such a special interdependence. At its simplest, it is surely important to remind ourselves that black society in the New World (and now, indirectly in Britain itself) was a result of the white man's rapacious need for cheap, malleable labour in the American colonies. Without slavery there would have been no black communities throughout the Americas on anything like their present scale. As we have seen, slavery spawned a complex set of attitudes of white to black; freedom in the nineteenth century generated new (and not always more benign) reactions. The subsequent expansion of British imperial power itself encouraged a complexity of racial attitudes which, though appropriate in an age of imperialism, have been swiftly made redundant since the Second World War. Thus, both black and white have inherited a historically determined skein of attitudes (towards and among each other). And we have scarcely begun to unravel the complexities of these attitudes. Current preoccupations with present-day relations between black and white demand that we know much more of the history and sociology which shaped them. As the problems of contemporary black life in Britain multiply, there will be, without question, a growing demand to know more about black history, both recent and long-term. Moreover, this is a history of great importance for both black and white.

For well over two centuries, the British were among the Western world's leading slave-trading nations, ferrying millions of enslaved Africans from their homelands into the Americas. In a number of North American, but especially Caribbean, settlements black slavery became a major institution. And yet within a very short span of time the British turned their back first on the slave trade (1807) and later on slavery (1833). The qualified form of slavery-apprenticeship – introduced in 1833 – was ended in 1838. Thereafter the British became the major driving force for international abolition and anti-slavery policies throughout the nineteenth century.

Such a transformation in British behaviour – from slaver to crusading abolitionist – was clearly a complex process, and it is one which has naturally attracted the attention of successive generations of historians. Since the Second World War there have been several revisionary studies of the economic determinants of abolition,[14] detailed analyses of the intellectual roots of anti-slavery ideas and exacting studies of the formal politics of the same movement.[15] More recently, historians have begun to pay attention (long overdue) to the role played by the slaves themselves in securing their own freedom.[16] Indeed the phenomenon of the British anti-slavery movement has generated a veritable academic industry of its own, with major international gatherings devoted to each and every facet of this perplexing historical conundrum. This book has obviously been influenced and shaped by that work and seeks in its turn to make a modest contribution to the continuing arguments about slavery and abolition.

It is important however to establish what this book seeks to do (and not to do). It does not aspire to being a definitive account of British abolition. It is instead an attempt to analyse the campaigns against the slave trade and slavery as a popular movement and to place those campaigns within the broader (and at times determining) context of black history both in Britain and the British West Indies. In addition, an attempt is made to suggest the possible links – some of the continuing cultural influences – between this distinctive epoch in British history and the more modern experience of relations between black and white.

Part I
Slavery and a Free Land

1 Slavery and a Free Land

Historians of slavery have long been curious about the relationship between slavery and freedom.[1] Many historians, and large numbers of modern students, have been particularly intrigued (and puzzled) by the mentality of people in past time who were able to justify the slavery of others while extolling their own rights of liberties and freedom. What, to the modern Western eye, might seem inconsistent – a contradiction in attitudes and behaviour – was not of course necessarily equally obvious to people in the past. In the British case, black slavery thrived for more than two centuries in the West Indian settlements and did so, for much of its history, with relatively few objections (of any kind). Yet the years when the British slave empire emerged and prospered were also the years when political life in Britain was characterised by a long-protracted, vocal and insistent struggle for a wide range of political and social rights. By the time the major Caribbean islands had been transformed into black slave societies producing tropical staples for the benefit of the metropolis, that same metropolis had witnessed – among other changes – the triumph of parliamentary over monarchical power, and the passing of the Habeas Corpus Act in 1679. However limited those political and social rights might now seem – however hemmed in by the restraints of property, and access to them limited by poverty – contemporaries took great pride in them; the liberties of the British were viewed as the achievements of (and justification for) the years of revolution and turmoil.

This contradiction in British experience in the seventeenth century – the parallel growths of slavery and liberties – was, at one level, easy to overlook since slavery was a colonial and not a domestic issue. Those blacks – slaves and free – who found themselves in seventeenth-century Britain were few and far between and offered no real substantive illustration of the clash between contemporary freedoms and slavery. A century later, by the mid-eighteenth century (when the slave colonies had reached their apogee), black society in Britain had grown substantially. It was at this point, that a number of contemporaries – black and white – began to recognise, debate and challenge the fundamental contradiction posed by slavery in Britain. By the 1760s slavery in a free land seemed contradictory and presented a challenge to those contemporaries anxious to secure and extend basic liberties to all living in Britain. From these small beginnings there was to emerge an abolitionist movement which challenged the whole of the British slave empire. Yet it needs to be stressed that the first effective and practical steps taken to tackle the problem of slavery in a free land occurred when this contradiction had become obvious and close to hand. And the resolution took the form of trying to grant slaves in Britain the rights of freemen. Thus in the 1760s there began the first effective agitation to secure equality of treatment for blacks (initially before the law). But this had strictly limited aspirations, and was restricted first to England, later to Scotland. Yet, within a relatively brief period, the whole of Britain's slave-trading and slave-owning empire came under fierce abolitionist attack. The abolitionist onslaught against firstly the slave trade and later slavery itself spanned a mere 50 years. Compared to the longer history of black slavery in the Americas, the story of British abolition – in the years 1787–1838 – was a brief though intense spasm of political agitation. Moreover there were few people, in the early days of abolition, who could have predicted the swiftness with which success would come.

By the last quarter of the eighteenth century Britain had established itself as Europe's pre-eminent slaving nation. The West Indian islands and their slave-grown produce were viewed enviously by European rivals (notably the French). And the whole uncertain edifice was kept in place by a complex web of military and naval regulation. The slaves, for their part, were overawed by a process of management and control which was, by turns, subtle in its daily regulation and division of the slave labour force, and crude in its persistent violence against slave 'short-comings' and resistance. The slave quarters were regularly augmented by new arrivals – African survivors from the horrors of the middle passage – and thereby ensured of a continuing cultural link with Africa. The slaves were the instruments of material progress in the sugar islands, yet they had little to show for their lifetime's labours, except to bequeath to their local-born children the stigma of their own slavery. Moreover the slaves were far-removed from the political or social considerations of contemporary British life. Before the origins of the abolitionist campaign, little attention – literary or political – was devoted to the conditions or lives of the slaves, although it is also true that many Britons, actively involved in the slaving empire, knew of their fate at first hand. Out of sight and mind, Britain's slaves toiled away unrecognised and unconsidered by their imperial masters. Indeed it was one of abolition's first and successful ploys to make the slaves more 'visible' and to bring them to the attention of the British public. This was, once more, easier to achieve by the late eighteenth century thanks to the existence of numbers of blacks in Britain whose personal testimony and experience authenticated the indictments levelled against the institution of black slavery by early abolitionists. From that point onwards, the slaves were to provide a continuing and vital element in the abolitionist campaign. Sometimes consciously, more often unwittingly, the lives and actions of British slaves (however geographically distant) materially affected the progress of the abolitionist cause in Britain itself. It is part of this book's ambition to integrate that story within the broader struggle for black freedom.

It is one of the most remarkable aspects of the long history of British slavery that, shortly after ending black slavery in 1838, the British rapidly purged their collective memories of much of what had gone before. Despite the fact that the British had carried perhaps 2.5 million Africans into bondage, and had established some of the most successful slave colonies in the Americas, that history was instantly overshadowed by the loudly-proclaimed virtues of ending the slave trade (1807) and slavery itself (1838). Clearly, few individuals or nations like to remind themselves of the more unpleasant episodes in their past, but in this particular case what compounded the immediate British amnesia about its slaving past was the subsequent and unflinchingly persistent emphasis upon British liberties, and the British love of freedom. No sooner had slavery ended, than

those related themes (the virtuousness of emancipation an
the British love of liberty) became a regular descant in all sort
of mid-nineteenth-century literature. In part this was a direc
result of the abolitionist campaign itself and of the insistenc
upon bestowing on blacks the full rights of Britons.[2] But th
assumptions about the British love of liberties go far deepe
than that and have, in the intervening years, become somethin
of an unquestioned and unchallenged assumption. This may b
explained in part by those aspects of British history used, i
political and educational circles, to present a distinctive (ofte
partisan) interpretation of the past, and thus of the future. Th
'lessons of history', learned formally through schooling an
informally via a plethora of popular cultural forms (books
magazines, comics and later, films) have succeeded in conveyin
an impression that the British not only enjoy a unique set o
liberties and freedoms but that their past is characterised b
liberty and the pursuit of liberty.

Over the past century, successive generations of schoolchildre
have been exposed to a Whiggish view of British history i
which each successive epoch of the past was portrayed as a
improving step towards the unquestioned (and obviously
superior condition of contemporary life. The pride which th
British took in themselves and in their achievements was rooted
in a particular view of history, at the heart of which lay a serie
of assumptions about liberties and freedoms. Indeed to a ver
marked degree, the history and development of Britain wer
conveyed as a series of triumphs, of liberty over the threats o
despotism. The British invariably have been portrayed as
people to whom love of liberty was a natural, innate (an
certainly God-given) quality. And the words of grea
contemporaries were always available to be dangled before
credulous youthful readership. They learned from Macaula
that 'The history of England is emphatically the history o
progress':

nothing is so interesting and delightful as to contemplate th
steps by which the England of the Domesday Book, the
England of the curfew and the forest laws, the England of th
crusades, monks, schoolmen, astrologers, serfs, outlaws,
became the England which we know and love, the classi

ground of liberty and philosophy, the school of all knowledge, the mart of all trade.[3]

Untold armies of British children breathed in this ideological miasma. And why should they doubt its central principles when they glanced at the achievements of nineteenth- or twentieth-century Britain?

This is not to claim, however, that this historical interpretation is fundamentally wrong. On the contrary, there is a powerful case to be made that the most significant epochs in recent British history have indeed been characterised by arguments – and fights – about liberties and freedom. Indeed the liberties in which the British took such inordinate pride were themselves functions of particular historical circumstances, most notably during the confused troubles of the seventeenth century. That century witnessed not only the diminution of monarchical power but also saw a far-reaching and influential debate about political and social rights.[4] If the political system which emerged from those years of conflict provided the foundations for subsequent political development in Britain, the philosophical arguments attendant on that revolution were to have ramifications far beyond the limits of British life. Enlightened Europe and colonial America were to be heirs and beneficiaries of the political arguments generated by the seventeenth-century revolution in Britain. And yet, as we have seen, those same years also saw the development and perfection of black slavery in the new West Indian colonies. The society which established the primacy of parliamentary power, and confirmed individual liberties before the law, was equally responsible for the development of black chattel slavery.

When, from the mid-seventeenth century onwards, arguments revived about political representation and personal liberties, proponents tended, once more, to reach back to earlier epochs for precedent and legitimacy. This had also been true of the seventeenth century; historical precedent was commonly recruited to ensure political authority or to strengthen an argument. 'History' was invariably the handmaiden of the politically active (particularly the radicals) in the seventeenth, eighteenth and nineteenth centuries. And throughout, the historical precedents (real or imaginary) were used to safeguard and advance particular social or political liberties.[5]

The period 1776–1848 was, with a few exceptional periods of calm, a time of social and political turmoil not equalled in its intensity and influence since. This 'age of revolution' was one in which arguments once more raged about liberties and freedom – though now commonly couched in the new French terminology of liberty, equality and fraternity. Demands for liberties – of all kinds – were met by a resistant political system fearful of conceding change in an apparently unstable society, and ever conscious of the memories of 1789. Not since the seventeenth-century revolution had Britain been so taxed by passionate arguments about liberties and freedoms.

In the years between the outbreak of revolution in France (1789) and the demise of Chartism (1848), British debates about liberties became inextricably intermeshed with parallel arguments about slavery. It was in this period (during which the modern democratic tradition was securely established in British life) that the British slave system was destroyed. Indeed it was a notable triumph of abolitionists that, in these years, they succeeded in establishing as a universally accepted principle that black slaves ought to enjoy the rights and liberties of the 'true-born Briton'.[6] To that extent the fight for black freedom became part of the broader debate about British liberties. This is, however, far from claiming that securing black freedom was *merely* an extension of British rights. What differentiated the arguments about black freedom from the rights and liberties of contemporary Britons was, of course, slavery itself. However much contemporary Britons felt their ancient liberties to be denied them – to have been usurped or removed by their political masters – the plight of black slaves was incomparably worse. The problem for slaves was not that they were simply denied access to basic rights but that they were, as a matter of principle, denied even their common humanity. They were things: chattel and property, comparable (in law and to some extent in social practice) to other inanimate material objects. The degree to which this denial of humanity was visibly, demonstrably and logically flawed was, in essence, the 'problem' which was unmoveably rooted at the heart of the major slave-owning empires.[7]

The existence of a flourishing slave empire alongside a frequently repeated pride in domestic liberties and rights forms, at first sight, an apparent contradiction common to many slave societies. In the British case, however, (and unlike for example the USA in the early nineteenth century) it is a contradiction often overlooked for the simple reason that the institution of black slavery developed and thrived in the Caribbean, 5000 miles from the British metropolis. There were, it is true, a number of points at which black slavery impinged directly on domestic British life; in the slave ports, in the framing of laws to govern the slave routes and the slave islands, and in the (generally esoteric) philosophical debate about slavery. But these were, until the mid seventeenth century, matters of generally marginal interest; of concern (by and large) only to those with an active or material interest in the slaving empire. Despite its enormity (the vast numbers of Africans carried into the New World by, say, 1760), despite its unquestioned material benefits to the metropolis, and despite the growing numbers of Britons (sailors, merchants, planters, officials and the like) familiar with the human reality of black slavery, the slave empire was distant, in place, time and sensibility from contemporary British experience. It is true that certain forms of bondage — notably indentured servants — were common in the first half of the seventeenth century. But this was qualitatively different from the chattel status of the black slave.

The fundamental contradiction in British history in the years of slavery — the clash between slavery and freedom in the years from the late sixteenth to the late eighteenth centuries — lies, at heart, in the physical divergence between imperial (West Indian) life and domestic British society. As the British sought to safeguard a complex series of social and political rights in those years, a new society was brought into existence in the New World (by enforced migration) devoid of any semblance of rights and liberties. But those slave societies owed little of their shape and character to Britain itself. True, the finance, political support and rapacious colonial mentality were unquestionably British, but the slave islands derived their social structure and form from other colonial and legal entities, notably from earlier Iberian and Dutch settlers elsewhere in the Americas. There were, in fact, few aspects of life on the black plantations which late seventeenth-century Britons would recognise as familiar (or British). Black slavery was an utterly alien form of society, with no roots in British life and offering no point of contact for British observes. It was as different — as unfamiliar and hostile —

as any other alien culture could be. It is true of course that successive generations of British settlers in the Caribbean soon *became* accustomed to plantation slavery, but so too did traders and merchants in Africa and on the American frontier became accustomed to the alien world of local indigenous peoples. Yet few settlers pretended to see anything worthwhile in indigenous life. Black slaves were in effect merely another species (however unique) of alien and 'primitive' peoples who lived out their lives beyond the care or ken of contemporary Britain.

When in the years 1787–1833 slavery came under attack, much of the growing revulsion felt in Britain, derived from the evidence about the nature of black slavery and the slave trade brought before the British public. Thus, the British debate about slavery was informed by an awareness of black slavery which contrasted with the earlier ignorance and indifference. It was an abolitionist ploy – and success – to enlighten the British people about slavery. But the abolitionists also sought, from 1787 onwards, to convey the principle that blacks were men and brothers. When that principle came to be widely accepted, by the mid-1820s, the final barrier to black freedom had been breached. Of course, this involved a complex campaign, itself substantially shaped by the material transformations in British life. Much of what follows seeks to describe this fundamental shift in sensibility – to accepting blacks as men and brothers – and to locate that shift within its determining social context.

There is, however, a further complexity to this story. Although earlier historians have analysed in detail the political and intellectual progress of black freedom, too little recognition has been made of the immediate British black experience from which embryonic abolition emerged. When the first pioneering abolitionists sought to safeguard the material and legal interests of black slaves – and the wider black community – their initial efforts were directed at blacks in Britain itself. Their successes in the 1760s and 1770s (however limited) illustrated to a curious British public not only the barbarities of black slavery in its wider setting but also highlighted the contradiction (liberty versus freedom) in the very heart of British society. The problems of black slavery in mid eighteenth-century Britain were, in effect, to provide an entrée to a more thorough scrutiny of black slavery throughout the empire. Slavery in Britain thus provided the opportunity for the initial rehearsal of ideals and tactics which were, in time, to prove irresistible when flung at the institution of colonial and maritime slavery. Let us begin therefore by examining that most startling of contradictions: the existence of black slavery in a free land.

2 Slaves in England

By the late sixteenth century, Englishmen took pride in the distinctive liberties afforded in their realm. In 1577, for example, William Harrison wrote:

> As for slaves and bondsmen we have none; nay such is the privilege of our country by the special grace of God and the bounty of our princes, that if any came hither from other realms, as soon as they set foot on land they become free of condition as their masters, whereby all note of servile bondage is utterly removed from them.[1]

If true, this was a remarkable contrast to preceding centuries when bondage, notably serfdom, had been an elemental feature of English society; a social category and an essential foundation to the feudal order. In England, the decline of serfdom and feudalism were inextricably linked. Bondage was no longer needed, from the fifteenth century onwards, for the land-owning classes could secure their economic well-being more effectively by the use of free labour, itself cajoled and regimented not by the limitations of legal bondage but by the no less rigorous dictates of a free market.

Although the institutions of bondage had effectively disappeared, arguments about bondage and freedom were central to those political controversies which wracked Britain in the first half of the seventeenth century. During the Civil War there evolved a fierce debate about the nature of representation and about the complex forms of social rights. Throughout the ebb and flow of political upheaval it was widely assumed on all hands that freedom was the fundamental right and inheritance of the Englishman. Inside Parliament, within the Army and among a host of active political groups, there took place a remarkable debate about the very nature and definition of social and political rights. In the process, the concept of slavery became a recurring theme in contemporary political vocabulary. Those anxious to denounce their political opponents, or merely intent on promoting their own partisan case, referred time and again to slavery as the vilest and most degraded social and political institution. In the Putney debate in the autumn of 1647, for example, Colonel Rainsborough complained, 'He hath fought to enslave himself, to give power to men of riches, men of estate, to make him a perpetual slave.'[2] Among the seventeenth-century radicals, this was a theme which haunted their thoughts about the outcome of the conflict. John Lilburne the Leveller asked, 'Is not all the Controversy whose slaves the poor shall be?',[3] a theme he returned to on other occasions. Similarly the Diggers denounced the bondage imposed by the nation's landowners: 'We are resolved to be cheated no longer, nor to be held under slavish fear of you no longer, seeing the Earth was made for us, as well as for you.'[4] Winstanley, the Diggers' key spokesman, offered a blueprint for a form of government in which 'All slaveries and oppressions which have been brought upon mankind by kings, lords of the manors, lawyers and landlords and the divine clergy are all cast out.'[5]

However varied the political ambitions of these men, they shared the common assumption that slavery was the worst of human conditions; their worst insult was that their enemies sought to perpetuate or impose slavery. Such accusations involved, of course, a degree of political and verbal licence, for the very institution they denounced – slavery – was indeed buoyant and expansive, though not in Britain or among the British. What added piquancy to the mid seventeenth-century denunciations of slavery was the parallel development of slavery – black chattel slavery – in the European settlements in the New World. It was perfectly true that slavery *was* the most abject of human conditions, but it threatened not the rights of Englishmen, but the rights of those bands of Africans who fell prey, in rapidly increasing numbers, to the rapacious power and economic needs of marauding European colonial powers.

Englishmen had been profitably involved in the early slave trade from Africa long before they had settled their own outposts on the African coast or established their own New World colonies. The Spanish and Portuguese pioneers of the maritime slave trade had introduced English sailors both to the existence of the black slave market and had begun to tempt the adventurous with the profitable lure of trading in black humanity. By the mid sixteenth century Englishmen were making cautious forays into the slave markets. After a voyage to Guinea in 1554–5, the Captain, John Lok, returned with (among other things) 'certain black slaves, whereof some were tall and strong men, and could well agree with our meates and drinkes'. Nor surprisingly, however, 'The cold and moyst aire doth somewhat offend them.'[6]

Subsequent English trading ventures to Africa returned with small numbers of Africans, using them as interpreters on later trips. Initially, however, the Africans in sixteenth-century Britain were objects of curiosity. They had no important economic role in Britain – as slaves or freemen – but were merely fashionable acquisitions in the upper reaches of a society anxious to add to its status by joining the fad for employing and owning black humanity.

What transformed the role and nature of black society in Britain were events in the New World. Initially the British slave trade had been merely to sell Africans into the Spanish and Portuguese colonies. This was pioneered by John Hawkins in his voyage of 1562, when 'he got into his possession, partly by the sword and partly by other means, to the number of 300 Negros at the least'. Sailing into the New World, Hawkins 'made vent of the whole of his Negros'.[7] Such trips – prospective and innovative – were fraught with commercial and military risks. But the establishment of English colonies in the Caribbean and mainland America in the early seventeenth century was to transform utterly the English involvement in slave trading.

In the early seventeenth century the British – and other northern European powers – were able gradually to establish themselves in the West Indies. The economic and political power of the ascendant British enabled them to loosen the weakening grip of the Spaniards in the region. With political encouragement from home, pioneering adventurers, keen to tap the proven wealth of the New World, established a number of settlements in the Americas. Some proved a disastrous failure, but others flourished. By the time of the English Civil War, the English had made tentative settlements in St Kitts, Nevis, Barbados and Montserrat. Small-scale farming, with master, indentured servant and small numbers of black slaves working side by side on relatively small land-holdings formed the first phase of settlement. Following the introduction of sugar into Barbados in 1640, however, the nature of economic life in the region was transformed. Labour intensive and suited to large-scale cultivation, sugar encouraged the rapid proliferation of sizeable plantations worked by large gangs of praedial labour. The Irish and Scottish indentured labourers were not available in sufficient numbers; but the Africans were. As sugar became the region's dominant tropical staple, the island's population became progressively more African, and the growing number of British slave-traders ferried their black cargoes into the islands. For instance, in 1640 there were some 6400 slaves (and 25,000 whites) in Barbados; by 1650 the slaves had increased to 20,000, and to 37,000 by 1680. The pattern was repeated in Jamaica, which was taken from the Spanish by Cromwell's army in 1655. Jamaica quickly became a black society; in 1670 there were 7000 slaves (and whites), but by 1700 there were 45,000 slaves on the island, and 80 years later the number had risen to almost a quarter of a million, yet by then whites numbered only 18,000.[8] In the North American colonies (where the economic demand for slaves was less pressing than in the Caribbean) there were upwards of 20,000 slaves by 1700, most notably in Virginia.

Both in North America and the West Indies, the increasing numbers of blacks had the effect of raising the social and economic status of poor white indentured labourers. They tended to become freer as blacks became ever more enslaved. By the late seventeenth century black slavery was firmly entrenched throughout British colonies in the Americas, both in law and economic practice. The law – of the colony and the metropolis – had transmuted the Africans into a thing, a chattel and property; 'to be bought and sold, a status applicable only and necessarily to blacks and to their descendants'.[9] But it was in the West Indies that British black slavery flourished to a remarkable degree, thanks to the voracious European appetite for sugar and because British maritime interests were able to supply increasing cargoes of African slaves. One man wrote of Barbados in 1645: 'I believe they have bought this year no lesse than a thousand Negros, and the more they buie, the better able they are to buye, for in a yeare and a halfe they will earn (with God's blessing) as much as they cost.'[10]

Supplies of slaves were not however merely a matter of

private initiative and commercial dealing (though the trade needed both qualities in abundance). Like the colonial settlements themselves, the slave trade was approved and regulated by King and Parliament. Initially the English slave trade was controlled by a number of monopolistic companies, led by the Royal African Company (1672) in which royal investors sank their money. Monopoly companies were, however, resented by those excluded from the obviously lucrative trades and by the slave owners in the colonies whose appetite for Africans simply could not be sated by the monopolies. There was a fierce economic and political argument in England in the late seventeenth and early eighteenth centuries *pro* and *con* the monopoly companies; ultimately the African Company's monopoly was ended in 1712 and the trade opened to other British slave traders. The point to be stressed here, however, is that the *issue* of slavery was a matter of political and social debate in England itself. In the century spanning the early settlement of the American and Caribbean colonies from the opening of the slave trade in 1712, the nature and role of black chattel slavery became progressively more important in domestic English politics. In the schemes to settle the colonies, the sanctioning and approval by King-in-Parliament of earlier colonial legislation, in the legislative controls over the development of the slave trade from Africa and in the encouragement given to the economic infrastructure of the Atlantic slaving empire, the English were intimately involved in matters of slavery. It is tempting to imagine that the slave trade and slavery were matters of colonial, and therefore distant, concern; in fact they were of immediate import to a wide range of English political and vested interest groups. When, in later years, the English began to shed the responsibilities of slavery and slave trading, it was seductively easy (but wrong) to imagine that the outrages of slavery were uniquely the work of wicked traders and planters. But without close metropolitan scrutiny and support, from the early seventeenth century, those groups could never have secured their position of economic dominance.

To reinforce this point, black slaves were an increasingly common sight in seventeenth-century England. Indeed, from John Lok's return from Africa in 1555 through to the ending of slavery in 1833, blacks became progressively more visible in all walks of life, though notably in the major slave-trading ports.

Until the late seventeenth century, slaves were imported, normally via the New World, but sometimes direct from West Africa, in relatively small numbers.[11] This situation changed dramatically in the course of the eighteenth century largely because the rise of the sugar colonies and the massive consequent expansion of the slave trade led to a marked increase in the importation of Negro slaves into England. They often came as surplus slaves on board the slavers, to be sold in English ports as a bonus for the crew. In Bristol, for instance, it was accepted practice that 'commanders of slaving vessels were allowed to transport a few slaves in each cargo for their personal profit'.[12] In fact this practice became so important that it led to a series of legal wrangles between sailors and ship owners.[13] Other slaves arrived in England in the retinue of returning absentee planters or as the attendants to returning military and colonial officials.[14] Thus, the black slave arrivals were haphazard and spasmodic; they were in fact the human flotsam and jetsam of the expansive Atlantic slaving empire.

In England, black slaves obviously did not occupy the crucial economic role created for them in the slave colonies. From their initial settlement however, in England and other western European countries, they became a popular and prestigious acquisition as domestic servants. Black domestics were common in royal and aristocratic circles by the late sixteenth century, despite belated and unsuccessful attempts by Queen Elizabeth's Government, in 1596 and in 1601, to expel such 'Negroes and blackamoores which . . . are carried into this realm'.[15] This antipathy clearly changed in the next half century, for the first two Stuart monarchs gave royal sanction to the employment of blacks as servants. What ultimately determined the expansion of black importations, however, was not the precedent or example of royal employment, but the settlement and development of the West Indian and mainland American colonies. The great majority of blacks brought to England came not direct from Africa but via the New World, including some born in Africa.

Unlike their fellow white servants, many black menials who found themselves in England were enslaved. Imported blacks were bought and sold much as they would have been in the colonies (the restored Charles II, for example, paid £50 for a black servant) and by the mid seventeenth century public advertisements offering slaves for sale or seeking information about runaways began to reflect the development of black chattel slavery in England.

In 1765 a Liverpool newspaper contained the following advertisement: 'To be sold at George's Coffee-house, betwixt the hours of six and eight o'clock, a very fine negro girl about eight years of age, very healthy, and hath been some time from the coast.' A London paper, the *London Advertiser*, offered in 1756: 'To be sold, a Negro Boy, about fourteen years old, warranted free from any distemper, and has had those fatal to that colour; has been used two years to all kinds of household work, and to wait at table; his price is £25.'[16]

By the mid eighteenth century such advertisements readily appeared throughout London and provincial newspapers; slaves were available in towns and cities far from the slave trade ports where they made their initial entry to English life. Although most seemed to live in London, from the late seventeenth century many could be found throughout the country, living as servants to provincial or rural aristocrats and gentry. Indeed their physical presence often survives to this day in contemporary portraits of landed families and their servants; blacks are sometimes represented sporting a padlocked collar.[17] With the rapid expansion of slave trading after the Restoration, contemporary terminology, reflecting the economic facts of empire, increasingly referred to the African as a commodity, merchandise or thing. Because the Navigation Acts insisted that commodities carried to and from the colonies should be carried in English ships, it was important to give slaves a specifically commercial classification. In 1677 the Solicitor-General decided 'that negroes ought to be esteemed goods and commodities within the Acts of Trade and Navigation'.[18] Coincidentally, in that same year an English court of law also accepted the view that the black was a commodity.[19] When, in 1700, Thomas Papillon of Kent died he left a Negro in his will declaring 'I take [him] to be in the nature and quality of my goods and chattels.'[20] Thus at the dawn of the eighteenth century there was irrefutable evidence of the chattel status of the black in England. But this had emerged, accidentally, as an inevitable by-product of the growth of the slave empires. There were, however, serious problems involved.

The legal position of black slaves in England – and therefore of their owners – was very uncertain. While imperial legislation and court judgements conceded the economic facts of empire, the approval given to the chattel status of the black was concerned primarily with the colonies or with the slave trade on the high seas. There were certain practical and legal obstacles to the introduction of black slavery into England. As we have seen, by the time black slaves were imported into England, the most common form of English bondage – serfdom – had long been extinct. The institution of black slavery which rapidly evolved in the colonies, and which was supervised and modified from London, could not easily be grafted onto existing English institutions and practices. Equally there was no specific legislation to buttress the developments of slavery in England, although the courts were prepared to listen to arguments in favour of (or against) slavery, based on common law.

It was ironic that as the West Indian slave empires were established in the seventeenth century, the same period in England saw the assertion of important political and human rights, at precisely that time Englishmen constructed a fabric focus in the Habeas Corpus Act of 1679. As more and more Englishmen came to pride themselves on their newly won rights, at precisely that time Englishment constructed a fabric of colonial slave society which was specifically designed to relegate the black below the level of humanity. Furthermore, because of the economic and political ties between metropolis and colonies, the two systems of law – English and colonial – often overlapped and frequently clashed. Nowhere was this more apparent than on the question of slavery. On the face of it the chattel status of imported slaves was at variance with the spirit and even the letter of English law. It was this problem which was to tax English courts until the early nineteenth century.

In dealing with the frequent slave cases, English judges found themselves unable to maintain a consistent position or to apply a consistent principle. This was largely because the legal arguments about chattel slavery called for a choice between two hallowed legal principles: the defence of property rights (in this case the slave owners' property rights in their slaves) and the defence of personal liberties (the slaves' freedom). In 1677, for instance, it was ruled in an English court that 'Negroes being usually bought and sold among Merchants, so Merchandise, and also being Infidels, there might be property in them.'[21] Twenty years later another court ruled that the black was *not* to be treated as chattel, 'for he is no other than a slavish servant'.[22] Similar confusion marked the major slave cases throughout the eighteenth century, as courts found themselves pulled between the contradictory demands of defending property and freedom.

In 1706 the Lord Chief Justice ruled that 'By the common law no man can have property in another . . . there is no such thing as a slave by the laws of England.'[23] Twenty-three years later the Attorney- and Solicitor-Generals, Philip Yorke and Charles Talbot, offered their famous opinion, in response to a petition from West Indian merchants and planters, which was completely at variance with the 1706 ruling: 'We are of the opinion, that a slave coming from the West Indies to Great Britain or Ireland, with or without his master, doth not become free and that this property in him is not thereby determined or varied.'[24] In 1749 this view was given added strength by Lord Hardwicke (the former Philip Yorke) who declared the slave in England to be 'as much property as any other thing'. Like other pieces of chattel, declared Hardwicke, Negroes 'wear out with labour, as cattle, or other things . . . they are like stock on a farm'.[25] Here, Hardwicke was doing more than describing colonial reality; he was defining a legal status by fashioning his judgement on the social reality of black slavery. A mere 13 years later however, in 1762, the legal pendulum swung the other way when the Lord Chancellor declared 'As soon as a man sets foot on English ground he is free.' Furthermore, Lord Henley suggested an escape route for the enslaved black in England who 'may have a Habeas Corpus if restrained of his liberty'.[26] From the late 1760s this suggestion was to prove a godsend to the small band of English humanitarians, led by Granville Sharp, who sought to assert black freedom by securing writs of Habeas Corpus.[27] Thereafter – and until all blacks in British possession were emancipated in 1833 – it was the writ of Habeas Corpus, and not the capricious decisions of English judges, which offered the best and most reliable source of legal redress for black slaves in England.

The social experience of blacks in England was not always congruent with legal judgements in their favour; the legal theory and social reality did not always correspond. For example in the early editions of his classic *Commentaries on the Laws of England*, Blackstone, who was deeply influenced by Montesquieu's attack on slavery, expressed the view that 'the spirit of Liberty is so deeply implanted in our constitution, and rooted in our very soil, that a slave or negro the moment he lands in England, falls under the protection of the laws and so far becomes a freeman'. A brief glance at contemporary newspaper advertisements would have warned Blackstone against too theoretical an approach.[28] Blackstone soon appreciated the gulf between his theory and daily practice. It was claimed that Lord Chief Justice Mansfield was instrumental in encouraging Blackstone to qualify his earlier, bold assertion and there was added to the third edition the proviso 'though the master's right to his services may possibly continue'.[29] Legal arguments in support of black freedom did little to arrest the progress of black slavery in England. Indeed while Blackstone was, initially, heralding the liberating qualities of arrival in England, newspapers regularly offered blacks for sale. Slave owners were much less confused about the matter than English judges. In the words of Lord Mansfield in 1772, slaves in England 'were sold in the exchange and other places of public resort by parties themselves resident in London and with as little reserve as they would have been in any of our West Indian possessions'.[30]

As the West Indian slave empire reached its apogee, and as the pace and volume of slave trading across the Atlantic increased, it was natural that ever more blacks should find their way to England. The numbers involved remain, inevitably, impressionistic but they unquestionably increased during the American War of Independence, when numbers of loyalists fled to England, with their slaves, to escape the conflict. The overall size of the black population in late eighteenth-century England is very uncertain. But, whatever its exact size, it is clear that not all blacks were enslaved. While critics were anxious that 'some restraint should be laid on the unnatural increase of blacks imported', particularly after 1783 when large numbers of former American slaves were brought to England, as the black population grew in size, a substantial proportion of them were able to gain their freedom.[31] Early in the eighteenth century the number of free blacks in London, for instance, was apparently small but by the middle years of the century their numbers had become a matter of frequent comment by contemporaries. The most obvious avenue to freedom was escape, initially into the poor warrens and alleyways of the capital, and later, as the free black population grew, into the 'subterranean' society of fellow blacks. Escape, given the legal impediments to effective black freedom, became the common recourse of imported slaves. Indeed a majority of newspaper advertisements in the late eighteenth century were concerned, not with slave sales, but with the recapture of runaways: 'Runaway, some time since, A NEGRO LAD about 18 Years of Age, near five feet two inches high, answers to the Name of Starling, and blows the French Horn very well. . . . Now the Property of Ralph Cook, at the Sign of the Rising Sun.'[32] There is no way of expressing the incidence of slave escapes numerically, but it finds frequent reflection in newspaper advertisements and contemporary comments. The runaways were invariably imported slaves rather than English-born, a fact which may be explained by reference to the demographic structure of the black population. We know that while some blacks were born in England, the very great majority were African-born males, itself perhaps an indication of the West Indian sexual imbalance. The obvious consequences of this was that there were few black marriages and few English-born Negroes. (An important though secondary consequence was the development of a strong local antipathy to miscegenation.)

As the eighteenth century advanced it became increasingly common for imported slaves to run away. In part these escapes were due to the loosening of the slave–master relationship by the solvents of simply living in free English society. Soon after arrival Negroes 'cease to consider themselves as slaves in this free country nor will they put up with an inequality of treatment'. The London magistrate, Sir John Fielding, writing in 1768, explained this by claiming that Negroes 'put themselves on an equal footing with other servants, become intoxicated with liberty [and] grow refractory'.[33] The attractions of freedom apparently proved irresistible for many slaves. Because the imported slaves were immersed in a society where freedom, as opposed to colonial slavery, was the most noticeable social characteristic, the incidence of escapes among English slaves was almost certainly higher than it was in the West Indies (although even there it seems to have been higher than many historians have hitherto allowed).

Most imported slaves in England were unskilled. The skilled minority in the colonies were presumably too valuable to remove from the tightly worked economy of the plantations. Those imported into England, said one planter, were 'neither husbandmen, manufacturers, nor artificers'.[34] In fact there were a few cases of black artisans living in England.[35] Very few were agricultural workers – the main task of West Indian slaves. Some were sailors, who inevitably tended to be transient, but the great majority of those imported into England were employed as domestics.

Servants constituted one of the largest occupational groups in eighteenth-century England; as the century advanced black servants became more fashionable and available. As in the seventeenth century, royalty set the social tone; George I, II and the sons of George III employed black servants, and inevitably nobles followed the royal lead. In fact, black servants became so common that the Duke of Dorset abandoned the practice in favour of Chinese servants. Two taverns at Wapping, in London, for instance served as sale rooms for black servants; in Liverpool there is evidence of blacks being sold by lot in auctions. The qualities required of a black servant are again reflected in newspaper advertisements. Ideally the black ought to be pocked-marked (and therefore immune), with some command of English, docile and 'fit to serve a gentleman'. By one of the ironies of history this source of information – advertisements – while resting upon the chattel status of the black, is one of the few sources of pre-modern black history which provides us with the human characteristics of these lost people.

> Ran away the 7th instant, from Capt Thomas Eaton, of the Prince William, a NEGRO MAN named MINGO, of a good black Complexion, smooth FACE, wears a Whig; had on two short blue Waistcoats, and brown Breeches; about 5 foot two inches high, his legs a little bent, his upper Teeth scagg'd and broken, has a Cut on his Right Wrist which stands up in A bunch. He speaks very good English.[36]

Often, however, it is difficult to distinguish between the black who was a free servant and one who was enslaved, for not all enslaved domestics ran away. Some worked faithfully until manumitted by a grateful master, others found a lifetime's loyalty rewarded by a mere change of owner on the death of their first master. It is thus difficult to analyse the blurred line which separated black slave from black servant. There are, however, numerous examples of slaves imported by military and colonial officials, who worked on the basis of equality with fellow white menials and who give every appearance of being merely black servants but who were, in fact, slaves whose status was not affected either by escape or manumission.

The often ill-defined relationship between English masters and their black slaves was sometimes further confused by the anxiety of many masters to convert their slaves to Christianity. Throughout the West Indies, black baptism, as the first step towards Christianisation, was bitterly resisted by the whites. Barbadian planters in 1680, for instance, complained that 'conversion of their slaves to Christianity would not only destroy their property, but endanger the island'.[37] West Indian planters, in general, bitterly resisted the conversion of their slaves, regarding the institutions of organised religion and the message of the preachers as fundamentally corrosive of their hold over their slaves. In England, however, slave owners seemed positively anxious to give their imported slaves the rudiments of religion, and sometimes even literacy. Of course the contagious egalitarianism and political dissent which colonial whites feared to be implicit in literacy and religion could indeed have devastating effects in a slave society (as Jamaica discovered in the early nineteenth century).[38] Among faithful black domestics living in white society, however, it could have quite the opposite effect and act as a brake on wordly action. For the importance of religion to the individual black we need only look to the writings of Ignatius Sancho, Olaudah Equiano and Ottobah Cugoano where religion so often seemed to redirect their aspirations towards the hereafter.[39] All three were weighed down by a sense of guilt, and looked to the next world for relief of their earthly cares. In England, Christianity among imported slaves may have been deliberately used and encouraged by white masters. Comparative analysis suggests that, whereas in the West Indies in the early nineteenth century fundamental Christianity became the cutting edge of emergent black self-awareness, in England it was but another factor in the generally smooth absorption of the blacks into local society.

Much of the impetus behind conversion of English slaves came from the blacks themselves who widely – but mistakenly – believed that baptism or marriage bestowed automatic freedom. Indeed part of the 1729 Yorke–Talbot opinion was designed to refute this view: 'baptism doth not bestow freedom on him [the slave] nor make any alteration in his temporal condition in these kingdoms'.[40] None the less the myth remained a powerful force in the black community. From the masters' side, baptism was often reserved for a favourite or faithful servant and naturally enough the master's domination would determine the black's particular faith. The Earl of Chesterfield, Ambassador to the Hague, described how, in 1728

> I treated the people here with an English Christening, in my chapel, of a Black-a-Moor boy that I have; having had him first instructed in the Christian faith by my chaplain, and examined by myself. The behaviour of young Christian was decent and exemplary, and he renounced his likeness [i.e. the devil] with great devotion, to the infinite edification of a very numerous audience of both sexes.[41]

Furthermore, without the approval of the master, English ministers were unwilling to baptise Negroes. None the less a significant number were baptised.[42] Some indication of this can be seen in the frequency with which blacks were given both Christian and surnames (in the West Indies a single slave name generally sufficed). Generally the black took the master's name or the name of the locality, though there are instances of Africans retaining their African name with the addition of a Christian name. Thus those blacks who lived in England were often brought much nearer to that ideal of the black Englishman which their white masters sought to cultivate than any similar group of servants or Africans in the slave colonies.

Conversion and renaming was (like the clothing the blacks were given) part of the attempt to transform them into black Englishmen. Similarly, blacks in England, both enslaved and free, generally had a more complete command of spoken English than colonial slaves, for English, rather than patois was vital to their work. Whereas in the colonies patois became the lingua franca of Africans of diverse language groups, all of whom needed to communicate through a common medium, English blacks needed to speak their masters' language. Once again, newspaper advertisements suggest the importance of spoken English among slaves.[43] While literacy was, naturally enough, rarer than spoken English, it was more pronounced among blacks in England than in the West Indies. Those who mastered the mechanics of literacy – Sancho and Equiano are among the best examples – lifted themselves from the general level of their poor fellow blacks, though literacy may have been a function rather than a cause of this improved status. On the other hand, the West Indian field slave and even the West Indian domestic slave, adopted the local patois which, as visitors to the islands were horrified to discover, was used even by West Indian whites. While English slaves undoubtedly maintained African intonations and accents (as evidenced in the 'bubbles' inserted in contemporary cartoons and caricatures)[44] they spoke the language of the host society.

There is a category of English black slave which defies simple analysis, for it consisted of blacks whose status was invisibly transmuted. It is easy to note those slaves who ran away and those who were freed. More difficult to calculate are those who never challenged their enslaved status but who lived as faithful – but none the less enslaved – domestics. Because of their fidelity such people were undistinguished by role and behaviour from their white workmates. While they appeared to be simply black domestics, many were, legally, slaves. If they or their masters failed to break the master–slave relationship it would effectively remain in abeyance. Thus there are deceptive instances of black 'servants' who were slaves, a fact which only came to light when the master died or wished to sell the 'servant'. Apparently many of these slaves imagined their bondage to have lapsed; to have been transmuted into free domestic work. An example of the shock of rediscovering their bondage can be seen in Equiano's autobiography.[45] After working faithfully for some years Equiano found himself sold by his English master to the captain of a ship bound for the West Indies. Furthermore there are frequent instances of both free and enslaved blacks being exported in this way. It was opposition to this particularly crude and obvious violation of English liberties which first agitated English humanitarians and proved to be the genesis of effective English political abolitionism.

The most famous of such incidents was the one leading to the

Somerset case of 1772. The details of this case, and of its legal and historical importance, are complex. More importantly, however, they have been widely misunderstood, largely because both lawyers and scholars have placed too great a trust in the surviving, but fragmentary and partial, law report, which was drawn up four years *after* the case. The Somerset case in fact provides us with a good example of historical myth displacing truth and developing an importance of its own.[46]

Stated briefly, the case involved a group of English humanitarians, led by Granville Sharp, who challenged the legality of the action of the master of the slave James Somerset in forcibly trying to dispatch the slave back to the colonies. The case staggered through eight hearings between December 1771 and June 1772, gathering public and political interest as it progressed. In the process – and afterwards – popular journals simplified and distorted the issue at stake as, indeed, did both defence and prosecution who used the occasion for a setpiece debate about the legality of slavery in England. When his months of attempted compromise had failed, the Lord Chief Justice, Mansfield, finally ruled that the master did not have the right forcibly to re-export his slave. What Mansfield did *not* say was that henceforth all slaves in England were free (the most commonly repeated consequence quoted in historical studies). Benjamin Franklin was bemused by the English self-congratulation about the decision. The country, he wrote, 'piqued itself on its virtue, love of liberty and the equity of its courts, in setting free a single negro'.[47] Thirteen years later, Mansfield went out of his way to correct the mistaken popular impression. The public, he claimed, 'were generally mistaken in the determination of the court of King's Bench, in the case of Somerset the negro, which had often been quoted, for nothing more was than determined than that there was no right in the master forcibly to take the slave and carry him abroad'.[48]

The proof of Mansfield's point lies in the clear evidence of the existence of slavery in England long after 1772. Slave cases continued to come before the courts. Newspapers continued to carry slave advertisements. In 1778 a group of humanitarians *bought* an African chief in order to free him, surely an unusual step had slavery been outlawed. Moreover even the specific ruling made by Mansfield was regularly flaunted, as slave owners continued after 1772, to dispatch slaves back to the colonies.[49] Few slaves could expect Somerset's luck in gaining access to the legal process.

The most immediate legal consequence of the Somerset case was to promote a similar case in Scotland. In *Knight v. Wedderburn* (1778), however, the decision did free local slaves (to Boswell's great delight). It was ruled that Wedderburn the master 'had no right to the Negro's service for any space of time, nor to send him out of the country against his consent'.[50]

In England there was no such legal loosening of the slaves' shackles, and the degree to which English courts continued to concern themselves with the chattel status of the Negro was well illustrated by the *Zong* case of 1783, presided over, ironically, by Mansfield. The Liverpool slave ship, the *Zong*, sailing from Africa to Jamaica, had begun to run out of supplies and the Captain ordered 132 sick slaves thrown overboard in order to conserve dwindling supplies for the rest. This atrocity came before the court as an insurance case – not a murder case – because the owner's insurance claim for the murdered slaves was disputed by the insurance underwriters. The case caused a great deal of public revulsion and was instrumental in rallying opinion to the initial abolitionist cause, especially as, a point of law, the *Zong* case was concerned with property. It seemed to have been Lord Mansfield's fate (in addition to having his house burnt by the Gordon rioters) to have been Lord Chief Justice at a critical juncture in the legal history of slavery. In the four slave cases he heard, on only one occasion did he side with the slave.[51]

However limited the 1772 judgement, it nevertheless contained a potential for black freedom in allowing them access to Habeas Corpus. Slave owners however quickly learned how best to circumvent the restrictions placed on them. Thereafter, on leaving the colonies, the master simply forced the black slave to sign, or mark, an indenture. Under the terms of such indentures the slave was transformed, for the purposes of English law, into an indentured servant on arrival in England and was thereby obliged to accompany the planter back to the colonies, where, naturally, the 'indentured' worker reverted to his former bondage. This arrangement was approved by an English court.[52] In addition, in 1799 it was decided that such 'indentured' workers could only receive wages if they were specified in the original indenture.[53] The result was that, in the last two decades of the eighteenth century, imported slaves were held in a legally approved subjection to their masters which was almost as complete as it had been in the West Indies. By using the technique of indenture, masters were even able to avoid the regulations forbidding the trade in slaves after abolition in 1807, for the slaves they shipped out of the islands were, technically, not slaves but indentured workers. Thus, slave owners used the law to outflank the legal efforts of abolitionists to outlaw slavery in England.

In the last years of the eighteenth century, while the legal position of the slaves in England may have worsened, their overall social position improved, primarily because of the dramatic change in public opinion about slavery. More and more help was available to blacks in the form of legal assistance and simple protection for runaways. Slave owners, given legal sanction to tighten their grip on 'indentured' slaves, found themselves faced by severe, hostile social pressures to free their slaves, or to treat them humanely. They were, in fact, confronted by an increasingly popular and influential abolitionist movement.

None the less, some slave owners were able to maintain their slaves' loyalty well into the nineteenth century.[54] Furthermore other slave owners did not need to threaten their blacks into obedience, for escape into a hungry freedom, involving a constant struggle for survival in an alien world, was an unhappy and intimidating prospect. 'I knew I was free in England but I did not know how to get my living; and therefore I did not like to leave the house.'[55] Thus up to the eve of emancipation the major problem facing newly imported slaves was precisely that which had faced earlier generations of slaves, namely how best to gain access to the legal safeguards of Englishmen or, failing that, how best to make good their escape. That great numbers did escape speaks for their desperation and for their emergent self-awareness.

Between the Somerset case of 1772 and emancipation in 1833, slaves imported into England were caught in a paradoxical position, for while public sentiment undoubtedly swung behind their cause, the law actually strengthened the hands of the slave-owners. Indeed, throughout the period under discussion here, on those rare occasions when the law failed to support the slave owners, the existence of slavery in England continued *despite* the law. Overwhelmingly, however, the process of law was weighted against the black slave; English law was in essence but a reflection of the imperial economic system. Fundamental safeguards of liberties, notably Habeas Corpus, were for long periods beyond the ken and the reach of enslaved blacks. Not until 'positive law' was introduced, in the form of emancipation in 1833, were slaves in England given the legal protection of Englishmen. Even when the slaves were emancipated the compensation awarded to their owners was a concession to the continuing power of the blacks' chattel status. Furthermore it would be a mistake to think that this status was merely a matter of colonial significance, for both in social and legal practice it was fundamental to the relationship forged between black and white society in eighteenth-century England.

The law, at its various levels, was a vital factor in the subjection and enslavement of generations of Africans. Statute law controlled the slave trade; the King-in-Parliament supervised the evolution of colonial slave laws; generations of English judges denied blacks in England any meaningful legal protection. While it is true that to a large extent the law reflected economic fact, in its turn it paved the way for further oppression of the black and assisted his relegation to the level of commodity.

Slavery in England was clearly an alien institution, a mutation of colonial bondage, kept uneasily afloat by certain English traditions about property which were ill-designed to cope with the concept of property in human beings. While it is relatively easy to state the existence of slavery in England and to delineate the major economic and legal determinants of its evolution, it is virtually impossible to assess the numbers of blacks involved. Slavery in England was clearly not as sizeable or as important an institution as in the New World. But in some respects slavery in England was a subtle institution, susceptible to change and able to develop a deceptive chameleonic appearance. Perhaps its most important result was the growth of a substantial black minority in London by the late eighteenth century, and the exposure of important contradictions within the English legal system. When, late in the century, English humanitarians began seriously to challenge the morality of slavery, many of them first came to the wider philosophical problem by having to cope with the human problems created by slavery in England. It would not be an exaggeration to say that the English brand of black slavery, hitherto largely unconsidered, was an important catalyst in directing the public gaze towards the even more abominable institution in the colonies.

3 Black Society in England

In 1764 the *Gentleman's Magazine* reported: 'The practice of importing Negro servants into these Kingdoms is said to be already a grievance that requires a remedy, and yet it is every day encouraged, insomuch that the number in the metropolis only is supposed to be near 20,000.'[1] This was in a total population of three quarters of a million. Over the next twenty years, there was a flurry of estimates about the size of the black population. Many of the estimates were politically inspired; ammunition in the increasingly bitter fight between slave-owners and humanitarians. Planters and their supporting scribes deliberately raised their estimates of blacks in England in order to alarm their readers. Then, as in the 1980s, the size of the black community had established itself as a fierce political issue. However imprecise the estimates, there can be little doubt that black society, by the late eighteenth century, had become a striking, unavoidable feature of metropolitan life. The *Universal History* went so far as to claim that 'every man who has ever stepped beyond the place of his birth has seen them'.[2]

Although blacks were to be found scattered throughout England in the late eighteenth century – in provincial towns and in rural communities where they were, generally, employed as servants – they were to be found in their greatest numbers and concentration in the capital. This was perfectly understandable; London was, after all, the nation's foremost seaport – the greatest entrepôt for exotic goods and peoples – and the centre of political and social life where the fashion of employing black servants was most pronounced. Blacks found their own distinctive communities in a number of other slaving ports, in France as well as England. Indeed, in precisely these same years, the French had a parallel debate about black settlement in the major French slaving ports. In 1777 a prohibition on further black settlement in France declared:

The Negroes are multiplying every day in France. They marry Europeans, the houses of prostitutes are infected by them; the colours mix, the blood is changing . . . these slaves, if they return to America, bring with them the spirit of freedom, independence and equality, which they communicate to others.[3]

In the varied and expanding debate about black society all these allegations were similarly levelled against the blacks in England. In fact the arguments about black society were, in essence, a species of the wider and more important debate about the morality and economics of the slave trade and slavery. Indeed, blacks in England stimulated the origins of that opposition to black slavery which, by 1833, had shattered the ediface of black bondage throughout British possessions. But before we can appreciate the long-term political ramifications of the black community, we need to explore in more detail the nature of that community.

The size of the black community in England was, as we have seen, uncertain. Estimates varied between 3000 and 20,000; those close to the blacks put the figure at the higher rather than the lower level.[4] Not only had it grown in size in the eighteenth century – notably since mid century when slave trading had reached its peak – but it had changed quite markedly. Whereas in the late seventeenth century, blacks tended to be found in more fashionable and prosperous houses, a century later they were ubiquitous. As the numbers of blacks increased, they became less exotic – more mundane and more visible – and were employed increasingly lower down the social scale. Of course there was never really a shortage of white servants – normally in the form of country people seeking work in the capital – but black domestics continued to have the lure of the unusual. But the increase in their numbers rendered them unexceptional where they had once been remarkable. There were fewer black women than men. Ignatius Sancho, the Westminster shopkeeper and correspondent with Sterne, was unusual in having a black wife. Other similar examples can be found of black families in eighteenth-century London. In 1726 a London newspaper contained the following account of a black baptism:

1st came the reputed Father, A Guiney Black, a very clever well-drest Fellow, and another Black who was to be the Godfather. 2ndly, The Midwife or rather her Deputy, a White Woman, carrying the little sooty Pagan, who was to be metamorphosed into a Christian. 3rdly, The Mother, who was also a Black but not of the Guiney Breed, a well shap'd well dress'd woman. 4thly, The Two Intended Godmothers, attended by 6 or 8 more, all Guiney Blacks, as pretty genteel girls as could be girt with a girdle, and setting aside the Complexion, enough to tempt an old frozen Anchorite to have cracked a Commandment with any of them.[5]

As far as we can tell, such black families were unusual. Olaudah Equiano, the African writer and spokesman, was more typical in marrying a white Englishwoman. 'I now mean as it seem Pleasing to my Good God to leave London in about 8 or 10 Days more, and take me a Wife (one Miss Cullen) of Soham in Cambridgeshire.'[6] Charles Morett, a free black, married a white woman and raised a family in the Oxfordshire village of North Ashton. Similarly the landlady of a tavern in York was married to a black. Rarer, but not unknown, were marriages between white men and black women.[7] Marriage, of course, bestowed a certain respectability on a black–white liaison which, if more informal, was widely denounced. Indeed in the eyes of many whites, one of the most troublesome aspects of black society (and the predominance of black males) was the unavoidable fact of inter-racial sexual activity and miscegenation. Yet what is surely most remarkable of all is the fact that liaisons between black and white were traditionally portrayed as *sexual* relations. Whenever discussion took place in print about black men and white women the argument was quickly reduced to its lowest sexual denominator; rarely were such liaisons described as others were, in which love, affection, respect or endearment might also be characteristic of the relationship. It was an assumption on the part of observers that black–white relations were, first and foremost, *sexual* relationships. And while it may seem appropriate to dismiss such commentary as merely prurient curiosity, it is too persistent and recurring a theme to ignore.

Curiosity about black–white sexuality was, even in the eighteenth century, of ancient lineage. More immediately, interest in black sexuality had been revived by the English explorations of West Africa from the sixteenth century and the creation of black, enslaved populations in the Americas. Faced by people whose kinship and marriage ties did not approximate to recognisable European models and among whom varying degrees of public nakedness were common, English travellers and writers began to speculate about the peculiarities of African morality and sexuality. The lascivious blacks – and the black male endowed with an unusually large phallus – rapidly established themselves among the more durable and pervasive of popular myths; myths which provided Shakespeare (and others) with rich material. Generations of English people – including those who had never seen a black person – came to share the belief in the enhanced sexuality of blacks.[8] It was, then, scarcely surprising that the predominantly male black population in mid and late eighteenth-century England found themselves the object of an increasing volume of sexual jibes and insults. So, too, were their consorts and friends; one observer denounced the 'strange partiality shewn for them by the lower orders of women'.[9] Edward Long, the Jamaican slave-owner who became the most acerbic of anti-black writers in the 1770s made precisely the same point: 'The lower class of women in England, are remarkably fond of the blacks, for reasons too brutal to mention; they would connect themselves with horses and asses, if the laws permitted them.'[10] In fact some of the more 'scandalous' liaisons between black and white were not with poor women but with wealthier, even aristocratic, ladies, none more daring and shocking than the Duchess of Queensbury's overt affection for her black servant Soubise. A shocked friend, visiting the Duchess in 1768 found her 'half-dressed and half-undressed. She was talking to her Black Boy.'[11]

Historical patterns can of course prove very misleading, but the common denunciation of black–white relations – and the discussion of such liaisons as merely sexual – has proved a remarkably resilient English response to black society over many centuries. In the late eighteenth century, in the British race riots of 1919 and in the more extreme denunciation of black immigration since 1945, black–white sexual relations – and their offspring – have been singled out for the most venomous and persistently reviled denunciation. And yet, if we consider the demographic nature of English black society in the late eighteenth century it is impossible to see how else friendly, loving or sexual relations could develop unless it was primarily with poor white women.

Not surprisingly, the offspring of these liaisons were denounced not merely as the physical reminders of 'scandalous' sexual improprieties but, perhaps more crucially, because of a number of prevailing racial myths. Throughout English colonies, in the Caribbean and North America, miscegenation was common place, particularly by the mid eighteenth century when the rise of black enslaved populations, the geographically isolated position of many white males and the ubiquity of black female servants made likely (and in some cases irresistible) the development of regular sexual relations between black and white. And wherever miscegenation was to be found, it was generally denounced by the same white class so responsible for it in the first place. Moreover it was, overwhelmingly, the consequence of liaisons between white men and black women; the reverse was rare, frowned upon and in some cases viewed with a dangerous hostility, more especially in the West Indies where white women were greatly outnumbered by white men. This was not simply a question of a double sexual standard so much as a complex threat, as perceived by white males, which corroded their social and economic dominance. But the very existence of black–white liaisons had wider, philosophical consequences: for white males to sleep or live with black women who by law and economic usage occupied the status of property, was to indulge in a basic contradiction. How could black women – the object of so much passion, lust, love and endearment on the part of white men – be *things*? Of course it could be argued that even within such liaisons we are merely witnessing another form of brute white power; of the extension of white dominion over black even in their beds.[12] Yet there is ample evidence – notably in the form of affectionate and considerate testamentary bequests in masters' wills for their black concubines and offspring – that such liaisons could also be as caring as any other.

Miscegenation clearly occupied a different social and political role in colonial society than in England where, because of the small numbers involved, it was more an object of, at best, curiosity, at worst plantocratic denunciation. The most strident of anti-black commentators were those with West Indian interests and plantocratic support. It is surely ironic that scribes writing for the planters – men more especially responsible for miscegenation in the colonies – took great exception to miscegenation in England. To outlaw it would be to 'preserve the race of Britain from stain and contamination'.[13] Indeed the planters and their friends had the affrontery to express the hope that miscegenation would be banned: that Parliament 'will provide such remedies as may be adequate to the occasion (by exporting blacks) . . . and save the natural beauty of Britain from the Morisco tint'.[14] Edward Long expressed the point more maliciously than most:

> In the course of a few generations more, the English blood will become so contaminated with this mixture, and from the chances, the ups and downs of life, this alloy may spread so extensively, as even to reach the middle, and then the higher order of the people, till the whole nation resembles the Portuguese and Moriscos in complexion of skin and business of mind.[15]

Miscegenation in England – for entirely demographic reasons – took the form of the most despised liaison in the West Indies; sex between black men and white women. Clearly, what horrified planters in their mother country was the flagrant – and even 'normal' – flourishing of liaisons which flouted one of the most precious of colonial taboos. Blacks in England were actively turning the planters' world upside down; running away from their owners, securing legal support for their freedom, working and flourishing independent of their former owners and indulging in affectionate or merely sexual liaisons with white women. Each of these features of black society in England was corrosive to the system of black chattel slavery as it had evolved in the New World. And, of course, they were also destructive of the limited version of slavery which had grown in England itself.

Equally unusual – at least in the eyes of slave-owners from the Caribbean – was the marriage of blacks. In the Caribbean islands slave marriages were, in general, not allowed; part of that all-embracing limitation on slaves' social lives, particularly the denial of access to Christianity. From the early days through to the end of British slavery, Christianity struggled to make inroads among the slaves, largely because of the hostility of planters who viewed it as the solvent of slavery itself. In 1680 for example certain 'Gentlemen of Barbados' declared 'that the conversion of their slaves to Christianity would not only destroy their property but endanger the island, insomuch as converted slaves grow more perverse and intractable than others, and hence of less value for labour or sale'.[16] Until the late eighteenth century, however, British planters had few problems since British churches made only feeble attempts to convert the slaves. As late as 1788 the Barbados slave system, described to Parliament, had no place for religion among the slaves: 'I do not know that there is any religious ceremony in the Marriage of Negro slaves in Barbados. There is no Law respecting it.'[17] Needless to say there was a fully developed social structure within the slave quarters; informal marriage was the norm and not, as many historians have previously claimed, the exception.[18] But the relationships were confirmed by usage and custom (and the slaves' own rituals) rather than the formal religious trappings recognised by whites. The obduracy of the planters, in conjunction with the initial lethargy of the churches (until the Nonconformists emerged in the late eighteenth century), effectively denied the slaves access to Christianity.

The situation was quite the reverse in England where local blacks were commonly converted to Christianity. In the early days of black settlement, black Christians were unusual. The Church of Christ in Bristol had one such: 'namely a blackamoor maid, named Frances a servant to one that lived upon the back in Bristol, which thing is somewhat rare in our days and nation, to have an Ethiopian, or blackamoor to be truly convinced of sin, and of their lost state without the Redeemer, and to be truly converted to the Lord Jesus'.[19]

While slaves undoubtedly believed that baptism conferred freedom, there is abundant evidence that slavery continued after conversion and baptism. John Caesar, baptised in London in 1717 'served as a slave to John and Benjamin Ward of Whitechapel though baptised into the Church of England'.[20] Another slave, baptised in Berkshire in 1769, was 'a Negro boy belonging to ye Earl of Kerry'.[21] Despite such evidence, blacks continued to seek baptism as the most likely route to freedom in England.[22]

Slave owners (other than emigré planters) were, in many cases, anxious to baptise their slaves. Black favourites were often rewarded for their faithful service by encouragement to join their owners' church. Indeed the available fragmentary baptismal evidence helps to throw additional light on England's black population. The very great majority of converted blacks were, for instance, male; a clear reflection of the sexual imbalance within the black population so often commented upon by observers. Furthermore, blacks – the great bulk of whom were 'immigrants' – were baptised at all ages and not, as was usual with whites, in infancy. Those born in England, however, tended to follow the local pattern and to be baptised as babies. In the 1730s and 1740s Mario Sambo, a black from Earls Colne near Colchester, had her three children baptised in the local church.[23] More common, however, was the baptism of young black servant boys. William Diego, baptised in Sunninghill, Berkshire, in 1755 was four-and-a-half. Jack London baptised in Norham in 1763 was eight years old, as was Timothy, the Duke of Richmond's black boy, baptised in 1728.[24] Prince Crofton was baptised at 12; John Weavan and Charles Hector were ten.[25] Olaudah Equiano, perhaps the most famous black in London in the 1780s was 14 when baptised at St Margaret's, Westminster. Equally common, however, were adult baptisms. In 1760, for example, at Warfield, Berkshire, 'three adult Negroes [were] converted to Christianity and baptised'.[26] William Williams was 23 when baptised in Devon; George Pompey was 20, while John August, 'an American black' was relatively old at 32 when baptised in Kent.[27] Between 1759 and 1764, 12 blacks were baptised in Lancaster parish church. Of these only one was female and all were adults.[28]

The timing of the black's baptism depended on a variety of factors; the rank and position of the parent, the time spent in England and, most important of all, the relationship with the white master or mistress. Without the formal approval of the master, English clerics were unwilling to baptise blacks. Ministers in Yorkshire for example sought the prior permission of their Archbishop. One such Yorkshire slave, Beswick, 'a Youth of no learning, and but of slender capacity', was the only regular parishioner to remain unbaptised, although both local ministers had 'instructed him to be baptised, if your Grace shall so order it'.[29] These hesitations felt by ministers about black baptisms give some indication of the social and political problems attendant on the emergence of black Christianity. In its turn this is a clear reminder of the complications which black slavery intruded into English life. The ramifications of black slavery spread well beyond the difficult relations between master and slave, and well beyond the English courts.

Inevitably a master or mistress exerted great influence over the choice of a particular religious persuasion adopted by the black. Parish records, and the headstones of blacks' graves in parish churchyards reflect, for example, black adherence to the Church of England. (Indeed one black was ordained into the Church of England in 1765.)[30] But this in its turn may tell us more about the religious inclinations of the white master class (the planters, colonial and military officials, gentry and nobles) who owned black menials in England and who effectively dictated their religious lives, than it does about black religion. John Wesley, for example, was able personally to convert blacks simply by knowing their masters. Visiting a house in Wandsworth, Wesley noted 'Two Negro servants . . . and a mulatto appear to be much awakened.' Within the year, Wesley had returned and 'baptised two negroes belonging to Mr Gilbert . . . one of these is deeply convinced of sin; the other rejoiced in God her saviour and is the first African Christian I have known'.[31] In fact 'African Christians' were more common than Wesley assumed, for trading companies and missionaries had long been active in bringing Africans to England for education and conversion. In 1754 three 'fine negro boys' were brought to London by the Society for Propagation of the Gospel. Within seven weeks 'one of them could say the Lord's Prayer and the Apostle Creed and the others answered well'. By 1789 it was estimated that 50 boys and 28 girls from the Sierra Leone region alone were being educated in London, Liverpool and Lancaster.[32]

As the English trading presence developed in the eighteenth century into fairly permanent settlements, African leaders were encouraged to send their sons to England for education. In part this was to assist British interests by having educated African middlemen in the trading areas but it was also partly due to that missionary zeal which, though in its infancy in the early eighteenth century, was already focussing on the 'heathenism' and idolatory of blacks. Transient black sailors were often converted by ministers living in dockside communities.[33] A chief from Sierra Leone sent his son to an English school and he 'learned in the space of a year and a half, to read fluently, and to write a letter in English without much difficulty'.[34] Another African, Philip Quaque, educated in England, later became a chaplain on the Gold Coast in his turn sending his children to school in England 'in order to secure their tender minds from receiving the bad impressions of the country, the vile customs and practices and above all, the losing of their mother's vile tongue'.[35] It would be hard to find a better illustration of the deliberate deracination of an African in the interests of the British. Yet it is also important to recall that planters in the Caribbean, faced by hundreds of thousands of black slaves, resolutely refused to educate or convert their slaves. It was one thing to have polite and educated black servants in England, or middlemen in Africa, but quite another to expose armies of praedial labour to the unpredictable influence of the printed word, or biblical message.

The conversion and baptism of blacks involved much more than the mere adoption of an alien religion (as the resistant colonial planters fully realised). At a simple level, Christianisation generally led to the giving or confirmation of new names. As part of the process of deracination and de-Africanisation in the slave colonies, planters gave their slaves a single name; many blacks inevitably arrived in England with their slave names. The classical, and sometimes absurd, slave names common in the West Indies could be found among English blacks; Pompey, Cato, Starling, Little Ephraim, Othello, Robinsoe Crusoe, and even Pan Ran Ratto Skinner. Baptism sometimes confirmed these names; sometimes however it was the occasion for the replacement of what were regarded as unmanageable names by anglicised names. When African names were retained, English masters usually added a new Christian name. By and large, however, baptism confirmed the blacks' adopted names, for some had already taken as their own name the name of their master or of their locality.[36]

Even more difficult to assess than the fragmentary details of black baptism, is the evidence about black marriages. Any discussion of marriage or mating patterns in the black community has to be set in its demographic context, for most blacks arrived in England accustomed to utterly different

societies in West Africa and the Americas. It is, for example
difficult to assess the degree and extent of African survivals in
marriage patterns among blacks of diverse tribal and Creole
backgrounds who now found themselves pitched into yet another
social environment in England. Moreover since most blacks –
particularly free blacks – were desperately poor it is likely that,
like many poor whites around them, formal marriage was an
institution to which they did not even aspire.

By the late eighteenth century, when the black population
had become an object of political controversy, the great majority
of blacks were free, though their freedom had been secured not
by legal redress, but rather by the simple (and contagious)
expedient of running away. But those who fled their bondage,
invariably sought refuge in the safety of the capital, poor
warrens and communities. Such secure redoubts were relatively
safe from the scrutiny and searches of propertied white society.
But, for the same reason, poor blacks were unlikely to have
access to formal or organised religion. They were, however, in
contact with other blacks who stayed on as servants loyal to
their employers and devout to their new faith. Devout blacks
often took great pains to press their faith on their fellow blacks,
few more incessantly than Ignatius Sancho, whose letters
published posthumously in 1782 reveal a remarkable missionary
zeal; he constantly urged his own godliness on others: 'let me,
as your true friend, recommend seriously to you to make
yourself acquainted with your Bible. Believe me, the more you
study the word of God, your peace and happiness will increase
the more with it'.[37] Equiano, who inherited Sancho's public
prominence was equally devout. Baptised in 1758, Equiano had
to wait a further seven years for his freedom.[38] Throughout a
series of personal crises Equiano, like Sancho, found great
comfort in his Bible. 'Now the Bible was my only companion
and comfort', he wrote, 'I prized it much, with many thanks to
God that I could read it for myself and was not left to be tossed
about or led by man's devices and notions.'[39] Here Equiano
touched upon a crucial point. Full access to the Bible necessarily
involved a degree of literacy which, for obvious reasons, planters
were unwilling even to contemplate in the colonies. It was
inevitable, given the nature of late eighteenth-century black
society in England (characterised by black servants and a core
of devout and prominent spokesmen), that literacy would be

common, if not exactly widespread. In England, literacy and religion were positively encouraged by numerous slave owners and employers; in the slave islands both social qualities were fiercely resisted, as long as slavery existed, as unknown and dangerous agents helping to weaken the planters' grip.

When, in the 1780s, the abolitionist campaign against the slave trade was launched, the publications of contemporary black writers provided an unusual and particularly influential argument; black voices speaking out against the inhumanities of slavery. Equiano was, without doubt, the most prominent black spokesman but his friend, Ottobah Cugoano, played his part, through his book *Thoughts and Sentiments on the Evils and Wicked Traffic of Human Species*, (which was substantially revised and rewritten by Equiano). Cugoano was keen to convert his fellow blacks, proposing in 1791 to open a school in London; 'for all such of his Complexion as are desirous to being acquainted with the knowledge of the Christian Religion and the Laws of Civilisation'. His school would pass on his religion to his fellow blacks; 'to have them educated in the Duties and Knowledge of that Religion which all good Christian People enjoy'.[40] Like Equiano, Cugoano was active in local black politics; both in the campaign against the slave trade and in the bitter arguments about the ill-fated Sierra Leone scheme. If planters wished to see proof of their latent fear that black religion and literacy would encourage dissatisfaction in the black community, they had only to look at London's black community and its spokesmen in the 1780s to see confirmation of their worst fears. Indeed when nonconformity made its early and seminal impact among West Indian slaves a very similar sequence of events unfolded. Black Nonconformists led the way in revitalising black politics, providing the leadership, organisation and biblical imagery, all of which became a potent solvent of black bondage. It was no accident that the slave revolts of 1819, 1823 and 1831 were associated at a number of levels with black christianity.[41] It was as if the planters' old nightmares had come to living fruition; articulate, literate and charismatic black christians led the assault against the (already crumbling) ediface of bondage.

It would be wrong, however, to imagine that there was a simple and automatic equation at work; that conversion and/or literacy necessarily created a radical black. Equiano, for instance, notwithstanding his important political activities, espoused a religion with powerful overtones of other-wordliness. In many respects, Equiano saw his faith as an escape from the trials and tribulations of black life in a white world. He frequently retreated into the security of his faith, surrendering earthly efforts in the sure knowledge that all would turn out well in the hereafter. In one instance, unable to convince his captors of the evils of their actions, Equiano 'told them that as I could not get any right among men here I hoped I should hereafter in Heaven'.[42] He took his punishments stoically. 'I considered that trials and disappointments are sometimes for our good, and thought that God might perhaps have permitted this in order to teach me wisdom and resignation.'[43] Such an open confession that at least one prominent black sublimated earthly cares in the healing balm of religion did nothing to ease the worries of planters. There could, after all, be no guarantee that black christianity would not upset the precarious equilibrium in the slave islands. In England, of course, the consequences of black Christianity and literacy could only be marginal.

Black religion in England has to be studied in the context of the broader debate about slavery and the slave trade, for religious objections to black slavery proved one of the most ubiquitous and powerful attacks on the planters and slave-traders. Again, it is an extremely complex problem which continues to excite fierce historical argument. It is possible however to assert a number of basic points. First, in an English society increasingly influenced by the wider ramifications of the evangelical revival, the fact that slaves were denied access to christianity was viewed by ever more English people as an intolerable scandal. Edmund Burke, for example, in drafting his reforming 'Sketch of a Negro Code' (1792) was insistent that the right to religious freedom was a fundamental social right to be enjoyed by slaves in the Caribbean.[44] Secondly those churches active among the slaves were obstructed by the planters; a fact which caused growing offence in England. Thirdly, English blacks, notably Sancho, Equiano and Cugoano, provided literary evidence of the virtues to be seen among black Christians. Indeed their books were part of the abolitionist case, trying to convince the English people that the black was indeed a man and a brother. The piety, loyalty and steadfastness of these men – to their religion and their role in English life – was thus important political ammunition in the mounting political debate about black slavery within the British empire. As with the existence of black slavery itself, the English first encountered black christianity, not in the abstract (as a distant, colonial issue) but as an immediate, local English institution and problem. Indeed the problems – and potentials – of black life were to be seen not only in the distant colonies, but in microscopic, detailed form, in England itself.

By the late eighteenth century, growing numbers of English people began to give serious consideration to the task of converting blacks to Christianity, both in England and the colonies. There emerged a distinct species of faith; simple, direct, other-wordly and fashioned in the belief that the 'capacity of a Negro is so mean, and the things he learns so very few and of so ordinary a sort'.[45] The outcome was a simplified Christianity, 'better adapted to their capacities and conditions' and much of the religious material written specifically for blacks was obviously based on this principle. 'The better you grow yourself, and the more Negroes you teach their daily duty to God the more happy you will be when you die.'[46] Instructions for the religious education of blacks so often centred on producing a peaceable temperament; 'may god keep you in this good disposition, and give you a teachable temper'. Hope lay in the future; 'This is not the world for which you were chiefly made; nor must you look for any true and lasting happiness here.' The black was expected to greet the day with a suitably docile prayer; 'O, merciful father, grant that I may perform my duty this day faithfully and cheerfully; and that I may never murmur, be uneasy or impatient under any of the troubles of this life.'[47] This prayer was to be followed by the hymn:

> Awake my soul and with the sun
> Thy daily stage of duty run
> Shake off dull sloth and early rise
> To pay thy morning sacrifice.[48]

It was widely felt that hymns provided a perfect way of encouraging black Christianity, for music was generally regarded as a distinctively black quality; 'The Negroes in general have an ear for music, and might without too much trouble be taught to sing hymns.'[49] Wesley, too, appreciated the opportunities afforded by black musicality; 'I cannot but observe that the Negroes above all of the human species I ever knew have the nicest ear for music. They have a kind of ecstatic delight in psalmody.'[50] Equiano seemed to confirm this for his English readers; 'We are almost a nation of dancers, musicians and poets. Thus every great event . . . is celebrated in public dances which are accompanied with songs and music suited to the occasion.'[51] This belief in innate black musicality was derived largely from the perceptions of travellers and slave owners about the role of music within African and American black societies. Although it was, on the one hand distrusted and even banned by slave owners – drumming in particular was feared as a means of slaves communicating subversively – black musicality was also encouraged. In Europe blacks were taught to play contemporary instruments and to provide entertainment while simultaneously offering a striking spectacle. It was also seen as a means of encouraging black Christianity.

Evidence about eighteenth-century black Christians can be seen readily, throughout the country, on the decaying headstones in English graveyards. At the point of death we are provided with a brief guide to an otherwise anonymous life. Rasselas Belfield was one such black. He died near Windermere in 1822 at the age of 32, leaving his sole yet ellusive record on the headstone.

> A slave by birth, I left my native land.
> And found my freedom on Britannia's Strand.
> Blest Isle! Thou Glory of the Wise and Free,
> Thy Touch alone unbinds the Chains of Slavery.[52]

A century earlier the mortal remains of another African had been laid to rest in the parish churchyard of Henbury near Bristol.

> Here Lieth the body of Scipio Africanus, Negro Servant to ye Right Honourable Charles William Earl of Suffolk and Bradon who died on Ye 21 December 1720 Aged 18 years. I who was Born a PAGAN and a SLAVE NOW sweetly sleep a CHRISTIAN in my Grave.

In the churchyard of the village of Elvington near York lies buried the remains of another black servant, Fisher Murray.

A faithful black servant who came from Madeira with Thomas Cheap esq., who was Consul there and after living 60 years in the family died 18th December 1821

Even more remarkable is the gravestone known as 'Sambo's grave' to be found at Sunderland Point near Lancaster.

Here lies poor Sambo A faithful Negro
Who Attending his *Master* from the *West Indies*
Died on his Arrival at Sunderland

Full sixty years the angry Winter's Wave
Has thundering dashed this bleak and barren Shore
Since SAMBO's Head laid in this lone GRAVE
Lies still and ne'er will hear their turmoil more

Full many a Sandbird chirps upon the Sod
And many a Moonlight Elfin round him trips
Full many a Summer's Sunbeam warms the Clod
And many a teeming Cloud upon him drips

But still he sleeps – till the awakening Sounds
of the Archangel's Trump new life impart
Then the GREAT JUDGE His Approbation founds
Not on Man's COLOUR but his – WORTH OF HEART

Such traces of forgotten blacks stand as monuments, across the country, to the devotion of some eighteenth-century blacks to their masters' religion. A decent church burial, attended by a mourning family, was clearly a fitting reward for a lifetime's service. It would be tempting to see black Christianity in England as a process of social consolation; deflecting blacks from their immediate and daily problems towards expectactions of a better life in the hereafter. While many seem to have taken that option afforded by Christianity, there were others for whom Christianity provided a social and political awakening. Indeed, throughout the slave islands the rapid diffusion of Christianity – notably nonconformity – by the late eighteenth century had a dramatically disruptive and radicalising effect among the slaves. Such consequences were, clearly, quite impossible among blacks in England; a small black minority in a white society. None the less, there were numerous examples of Christian blacks who openly challenged the lot and the sufferings of themselves and their fellow blacks. However pious Sancho and Equiano, they were also men who had strong views about the oppression of blacks by whites. Indeed there is a case to be made that their respectable piety *strengthened* their social and political utterances. Thus the impact of Christianity among English blacks defies a simple – or single – explanation.

As the black population grew in size – and as more of them were converted – freedom and not slavery came to characterise black society. Blacks simply ran away from their English owners, preferring the uncertainty and hardship of life in the capital's poor quarters to the life of an enslaved domestic. Poor, free blacks formed the core of the metropolitan black community which, in time, lured more and more slaves to its ranks. Indeed, slave-owners bitterly complained of the seduction of slaves to freedom. Arriving in England, slaves found themselves confronted by

> The ideas of liberty, the charms of novelty, and an ignorance of the country they had got to, where they found themselves upon a perfect equality, at least, with the inferior white people, could not fail of having pernicious effects upon their minds, and great numbers ran away from their masters.[53]

Indeed English newspapers began to carry more advertisements for slave runaways than slave sales. Slave runaways were of course a perpetual worry in the slave islands but the problem in England was of an entirely different order. Throughout the seventeenth and eighteenth centuries English slaves absconded. But from the 1760s the process accelerated, not merely because of the increase in the black population, but because of the convergence of social forces already mentioned. Black Christianity, the activities of free blacks, the mounting legal campaign for black freedom – and the assistance of white sympathisers – cumulatively made slave-holding increasingly difficult in late eighteenth-century England. Thus the English black community – though conceived and developed by slavery –

was becoming progressively freer. But it was a precarious freedom, secured by the difficult and risky act of physical escape and maintained only by dint of permanent vigilence and co-operation among blacks against the ubiquitous threat of re-enslavement and transportation back to the slave islands. In fact it was precisely this threat – and its legal complexities – which dominated the late eighteenth-century slave cases, and which ultimately provided blacks and their white friends with legal redress.

Black freedom had its undoubted limitations, for even free blacks faced the dangers of arbitrary harassment and kidnapping. For every case we know of where black and white activists were able to stop kidnapped blacks being transported back to the slave islands, how many more – unknown, unrecorded and lamented – were successfully re-enslaved? In 1794 *The Times* recorded the following incident: 'of the wife of a gentleman at Sheerness who had eloped with a black servant. They were pursued to the Nag's Head in the Borough on Sunday where *Blackey* fired a shot at his pursuers, for which he was taken and committed'. The story continued the following day: 'the husband took her three children, and all the property he found on the coach, desired his wife to go where she pleased (after she said she'd live with no man but the Black) and *Mungo* was taken by a press gang, and put on board the tender'.[54]

Understandably, English blacks, especially in London, gathered together from a need for collective security, to care for their own collective interests, to pursue an independent social life and to safeguard the well-being of new black arrivals cast adrift in the alien world of London. Blacks organised their own – exclusive – social events; they gathered together in private houses; they attended the slave cases in large numbers; they raised money for blacks in distress and they cultivated important political ties with prominent white sympathisers and abolitionists. Through the good offices of their leaders – notably Equiano and Cugoano – the black community conveyed crucial information about slavery and the slave trade to the pioneer abolitionists. Indeed, the first news of the infamous *Zong* case came from the black community, and was passed on to Granville Sharp, who promptly made effective political capital and public notoriety from the case.[55]

The problems of the English blacks did not end with the

removal of the threatening and inescapable shadow of slavery and re-enslavement. Black freedom was characterised by the burdens of poverty in a hostile and, generally, alien environment. But it is surely some measure of the black commitment to securing freedom in England that it was not deflected by the obvious and considerable physical and material hardships of life in London's poorest communities. Indeed blacks became an inescapable feature of late eighteenth-century London life because so many of them were poor: beggars, crossing-sweepers and the generally-wretched whose condition raised disturbing questions about the broader British relationship with black humanity.

The 'Black Poor' became a distinct social problem, in the years after the American War of Independence (the numbers of poor blacks swelled by ex-slaves fleeing the American conflict), which demanded a political solution. Black vagrancy and black crime – however smallscale and petty – provided evidence of the broader problems endured by large numbers of English blacks and which culminated in the severe winter of 1786. The abject condition of large numbers of the black poor prompted the formation of a 'Committee for the Relief of the Black Poor'. There was a generous financial response to this appeal, but the task of feeding and relieving black poverty was very taxing. The Committee, looking around for a more permanent solution to black poverty, was soon transmuted into an organisation actively promoting the repatriation of English blacks: 'to furnish the means of sending abroad these miserable objects, to such places as may put them in a condition of getting their bread in freedom and comfort'.[56]

In the spring of 1786 the Committee considered a proposal – submitted by an explorer Henry Smeathman – to repatriate the poor blacks to Sierra Leone. With government support and money this ill-fated scheme proceeded, through that year – but against the advice of prominent London blacks – to lure blacks for the scheme; 500 initially agreed to go. Many more simply refused to countenance the idea of returning to the area which continued to be dominated by slave traders.[57] To Press denunciation of those blacks who refused to volunteer, efforts were made to round up the black poor and oblige them to join the Royal Navy ships waiting to transport them back to Africa. The expedition itself was characterised by political confusion and local graft; in the end only 441 blacks sailed for Africa and the expedition proved disastrous. By September 1787 only 268 survivors remained alive in Sierra Leone. Black spokesmen in London, notably Cugoano and Equiano had been vindicated for, from the first they had objected to the purpose and management of the scheme. In the long term, the foundations were laid for the subsequent development of Sierra Leone, but the immediate result was disaster for the small band of pioneers and it reinforced distrust and cynicism among blacks in London towards official efforts at relief.[58]

The numbers of blacks involved were relatively small (though this is not to diminish the sufferings of those involved). This may be explained by a number of possibilities. First, the overall numbers of black poor may have been greatly exaggerated; most commentators, after all, had a partial political case to make and clearly had an interest in exaggerating the numbers of poor blacks in London. Secondly, the scheme may have been unattractive – for a variety of compelling reasons – to large numbers of blacks. Finally, the leaders of the black community may well have discouraged their fellows from joining – again from a series of compelling motives. It is also important to stress that the coverage given to the episode by the London Press was – with a few notable exceptions – conducted in critical and derogatory terms. The blacks were portrayed as a problem (with no explanation of the origins of their woes); they were dismissed as unco-operative and assailed by local and national authorities in order to dragoon them into leaving London. Moreover their leaders and spokesmen were similarly denounced as subversive. By the time the ill-fated expedition sailed, the episode had become the source of a revived and virulent antipathy towards blacks in England. Furthermore black society had come to be seen as one dominated by beggars and the poor.

Naturally enough, black society was much more occupationally varied than the discussion surrounding the Sierra Leone scheme might lead us to believe. In fact blacks were to be found in an unusually diverse and varied range of jobs and occupations. Black musicians were a common sight, from the highest to the lowest of levels (as indeed had been the case in England since the sixteenth century). Perhaps the most famous – on the streets and the stage – was Billy Waters, the one-legged fiddler who appeared in a host of contemporary cartoons and was popularly known as 'king of the beggars'. His funeral, in 1823, was followed by an extraordinary procession of admirers and fellow performers through the streets of London. At the other extreme was George Frederick Polgreen Bridgetower, friend of Beethoven and accomplished violinist whose English concerts from the 1780s through to about 1820 were invariably enthusiastically received. But by the time he died, in London in 1860, he was poor and almost forgotten.[59]

There were other blacks who gained a degree of contemporary notoriety, often because of their work. Molineaux and Richmond, two of England's most prominent boxers, were black, both born in America. Suartjie Baartman, the 'Hottentot Venus' was displayed, naked, in early nineteenth-century London to expose her peculiar physical characteristics. Some thought the display 'contrary to every principle of morality and good order'.[60] Less exotic, but no less important for asserting the variety of black society, is the evidence of black actors, teachers, artisans, gardeners, nurses, sailors; indeed the whole span of occupations and skills, which ranged from the beasts of burden to the most professional and highly trained of occupations. It may well be true that the English came face to face with blacks more often as domestics or as mendicants in London; but there were, without doubt, large numbers of English people who saw, worked or had dealings with blacks in a great variety of occupations. It was obvious and irrefutable to large numbers of people that blacks were not necessarily suited and equipped uniquely for brute, physical occupations, an image assiduously disseminated for more than a century by the slave lobbies. Indeed it was remarkable just how varied were the daily toils and the long-term accomplishments of a people supposed to be consigned to a lifetime's physical toil for their white betters.

Clearly, black society in England was not 'natural'; it had grown not from natural increase, traditional migrations or immigrations, but from forced shipment and bondage as an international movement of black peoples. Indeed the origins and peculiarities of black society made it quite impossible that the economic and occupational structure of black life in England could even vaguely approximate the traditional or ideal models to which English people were accustomed. Black society in England was, like slavery, a mutation of a distant colonial phenomenon (itself of course bizarre and distinctive). But the blacks cast adrift in England had to make their way in life as best they could. Many, if not most, had already endured the traumas of enslavement and transportation; many had experienced the turmoil of the American War. Others had suffered the privations and suffering of praedial slavery in the West Indian or American colonies. Some blacks had suffered all these difficulties and more. Moreover it is worth stressing that all these sufferings had taken place *before* arrival in England, a fact which can be interpreted in a number of conflicting ways. It is possible for instance to argue that, after earlier troubles, even the most miserable of conditions in England formed an improvement, though this case is undermined by the response of the wretched volunteers to remigrate to Sierra Leone. But it is also possible that, for most blacks in late eighteenth-century England, life was merely a continuation, in a colder clime, of the problems blacks faced in the New World. It would, however, be wrong to equate too closely black slavery in England with that in, say, Jamaica or Virginia. Equally, and as we have seen, England (unconsciously) offered blacks the opportunity of securing their own self-improvement and well-being in a way unthinkable in the slave colonies. Ultimately however what made life in England better for contemporary blacks was their own individual and collective efforts. True, many were blessed with the material and domestic comforts of working as a servant for a friendly or considerate employer; but it was the flight to freedom, within London, the succour and comfort of fellow blacks and the security afforded by collective and co-operative endeavours which, above all else, helped improve the lot of England's blacks. Even then, they could rarely escape the fear of detection and harassment. As long as the slave empire flourished, as long as slave trading was tolerated and as long as slave-traders and owners lived and operated in England, blacks would face unremitting hostility and danger. And this was quite in addition to whatever antagonism they might encounter of a more personal (though not endangering) kind. Not until the slave trade and slavery were ended (1807 and 1833 respectively) would blacks in England be as free and safe as their white neighbours. We shall see, however, that even this security was to be partially offset by the emergence of new forms of racial antagonism. In the late eighteenth century,

however, the difficulties of blacks in England were not merely
physical. They were confronted by a chorus of abuse – much of
it racial – from a variety of men who disliked the black presence
in England.

4 Recurring Themes: Black Images in White Culture

From the mid eighteenth century until the ending of British slavery in the 1830s there was a broad literary and political debate about black society and black individuals. Much of that debate centred on specific issues about black freedom and slavery. But it is also true that the arguments were suffused with images of black life which were, at once, traditional and also unrealistic. Despite the presence of a significant black minority in England, and despite the presence of prominent black individuals in the abolition campaign, much of the debate about black life was concerned not with the physical and undeniable realities, but with stereotypical images. British responses to the black community were – inevitably perhaps – varied and often contradictory but it seems clear that British images of black life derived not so much from contact with the local community or individuals, but from much more indirect influences. Indeed by the mid-eighteenth century both black and white communities had inherited an ancient tradition of mutual observation and commentary; but much of it was mythical.

In the years before the establishment of maritime links with West Africa, Europeans had been more familiar with the mythology rather than the reality of black Africans. From classical authors, Europeans had acquired ideas about black humanity which, however bizarre and weird they may now seem, were none the less influential and pervasive. Of course, it is true that accounts of Africa – from classical or, later, from Renaissance sources – were not concerned uniquely with the humanity of the region; there was a great curiosity about the geography, the animal life and the natural wonders of black Africa. But white Europeans reserved their greatest curiosity for black Africans themselves. Naturally enough, it is impossible to know, in preliterate European societies, how widely such views were disseminated – to say nothing of whether the more extravagant claims about Africans were actually believed. None the less, it is clear that among the educated élite there were established marked, caricatured images of black life which owed little at all to the realities of African life.

Classical authors began the tradition. Herodotus described how Africans 'screech like bats' and how the whole of Africa was inhabited with people with dogs heads 'and those with no heads have eyes in their chests'. The catalogue of bizarre features alleged of Africans continued; sexual habits, social customs, family organisations and social life – all and more were reduced to a literature of fantastic grossness and repulsion. A third-century geographer, Solinus, wrote of the Africans' polygamy and of their gross physical appearance. Solinus proved influential among later writers who used his work as a source for information in Africa. It was thus hardly surprising that the most extraordinary claims about Africans were regularly repeated in European commentaries. Rabelais, for example, claimed that 'Africa always produces new and monstrous things.'[1] It is also true that similar unusual claims were made for 'exotic' peoples from other parts of the non-European world, but these images of black life were to prove especially important when Africa began to afford marauding Europeans a plentiful supply of slaves for the settlements in the New World colonies.[2] Indeed, by the time Europeans made their first effective contacts with black Africa, the inhabitants of the region had already been allowed a distinctive role in the European mind.

In the millennium between the collapse of classical Rome and the decline of European serfdom, small numbers of Africans managed to find their way to northern Europe. As soldiers, lovers, wives, court officials – or merely as eye-catching (because exotic) curiosities – black Africans made regular appearances, especially in the upper reaches of European life. A French aristocrat had a black Sudanese wife in the thirteenth century; later, Francis I had a black mistress. There were a number of black Africans in the Scottish court in the early sixteenth century, one of whom was celebrated in Dunbar's poem 'Ane Black Moir'.[3] In England, Africans were a common sight at the courts of the late Tudor monarchs, though by that time the Iberian links with black Africa were well established and

Africans were becoming a more regular sight in the major ports of Europe. Indeed by the late sixteenth century the black had become a common object both in courtly entertainment and, more crucially perhaps, had become a stereotype in English literature. In Elizabethan and Jacobean drama, for example, black characters were commonplace and, with few exceptions, they were normally portrayed as villains, both lascivious and untrustworthy.[4] *Othello* was a striking exception to this literary rule, but even in that case Shakespeare reflected a range of contemporary antagonisms towards the black. *Othello* was cast in a particular sexual role: 'an old black ram is tupping your white ewe', 'your daughter and the Moore are now making the beast with two backs'. This is just the most obvious and best-known example of contemporary British perceptions of black sexuality. Although it is likely that there was a multitude of attitudes towards black sexuality, it was widely believed that the black was a particularly sexual being. Indeed from a very early date British writers commonly described the black as characterised by lust; a man driven by powerful sexual urges, possessed of an unusually large phallus and – for both these reasons – especially attractive to certain white women. Shakespeare, of course, did not invent these popular beliefs; but he used them – and played upon them – throughout *Othello*. For the purposes of this study, however, it is worth recording that, from the sixteenth to the late twentieth centuries, discussion about black life has often resolved itself into an assertion – or assumption – about the distinctive and potent nature of black sexuality.[5] Normally, the discussion concerned itself with the black male and the white female. As we have seen, in Britain it is clear why this might be the case, if only for demographic reasons. But the issue transcended the particularities of population, for it had entered the realms of widespread and unquestioned mythology and relied for its strength, from one generation to another, not on hard data or provable evidence, but on the more indefinable but none the less potent force of oral tradition and popular cultural acceptance. People came to believe that blacks were lascivious, and this was a belief which recurred, from one generation to another, throughout the wide literary debate about black life from the sixteenth century onwards.

European explorers confronting black Africans from the

fifteenth century onwards, took some of these beliefs with them. But they also found confirmation of their views in a number of salient features of African life. African nakedness, 'savagery', polygamy and, to European eyes, an incomprehensible structure of family and kinship ties all, among other things, helped confirm the traditional images Europeans held of black community. The human and social reality of black Africa served not to dispel the more traditional beliefs, but rather to confirm and even to exaggerate them. In a series of notable accounts, published in collected form by Richard Hakluyt – and reissued many times since – English voyagers described their initial impressions of Africa and Africans. To modern eyes, the most striking impression is the pure fantasy of much of their accounts. It is true that travellers were often taken aback by the remarkable physical features of Africa and its inhabitants, and their accounts register that astonishment and amazement. But their descriptions record, in elaborate and exaggerated form, a number of the existing popular myths about black life, but now apparently given the added credibility of eye-witness confirmation.

The early English voyages to black Africa, by Thomas Windham (1553) and John Lok (1554–5) were described in the most colourful and inventive terms. In Africa, it was claimed, there lived people 'which we nowe caule Moores, Moorans, or Negroes, a people of beastly lynyage, without a god, law, religion or common wealth, and so scorched and vexed with the heate of the soone, that in many places they curse it when it ryseth'.[6] From the first, Englishmen assumed that Africans were bereft of those personal and collective virtues which were thought to be the hallmark of a civilised society. It is true, of course, that many other exotic peoples fell into the same category – indigenous people in North America for example – but the savagery and heathenism of the African was of a different order. Two factors above all else rendered African 'savagery' qualitatively different; first, the Africans were black – a colour possessed of remarkably potent cultural values to the English in the sixteenth and seventeenth centuries and, secondly, Africans were already being consigned to the status of chattel and to a lifetime's bondage, as black slaves to their Iberian conquerors and masters. It was a simple matter for Englishmen to follow the Iberian example and to treat and regard the black

African as a potential slave and thing. And it took no leap of the imagination to view the Africans' blackness as proof and confirmation of the wickedness, sinfulness and baseness alleged to be the natural qualities of black humans. To the English the colours black and white expressed the sharpest of contrasting cultural values and implications.[7] Cleanliness and dirtiness; virtue and sin; chastity and carnality; beauty and ugliness were all commonly expressed through the words – and the colours – white and black. At a time when the English clung to values of beauty and virtue expressed through concepts of whiteness and fairness, they began to encounter – in Africa and then, as we have seen, in England itself – human beings who were the human antithesis of contemporary English ideals. To English eyes, the Africans' colour (and it is significant that it was, initially, invariably described, starkly as 'black') was a representation of all that the English held to be wicked, sinful and ugly.

This argument (though it was, often, more an assumption than a reasoned argument) seemed confirmed when Englishmen sought an explanation for the Africans' blackness. Indeed the cause of different human colouring was an ancient philosophical and scientific conundrum, though it was later limited in scope by the scriptural insistence on the single origin of mankind. The most obvious, easiest and, at first sight, most convincing explanation was the heat of the sun. For all its persuasiveness, however, there were obvious and demonstrable objections to the argument. Less easy to challenge were the scriptural explanations commonly used from the seventeenth century, that the Africans' colour was the curse of God on Ham for having gazed on his father's nakedness. This, too, had a number of obvious flaws. None the less it provided a relatively simple explanation in an English society more strictly ordered by and aware of scriptural dictates than modern people can readily appreciate. The power of an alleged biblical explanation – however imperfect, garbled or distorted that explanation might be – was a potent force in a post-Reformation society where preaching and biblical exegesis took place in the contemporary vernacular.

Ultimately, however, the most potent force which shaped the English responses to blacks was the rapid development of chattel slavery and the resulting black community in England.

Basic to the British slaving empire was the property status of the black. Moreover the development of chattel slavery was a complex change which derived not merely from the simple economic growth of empire, but equally from the support given by English statute law. In the years after the Restoration of 1660 – when the English slave islands were securely settled and economically buoyant – the English came to view the black as a thing. The Charter of the Royal African Company (1672), for instance, lumped together Negroes with wood, elephant teeth, hides and 'other commodities'.[8] A mere five years later the Solicitor-General declared that 'negroes ought to be esteemed goods and commodities within the Acts of Trade and Navigation'.[9] Of course this was an inevitable by-product of the development of slave colonies whose economic rationale and legal framework were rooted in the black chattel status. In the words of one West Indian planter:

> A West Indian estate consists of two parts: lands with their adjuncts, buildings etc., and the living stock, *viz.* cattle and negroes, all of which are as much the property of the planter as it is possible for the most authentic statutes of the British Senate and Colonial Assemblies to make them.[10]

The law – no less than economic customs – demanded that the black slave be viewed as a thing. An official report on West Indian laws declared, in 1789, that

> The leading idea in the Negro System of Jurisprudence is that which was the first in the Minds of those most interested in its Formation: namely, that Negroes were property, and a species of Property that needed a rigorous and vigilant *Regulation.*[11]

These comments belong, of course, to the mature phase of British colonial slavery. None the less, the principle that the black slave was a thing was a fundamental and early principle of the slave colonies and had, in large part, been inherited from other European colonial powers (notably the Spanish, Portuguese and Dutch) whose slave-trading ventures predated the English settlements. Of course the unavoidable centrality of black chattel status in law and economic practice does not mean that it was universally accepted by the English themselves. None the less it was the black as a thing, as a non-human, which formed the main economic foundation of whatever economic benefits accrued to Britain from her slaving interests. The profits of the slave empire have long been a subject of controversy among historians but however one resolves this economic dilemma, the undisputed fact remains that the profits – or the prospects of profit-making – hinged upon the efforts of black slaves. Hypothetical questions about whether alternative kinds of labour – free, indentured, contracted or whatever – might have been equally viable are, for the purposes of this study, irrelevant. It was slave labour which tapped the wealth of the West Indies. And slave labour required, in its introduction, growth and consolidation, not merely the complex economic and military power of the ascendant European powers, but also a foundation of political support, legal justification and popular political backing. And it was to that end – to create and consolidate public support for black slavery – that much of the literature concerning blacks was written from the late seventeenth century onwards. Yet to express the point in this manner is, in some respects, to caricature a complicated and tortuous process. As we have seen, there was an ancient literary tradition of black stereotype – a tradition which fed into the renewed debate about black life from the mid eighteenth century onwards.

It is true that the alleged inhumanity of the black was a concept not universally supported throughout the long history of British slavery. From the early days of black bondage, there were critics who sought to defend the violated humanity of Africans and who consistently rejected the arguments that the blacks were less than human.

The Quakers were among the early critics of slavery and from the late seventeenth century onwards, communities of Friends periodically denounced slavery and its concomitant theories of black inferiority or inequality.[12] Recent historians of anti-slavery have documented the literary tradition which ultimately bred a growing intellectual (and ultimately, political) objection to slavery. Men of both the Scottish and French enlightenment pitted their wits against prevailing justifications for slavery and black inequality. However obtuse (and inaccessible) their arguments, enlightened writers provided both an intellectual stimulus and new lines of argument for men of more practical and popular bent.[13] But until the mid eighteenth century (that is until the apogee of this first British empire) such voices were isolated, unheeded and in the short term generally ineffective in the teeth of the economic benefits which seemed attendant on the growth of black slavery. The full expression of black equality – the growing acceptance that the black, far from being a thing, was indeed a 'man and a brother' – was in large part a tactic and a consequence of the expansive abolitionist movement, particularly in the 1820s and 1830s. But until the success of anti-slavery, it was the black *as a thing* which dominated British dealings with Negroes.

This was not merely a matter of political abstractions; blacks were, after all, bought and sold as things in England in the same way (though clearly not on the same scale) as slaves in the colonies. Despite the legal confusions surrounding the slave cases, blacks in eighteenth-century England were periodically displayed before the public in their guise as things; as objects to be bought, sold, bequeathed or inherited. Clearly, the law can never offer a perfectly sharp reflection of prevailing social practice, but enough is known of slavery within England to argue that one of the major English responses to Negroes was to view them as inhuman objects. But even so bold a statement must, by the nature of the topic, be flawed by contradictions and exceptions. It was perfectly possible, for example, to treat blacks in general as non-beings while simultaneously having fond or affectionate dealings with individual blacks. This was clearly the case in the slave colonies where white men whose lives and economic futures depended upon maintaining black inhumanity were none the less perfectly happy to live in conjugal harmony with their black concubines and their offspring. Men who hated (and feared) blacks *en masse* were quite capable of loving and caring for particular blacks.

From the first, the, British images of black life were not derived uniquely from direct or personal contact with Africans or Afro-Americans. More often they came from the stories, rumours and publications about Africa and Africans; all of which increased substantially with the massive expansion of the slave empires. By the late seventeenth century when travel accounts of Africa increased – the initial curiosity about Africa had been effectively replaced by a cruder (if none the less accurate) view that West Africa's prime contribution was to provide enslaved manpower for the New World. English publications, from the 1670s onwards, came to *assume* that there was an immutable link between blackness and slavery.[14] Time and again, authors discussed black Africans as uncivilised, barbarous, pagan – and beyond the ken of contemporary morality and civility. Mendacious and cruel, lazy and untrustworthy, the African was widely thought to be incapable of all but the most limited and simple tasks and creative energies. Understandably, later apologists for slavery made effective use of such accounts by arguing that the slave trade offered salvation; an escape route from the inhumanity and savagery of African life towards the more sophisticated societies of the New World.[15]

There were, it is true, contrary interpretations, accounts of Africa which conceded the corrupting impact of the slave trade. Equally there were descriptions – more associated with an early Romantic tradition – which saw in the Africans' simplicity the essence of the 'Noble Savage'. In general, however, accounts of Africa were remarkably varied, often describing the more peaceful realities as well as the more fanciful atrocities and barbarities. Within the voluminous pages of seventeenth- and eighteenth-century accounts of Africa it was perfectly possible to develop contrary images of African life. But it seems clear that the predominant and most seminal image was that of African savagery and barbarity. To quote the words of the Earl of Chesterfield to his son: 'the Africans are the most ignorant and unpolished peoples in the world, little better than the lions, tigers and leopards and other wild beasts which the country produces in great numbers'.[16] There was, then, a tradition which cast the black in the role, at worst, of inhuman beast, at best as a man generally inferior to the dominant white man. Moreover – and it needs to be reiterated because it is so often ignored – this image was congruent with the treatment of the blacks in the New World. For all its obvious and undeniable moral flaws, despite the evidence of humane treatment towards some slaves, and notwithstanding the clear evidence that black slaves were *Homo sapiens*, black slaves were things; objects and chattel, specifically stripped by law and economic usage of their humanity. English people of the eighteenth century were then long accustomed to the image of the black as a thing – an object – or of viewing him as a markedly inferior being; so distinct in fact from the sensibility of their English contemporaries as to be beyond the pale of fellow humanity.

By the late seventeenth century there was an emergent plantocratic literature; tracts and pamphlets from the pens of men with experience of, and interest in, the slave colonies. It was a literature which confirmed the bleakest accounts of African life. Furthermore, visiting Englishmen, sympathetic to the black and appalled at the institutional and capricious violence of black slavery, revealed the depths of plantocratic hatred of the black workers. Morgan Godwyn reported in 1680 that a Barbadian had told him '*That* Negros *were* Beasts *and had no more Souls than Beasts, and that Religion did not concern them.*' Among the planters, Godwyn felt that the belief had grown 'That the *Negros*, though in their Figure they carry some resemblances to Manhood, yet are they indeed *no men.*' Equally important, Godwyn reported that colour was widely accepted as the sufficient explanation for the slaves' bondage. Their colour 'being most obvious to the sight . . . is apt to make no *slight* impression upon rude Minds, already prepared to admit of any thing for Truth which shall make for Interest'. Thus did the planters use their slaves' blackness and their 'paganism' as an excuse for reducing them to the level of inhuman beasts of burden. Planters, in the words of Francis Brokesby (1690) widely argued 'That Negroes are Creatures destitute of Souls, to be ranked among Brute, Beasts and Treated accordingly (as generally they are) and whom Religion (apt only to make Subjects Mutinous) doth in no way concern.'[17]

This denigration of black humanity was not, however, uniquely a product of the West India lobby. There was, for example, a parallel tradition in British philosophy. The most prominent and original of contemporary thinkers repeated remarks about blacks which seemed more in keeping with plantocratic life than British intellectual circles. Sir William Petty, John Locke and David Hume all for example, openly accepted the inferiority of black humanity and employed their assumptions in developing a broader argument. It is, of course, a simple matter to extract their words and divorce them from their wider intellectual framework. But it is worth reminding ourselves that a belief in black inferiority was not the monopoly of planters, slave traders and their friends. Writing in 1748, David Hume noted

I am apt to suspect the negroes, and in general all the other species of man . . . to be naturally inferior to the whites. There never was a civilized nation of any other complexion than white, nor even any individual eminent either in action or speculation. . . . Not to mentioned our colonies, there are NEGROE slaves dispersed all over Europe, of which none ever discovered any symptoms of ingenuity.[18]

It was, however, the more popular literary tradition which repeated similar opinions about the blacks from the mid eighteenth century onwards. It was no accident that the crescendo of abuse against blacks coincided with the rise of an unavoidable, sizeable black community in England. Drawing empirical data (such as it was) from existing accounts of life in West Africa and the slave colonies, a number of writers purveyed images of black life which, in denigrating and dehumanising the black, were designed to promote the economic and social interests of the slave lobby. According to the *Universal History* (published in 23 volumes between 1736–65), the Africans were

proud, lazy, treacherous, thievish, hot, and addicted to all kinds of lusts, and most ready to promote them in others, as pimps, panders, incestuous, brutish, and savage, cruel and revengeful, devourers of human flesh, and quaffers of human blood, inconstant, base, treacherous, and cowardly; fond of and addicted to all sorts of superstition and witchcraft; and, in a word, to every vice that came in their way, or within their reach.[19]

Such evidence was ideally suited to the interests of planters and their scribes anxious, later in the century, to counter the criticisms of their inreasingly vociferous opponents. Thus, from the 1760s onwards, there was an outpouring of cheap polemical literature defending slavery and the slave trade, which drew its 'intellectual' sustenance from what was, by then, a well-established literary (and popular) tradition. What gave added credibility to such works was the personal experience of the authors, many of whom had lived and worked in slave communities; the traditions of the past were, apparently, given the confirmation of personal experience.

To William Knox, formerly in Georgia 'a *new Negroe* (as those lately imported from Africa are called) is a complete definition of indolent stupidity'.[20] It was, however, the phenomenon discussed above – black settlement in England – which provided a specific and local focus for the literary arguments about black life. Indeed the development of an English black community – and the legal and intellectual debate about slavery attendant on that community – proved instrumental in the initial campaign against slavery and the slave trade. In the process, the traditional images of black life were paraded before the English reading public. In the late eighteenth century, however, it was possible for the interested or informed reader to test what was said or written against the human realities of black life in England. But the emergence of the most overtly racist literature was designed to generate hostility to blacks in England and specifically to encourage restrictions on further black settlement. Thus, the intellectual and literary traditions towards black life fused with a domestic political debate (though one shaped to a marked degree by colonial problems and experiences) to produce an embittered argument about blacks in England. In the process there developed an increased awareness of black life in England, and greater attention was paid to black society.

From the 1760s onwards there were flurries of articles in a number of newspapers and periodicals denouncing (and then defending) the custom of importing black servants. But it was the question of the *legality* of slavery in England which brought black society its most widespread publicity. Slavery undoubtedly existed as an institution in England, but its legality was extremely dubious. Indeed from the seventeenth century onwards the law cases which concerned themselves directly with the legality of slavery in England were marked by confusion, a confusion which increased as more slaves found themselves in England. Not until the 1760s, however, was a concerted effort made to *use* the courts as a means of securing black freedom. In this, the inspiration and effort derived substantially from Granville Sharp, though even he hit upon the problem by pure accident (when a badly beaten slave was treated by Sharp's doctor brother). Sharp sought to undermine local slavery by the simple expedient of extending to blacks all the legal rights of Englishmen. The process was, inevitably perhaps, tortuous and protracted and the courts were uncertain and hesitant. But in the course of these legal cases, there was a great deal of contemporary publicity and published argument. In fact the arguments *pro* and *con* slavery in England were rehearsed not merely in the courts but, more widely, through the Press, Journals and in tract literature, all directing their conflicting claims to the maturing and widening literacy of the English public.[21] Thus, in the quarter of a century between the Peace of Paris (1763) and the outbreak of the French Revolution (1789) from these two related forces – black settlement (and opposition to it) and the initial legal and political drive for black freedom – there followed a unique and pervasive debate about black life and society. In the process, old stereotypical images were reinforced and reached a wider audience by the work of the political opponents of black freedom and black settlement.

The objections to black society were easily recited; the conflict with the interests of local white workers, dislike of miscegenation and fear of the contagion of ideas of freedom, not simply among blacks in England but, more dangerously, back to slaves in the West Indian islands. There is no doubt that such claims were genuinely believed, but it is scarcely a cynical view to suggest that these fears were, in essence, a plea for the continuation of slavery itself. Only the rigours and restraints of bondage would, it was felt, prevent the blacks from reverting to their natural traits and vices. It was perfectly clear, furthermore, that the intellectual and political arguments about slavery in England were, at heart, universalist and therefore directly threatening to slavery in the colonies. Arguments about rights could not easily be arrested at national borders (a point dramatically revealed, of course, in 1776 and then 1789) and the plantocratic interests in London were aware that the arguments for black freedom were corrosive of their wider slaving interests. Thus the fight to preserve slavery began in England just as the battle to secure black freedom was joined in London from the late 1760s onwards.

The legal arguments about slavery culminated in the Somerset case of 1772. The ensuing political argument saw the most overt of racist attacks on blacks, indeed it is possible to mark the origins of a recognisably modern racist perception of black humanity in the writings which followed the 1772 case. Samuel

Estwick (himself employed as the agent for Barbados) argued that restricting black settlement would 'preserve the race of Britons from stain and contamination' (a point made in almost precisely the same terms by contemporaries making a similar argument in France).[22] What is interesting here is the description of the British as a specific race, an account familiar in the nineteenth century, but unusual in the late eighteenth century. It was, however, the words of Edward Long which thrust the arguments about black life to a more extreme and racist point. Long's views derived both from his long years in Jamaica and from recent publications written about blacks and about Africa. But he gave established stereotypes a new and quite extraodinarily acerbic edge. Blacks in England were dismissed as a 'dissolute, idle, profligate crew', but in great demand among the 'lower class of women' for their sexual attractions. Blacks were, he claimed, unable to work effectively, especially in the British climate and the conclusion was simple; 'some restraint should be laid on the unnatural increase of blacks imported'.[23] In a subsequent book, his *History of Jamaica*, Long continued his negrophobic utterances, comparing the black to the orang-utan, and suggesting that sexual relations took place between the two. Wild and untameable, antisocial and animal-like, the black of Edward Long's accounts was closer to the animal kingdom than to the civilised world of man.[24] Slavery – needless to say – was the perfect and obvious restraint for people living in such barbarity. The harsher the image of black life, the stronger appeared the case for slavery. Yet there is a case to be made that the extremity of Long's black images was a reflection not only of his personal views but of the political troubles facing the slave owners. The more desperate their situation, the more extreme and bitter their attacks on the blacks. And we need to recall that, however limited the decision in the Somerset case of 1772, it was without doubt a defeat for the plantocracy. Thus the literary excesses of the plantocratic authors were as much a reflection of their frustrated anger at the defeat of 1772 as they were an insight into their morbid and prurient racism.

It is more difficult, however, to assess how popular – how widespread and commonplace – was the English belief in black inferiority. Fortunately we have the words of contemporary blacks as evidence of the treatment they received in eighteenth-century England. The evidence is, of course, mixed but there is incontrovertible data of widespread antipathy towards contemporary blacks. Ignatius Sancho, writing in 1766, described himself as 'one of those people whom the vulgar and illiberal call "Negurs"'. He thought that those English people who possessed 'charity enough to admit dark faces into the fellowship of Christians' were rare. Even when describing mundane events, Sancho provides clues to some of the hostility shown towards contemporary blacks. Taking his family out one day, Sancho wrote 'we went by water – had a coach home – were gazed at, etc. etc. – *but not much abused*'. On another occasion, 'they stopped us in the town and most generously insulted us'.[25] There was no doubt in Sancho's mind of the dominant English response to blacks; 'the national antipathy and prejudice towards their woolly headed breathern'. Sancho confirmed that contemporaries tended to deal with blacks as stereotypes: 'from Othello to Sancho the big – we are foolish – or mulish-all – all without a single exception'.[26]

It would, however, be quite wrong to suggest that such hostility was the only black experience. There were, after all, a host of examples of affectionate relations between black and white. Similarly, black and white worked amicably together, notably as domestic servants. And it was ruefully remarked that poor whites often safeguarded runaway slaves, preventing their owners recapturing their black property. Yet, however mixed and varied the white responses to black society, there was no doubt that the pre-eminent sentiment was hostility and distrust. It was scarcely encouraging that in 1787 the Government sought to encourage the relief of the black poor (swollen by refugees from the American war) by financing a repatriation scheme to Africa. The fact that few blacks joined the scheme tells us more about its dangers than it does about the need to flee the inhospitability of English life. After living in England for 50 years, Sancho wrote 'I am only a lodger – and hardly that.'[27]

Quite apart from the ancient traditions of curiosity – the literary and popular inheritance, absorbed by one generation after another, of imputing to blacks personal and collective traits which owed little to reality – the seminal force in shaping English treatment of the black was, of course, slavery. By the late eighteenth century the assumed causal relationship between blackness and bondage, the virtually unquestioned material well-being which accrued to England from its slaving empire and the commonplace existence of slaves in some parts of England itself all, among other things, provided the crucial determinants of English perceptions of, and reactions to, black life. It was to be the first – and most daunting – task facing the early abolition movement to establish a contrary framework of perceptions; it was to achieve this by the remarkably simple – but effective – assertion of principle, 'Am I not a man and a brother?' If the question mark suggests a potential uncertainty, the motto was in effect an original and effective philosophy of equalitarianism. No one could have envisaged how swiftly and universally the commitment to black equality would, apparently, dispel so much of the prevailing antipathy. But we need to recall two salient facts. Firstly the emergence of a commitment to black equality (in addition to flying in the teeth of British experience) became effective only when the demographic (and to a lesser extent the industrial) nature of English life had begun to change dramatically. And secondly, it took place when black life in England was in a state of relative demographic decline; a declining black population found itself in a society characterised by massive and unprecedented population growth and urban expansion. It was, ironically, this very transformation in economic and demographic life which was to prove crucially important in establishing a commitment to black freedom and in overthrowing the institutions of slavery and the slave trade.

The abolition movement between 1787 and 1838 was primarily a *political* campaign, and while of necessity it addressed itself to the difficult task of changing public opinion, it would be unrealistic to expect the traditions (and prejudices) of centuries to be universally or permanently dispelled. Indeed the revival of early Victorian racism soon after the ending of slavery, in the 1840s, is evidence of the durability and resilience of many racial stereotypes, even in the face of contrary and hostile forces. But even in the midst of the successful abolitionist campaign, the English continued to be beset by many of the old stereotypical images. Indeed, the *pro*-slave trade and slavery lobby persisted with the traditional denunciations and denigrations of black life and achievements as a central feature of their defence of slavery.[28] Alexander McDonnell, a man with slaving interests in Demerara, wrote of the African in 1833:

it is the vice, the barbarian habits, which obstruct the
progress of social improvement, and in common reason we
ought not to expect a different result until they are weaned
from their vicious customs, have tasted the artificial
enjoyments of life, and have been taught to regard the
conjugal bond as sacred.[29]

Such assertion, commonplace in the pamphlet war between
the abolitionists and planters, might be viewed as merely the
last throw of desperate men. But despite the declining power of
the plantocracy their views on black inferiority – however
politically redundant and ineffective – were shared by many
others. Indeed no sooner had West Indian slaves secured their
freedom than a revived racism in England began to look to the
Caribbean for *proof* of revived antipathy. The economic decline
of the plantations, the demise of the sugar industry and the
flight of former slaves from their house of bondage seemed to
many early Victorian commentators to vindicate all that the
planters had previously claimed. Lazy blacks, unwilling to
work, had allowed an industry to collapse, thus betraying the
faith placed in them by their English abolitionist friends. In
truth, the economic decline of sugar was in train *before*
emancipation. Although it might make political sense to portray
black potential in glowing terms, any failure to live up to such
idealist achievements could only create disappointment. Thus
in an ironic twist, one major consequence of the remarkable
abolitionist campaign culminating in black freedom in 1838
was to lay the basis for the subsequent revival of racism. Few
were more disappointed with the West Indian free blacks than
Thomas Carlyle. His 'Discourse on the Nigger Question' (1849)
denounced the efforts and ambitions which had preceded
emancipation. The black was, by nature, an inferior being.

> Do I then hate the Negro? No; except when the soul is killed
> out of him, I decidedly like poor Quashee, and find him a
> pretty kind of man. With a pennyworth of oil, you can make
> a handsome glossy thing of Quashee, when the soul is not
> killed in him. A swift, supple fellow; a merry-hearted,
> grinning, dancing, singing, affectionate kind of creature, with
> a great deal of melody and amenability in his composition.[30]

Here were many of the ageless stereotypes, rehearsed by English writers over the centuries; of the musical jackass able to achieve a certain acceptability in white eyes only through his natural musicality. When attacked for his assessment, Carlyle reiterated his case with even greater venom: 'One always rather likes the Nigger; evidently a poor blockhead with good dispositions, with affections, attachments – with a turn for Nigger melodies and the like. . . . The Almighty Maker has appointed him to be a Servant.'[31]

At much the same time, the same point was made by another essayist with even greater (though more offensive) clarity. 'The Negroes are made on purpose to serve the whites, just as the black ants are made on purpose to serve the red.'[32] The magazine *John Bull* neatly expressed the disillusionment felt with former slaves: 'There is no question, from what we have witnessed in the West Indies, but that the negro is disinclined to labour, and has not the disposition towards self-improvement manifested by the white man.' The American Civil War served, for many Britons, merely to compound the growing doubts about whether it was worth trying to help the black: 'is the negro worth all the trouble, anxiety, blood-shed and misery which his wrongs and rights have produced?'. If the black is 'left to himself and without white control he forgets the lessons he has learnt, and slides rapidly back to his original barbarism'.[33]

The major political upheavals within the British empire had provided Carlyle and others with ammunition for such racist attacks. The Indian Mutiny (1857) and the Morant Bay Rebellion (1865) in Jamaica – with their horrific violence (more especially in the form of reprisals against Indians and black Jamaicans by the local armed forces) – severely shook the complacent control of British imperial authority. But it also disillusioned large numbers of Britons with the peoples of the empire; apparently unwilling to accept the benefits of British imperial governance, they showed (in 1857 and 1865) their ill-disguised natural savagery, which only the restraints of British control kept in check.[34] After 1857 the word 'nigger' or 'nigga' entered common English usage, and appeared regularly in letters and newspapers; but it was used particularly to describe Indians. 'Every nigger we meet we either string up or shoot', one man wrote during the mutiny. Another wrote of 'the nigger – I mean the Oriental gentleman'.[35] Eight years later, the Jamaican uprising (a minor violent incident stimulated an outrageous repression orchestrated by Governor Eyre) created a political furore in Britain. In the process, the old racial stereotypes were resurrected and given a new life: 'The original nature of the African betokened itself in acts of horrible mutilation . . . the rabble of this rebellion were in all likelihood drunken and worthless savages scarcely responsible for their misdeeds.'[36] But what are we to make of the savagery of the colonial authorities who killed more than 400 blacks? None the less the 1865 rebellion confirmed many of the fears voiced in 1857; it convinced more people that the philanthropists had been wrong in their expectation of black freedom.

> Gentlemen of Exeter Hall, the game is entirely up. Ladies, given to 'presiding' over weak tea and tooth-endangering currant loaves, your ebony friend has fallen from his high estate and swings, by representation, for the delectation of the turkey buzzards of the Gulf of Mexico. It is high time.[37]

Evangelicals were in no doubt that public feelings about race had changed dramatically since the ending of slavery. The benign feelings, and even that sense of telescopic comaraderie showed to people so many thousands of miles away, had evaporated by the 1860s. In their place was to be found a malignant antipathy, born of political change (and imperial violence) informed by the crudest of traditional stereotypes which were now expressed in the coarsest of terms. Moreover this newly strident racism and negrophobia was all the more potent – and credible – because it coincided with and was influenced by, new schools of 'scientific racism'.

Much of the empirical data (such as it was) of traditional racism was based, as we have seen, on evidence from visitors to Africa and the slave colonies. But the rise of nineteenth-century science and of social sciences, notably anthropology, shifted the very nature, approach and articulation of the study of race. Science began to give the study of race a totally new rationale and framework, both of which were to be instrumental in explaining and justifying the subsequent development of a new – and more widely flung – British empire. Indeed the history of the British empire, and British imperial ideology, until it began to sag and then collapse dramatically from the 1940s onwards, cannot be fully understood without its attendant racism, and the intellectual basis for that racism. Increasingly, those intellectual roots flourished in the world of expansive Victorian science.

The origins of scientific racism can be traced to the eighteenth century, but it only became widespread – almost *de rigeur* – in the nineteenth when it was widely adopted as *the* natural and most obvious tool for categorising mankind. Marx was unusual in opting for social class as the key social category. In 1850, the Scottish anatomist, Robert Knox, asserted in his book *The Races of Man*, that 'human character, individual and national, is traceable solely to the nature of that race to which the individual or nation belongs'. Aware of objections to his arguments, Knox boldly continued: 'Nevertheless, that race in human affairs is everything, is simply a fact, the most remarkable, the most comprehensive, which philosophy has ever announced. Race is everything: literature, science, art – in a word, civilization, depends on it.'[38]

There were, of course, different (and often conflicting) views of race but all were united in the inferiority of the non-white and in conviction (scientifically proved of course) that their inferiority debarred them from enjoying the rights and benefits of white civilisation. The politics, administration, military control and social life of the British empire hinged upon this belief. Differing from one colony to another the British dominance of her subject peoples was specifically designed to exclude them from the equal enjoyment of all facets of imperial life. They were, naturally, inferior people consigned to inferior stations (however complex and confused the realities of the colonial pecking order). And that inferiority was a proven 'scientific' fact.

There was a congruence of opinion, among men working in diverse disciplines, that human society, its history and its contemporary forms, could only be fully and adequately explained by race: 'The comparative anatomist agrees with the historian in placing them [non-whites] on a lower level than the European. And the phrenologist agrees with the anatomist.'

The ambition of the Ethnological Society of London (founded in 1843) to enquire into 'the distinguishing characteristics, physical and moral, of the variations of mankind'[39] reflected contemporary racial perceptions: in time the society's findings were to confirm the racial hierarchy of mankind so central to the early Victorian world view. Moreover we need to recall that Victorian scientific bodies had a varied membership; men of letters, politicians, clergymen and civil servants attended in large numbers, imbibing and subsequently replicating the new scientific orthodoxy that race was the key and explanatory category in the history, division and future of mankind. Not surprisingly, men of science and their supporters vigorously supported the savage repression of Governor Eyre in 1865. The 1866 meeting of the Anthropological Society of London was told 'we anthropologists have looked upon, with intense admiration, at the conduct of Governor Eyre as that of a man of whom England ought to be (and some day will be) justly proud'. At another meeting, the Society enthusiastically heard a paper on 'The Negro and Jamaica' in which the black was described as an immoral savage, at best the equivalent of a child and for whom slavery had provided a civilising influence.[40]

The issue of slavery, and of black society and its potential, was, of course, particularly relevant in the early 1860s when the controversy about the American Civil War breathed new life into traditional racist arguments in Britain. Nor was the war viewed as a distant or abstract issue; the war and its attendant arguments *pro* and *con* slavery received widespread coverage throughout the British Press. For the purposes of this study, the war was grist to the mill for those individuals and organisations committed to propagating the newly found scientific orthodoxy of racial hierarchy; the Anthropological Society for instance became independent of the Ethnological Society in 1863 *specifically* to popularise its findings.[41] But perhaps more helpful to the task of promoting the new racism was the membership of both societies, drawn as it was from the governing and intellectual élite of mid-Victorian life. Authors were readily recruited, and so too were numbers of teachers and headmasters, notably from the revived and expansive public schools. Indeed it seems plausible that the strength and ubiquity of late Victorian (and later) racism derived substantially from the lessons, ideology and reading materials which dominated public school education. It was among the young that the seeds of racism were successfully implanted. Public school boys subsequently formed the governing élite of domestic and colonial society and were, without question, substantially inspired and informed by the images of race so assiduously dangled before them in their early life. The headmaster of Marlborough, Frederick William Farrar (also, of course, a successful novelist), argued in 1861 that the 'savage races' 'are without a past and without a future, doomed as races infinitely nobler have been before them, to a rapid, and entire, and perhaps for the highest destinies of mankind, an enviable extinction'.[42] Among the pupils of such men it was perfectly understandable that late Victorian racism was to be found in its sharpest and simplest form. Successive generations were taught to view the world – at home and abroad – in racial terms. The headmaster of Uppingham, Edward Thring (1853–87), argued that 'The learning to be responsible, and independent, to bear pain, to play games, to drop rank, and wealth, and home luxury, is a priceless boon. I think myself that it is this which has made the English *such an adventurous race*.'[43]

Such views, disseminated by verbal instruction, were reinforced by voluminous literature, books, magazines and 'comics' which fed the voracious literary appetite of children of all social classes (and both sexes). Of course, children's literature had long eulogised the superiority of the British in general and the English in particular.

> I thank the Goodness and the Grace
> That on my birth have smiled,
> And made me, in these Christian Days
> A happy English child.[44]

An illustrated alphabet for small children chose as its example of the letter 'Z' a black sleeping under a tree

> Sun so hot, O!
> Take it easy!
> That's the Motto
> In Zambesi![45]

Such views were commonplace in English children's books. Furthermore, the coming of compulsory schooling in the last quarter of the nineteenth century saw this racial view of the world make a rapid and universal impact throughout the nation's Board Schools. Moreover this took place at time of massive British imperial expansion, when the traditional lessons of superiority could apparently be confirmed by merely pointing to the map. One school text, looking back on Englishmen's achievements, asserted 'They all show the bold, frank, sturdy character which so strongly marks the Anglo-Saxon race.' S. R.

Gardiner, Fellow of Merton College, wrote that Lord Palmerston was 'cheery, high spirited and worthily representing the race to which he belonged'. Other races, inevitably, were less well-regarded. One text book described Hindus as 'an innocent race of men, whose only food is rice, and who are maintained for three half pence a day per man'.[46]

West Indians were often described in terms which had scarcely changed for a century. A text book of 1911 wrote that the black West Indian was

> Lazy, vicious and incapable of serious improvement or of work except under compulsion. In such a climate a few bananas will sustain the life of a negro quite sufficiently; why should he work to get more than this. He is quite happy and quite useless and spends any extra wages which he may earn upon finery.[47]

This could easily have come from the pen of an eighteenth-century planter, but the fact that it was a sentiment expressed in English schools in the twentieth century provides a glimpse of one way in which the values and outlook of empire were bequeathed from one generation to another, over a remarkably long span of time. Indeed the point can be represented thus: it is perfectly likely that an old person, alive today (1984) received lessons in childhood which were informed by racial assumptions which were themselves extremely close to the plantocratic propaganda of the late eighteenth century. Clearly, it would be absurd to suggest that nothing had changed. There was, for instance, a dissenting literary and educational tradition which sought to eschew the racial and political values of empire. But it was overwhelmingly a minority and ineffective view. The most influential changes had, in fact, served to *confirm* the assumptions of racial superiority by giving them the added strength of scientific and anthropological credibility. Moreover the *facts* of late Victorian empire – the undeniable expansion of British imperial, commercial and military influence and control, largely at the expense of innocent and weaker native peoples – seemed to clinch the educational and political arguments so assiduously propagated at all levels of British life. It was a theme to which successive generations of statesmen and politicians warmed in the years before 1914. Joseph Chamberlain was quite specific

> I believe in this race, the greatest governing race the world has ever seen; in this Anglo-Saxon race, so proud reaching, self-confident and determined, this race, which neither climate nor change can degenerate, which will infallibly be the predominant force of future history and universal civilisation.[48]

Governing élites clearly needed justification of some kind to give their governance credibility and sanction. What happened in the century between the apogee of the slave empire (*c.* 1776) and the 'grab for Africa' was the emergence of a racially based justification; the British governed their native peoples (and, as we shall see, their own domestic society) thanks to the blessings and qualities bestowed by their racial superiority. Furthermore, this view (though in truth it was a complexity of views) was shared by men on both sides of the Atlantic. Jamaica planters, early American leaders and the British cultural élite were united in their attachment to a belief in the racial superiority of the whites and the inferiority of the black.[49]

The triumph of the new scientific-racism clearly had profound consequences for the perception of non-white humanity well beyond Europe. But it had equally important repercussions for contemporary views of *domestic* society. Increasingly, British life – being transformed of course by the remarkable impact of population growth, urbanisation and industrial change – came to be viewed in racial terms. Just as the rationale for imperial government was presented in racial terms, so too did the strata of British life come to be seen in that way. The 'lower orders' were, increasingly, viewed and described as inferior beings, consigned to their helot-like existence by their racial characteristics. Working people as a 'lesser breed', 'a caste apart', 'a separate race' and similar expressions became common descriptions of English life by the mid nineteenth century. In 1864, for example, the *Saturday Review* wrote 'The Bethnal Green poor, as compared with the comfortable inhabitants of western London, are a caste apart, a race of whom we know nothing, whose lives are of a quite different complexion from ours.'[50]

Unknown England – that volatile, urban aggregation of humanity which seemed to pose such a pervasive threat to social stability – was described in terms which were equally applied to colonial peoples. Like blacks abroad, the urban poor lived beyond the pale and the ken of propertied society; immoral undisciplined and violent, black and poor white alike were thought of as 'vicious and shy, incapable of telling the truth, naturally lazy and unwilling to work unless under compulsion'.[51] In both cases, these assumptions underpinned the commitment to impose a firm discipline and control from above. But it was a discipline shaped by the authority of racial superiority.

Among the poor in British cities, few were more abject – or despised – than the Irish. By 1841 there was upward of half a million Irish in mainland Britain; a decade later many more had fled from the devastating famine. Throughout their long history in Britain the Irish had been the object of ridicule and antipathy; they had, in fact, long been victims of a stereotype which bore great resemblance to the English stereotypical views of the blacks. In literature, political debate and – most influentially – in popular culture, the Irish stereotype is recognisable because it remains with us; the ignorant labourer, too fond of drink for his own good, not too bright and as keen to fight as he was to drink. There were, of course, certain features of this stereotype which the Irish adopted for their own use (much as the blacks in the new world took on the assumed qualities of their own stereotype). Throughout, the Irish were widely thought to be inferior, a British *Untermensch* fit only for manual labour. But by the mid nineteenth century they were also described in *racial* terms. In 1869, for example, the Earl of Kimberley remarked: 'the true source of Irish unhappiness is the character of the Irish race: it must take many generations to alter the character for the better'.[52]

By the late nineteenth century, the popular Press normally referred to the Irish as a 'race'.[53] But so too were wide sections of plebeian life – a tendency accentuated by the emergence of late-century eugenics, the rise of social reforming movements concerned with the lot of the urban poor, and the military disasters of the Boer War. In large measure the analysis of mankind – domestic and foreign – in racial categories was, as we have seen, primarily a function of the triumph of Victorian science which itself attached such a key and seminal importance to race. But Victorian scientists – and social scientists – made free use of the broader cultural and political tradition inherited from an earlier society. Indeed it seems clear that many salient attitudes towards black life – more stereotype than reality – were bequeathed from slaving generations to those committed to black freedom but none the less prepared to accept and transform culturally determined attitudes to non-whites. Furthermore, the inheritance of racial attitudes – changing as they clearly did across time – was not merely a matter of intellectual debate and influence. There were broad channels of popular cultural inheritance which disseminated racial stereotypes throughout domestic society. Ironically, however, the lowest levels of British urban society themselves became the object of racial scrutiny and categorisation. The justification for the control over domestic urban life, and of wide stretches of the British empire, was overtly racial by the late nineteenth century. This was not, of course, the sole justification, but the strength and ubiquity of racial images and the extraordinary infusion of the language of race into everyday British vocabulary (in schools, in books, in politics) provides a revealing insight into contemporary British attitudes towards themselves and the outside world. The scientific and social scientific newness of much of that vocabulary ought not to deceive us for it formed an unbroken link with an historic epoch which, if lacking the vocabulary of race, bequeathed a number of essential stereotypes to later generations. Many of the images of black life proffered to the British in the mid and late nineteenth centuries bore the main ingredients so well rehearsed in Britain's heyday of slaving. The sins of the slaving father were to be found in abundance among their mid and late Victorian descendants.

Part II
Men and Brothers

5 Abolishing the Trade: Public Sentiment and Abolition, 1776–1807

The spread of anti-slavery sentiment in the last quarter of the eighteenth century was dramatic, swift and ubiquitous. Within a very short time a national organisation, the Society for the Abolition of the Slave Trade, sprang up to tap existing abolitionist feeling, to encourage its further growth and to exert abolitionist pressure on Parliament. Writing, in 1788, the *Annual Register* remarked that the slave trade 'does not appear, till of late years, to have been considered with that great attention, which a practice so abhorrent in its nature to the mild principles of modern policy and manners might have been expected to excite'.[1] And yet, the initial – and quite unexpected – public response to abolition suggests a reservoir of antipathy waiting to find expression and organisation. A few years after coming into being in 1787, the Abolition Society recorded in its Minute book: 'The Publick we believe are convinced of that there is something both in the principle and conduct of this Trade fundamentally wrong.'[2]

Long before the flowering of organised abolition there had existed an important intellectual critique of slavery which, by its very nature, remained the preserve of contemporary intelligentsia. It was an intellectual debate of genuinely international proportions, drawing on the arguments (and experiences) of men in Britain and France as well as the North American and Caribbean colonies. There was in a sense, an accumulating critique of slavery – primarily from men of the French and Scottish Enlightenment – which slowly but effectively began to erode the previously unchallenged assumptions and arguments in favour of slavery. Francis Hutcheson in the early and mid eighteenth century was specifically critical of prior justifications of slavery, proffering instead a doctrine of liberty which allowed 'little room for Negro slavery'.[3] Better known perhaps – and certainly more influential – was *L'Esprit des Lois*, published by Montesquieu in 1748. Most famous for its powerful advocacy of liberty (inspired in large measure by studying the English constitution) *L'Esprit des Lois* also (and perhaps inevitably) embraced a criticism of slavery, though couching its denunciation in ironic terms.[4] Montesquieu's contribution to anti-slavery sentiment at the broadest – and most international level – was crucial. More directly, however, it proved seminal among a host of British writers and philosophers, few more notable – or influential – than Edmund Burke. Indeed it seems clear that Montesquieu was the crucial intellectual force which propelled Burke towards an advocacy of reform in colonial policy, especially in British India and in the slave empires.[5] As early as 1780 Burke drafted a plan for ameliorating the slave trade and colonial slavery. It was later claimed (by Wilberforce's sons) that Burke abandoned the idea 'after mature consideration' because of 'the conviction that the strength of the West Indian body would defeat the utmost effort of his powerful party, and cover them in ruinous unpopularity'.[6] Twelve years later, in 1792 (despite his famous hostility to the Revolution in France), he submitted a detailed 'Sketch of a Negro Code'[7] to the Home Secretary, Henry Dundas. Unquestionably influenced by Montesquieu (whose work Burke had translated into English) this 'Sketch' was a remarkably advanced – and comprehensive – blueprint designed to ease the transmutation of Britain's slaves into free people. By that date, abolition had secured a powerful hold over both public and parliamentary opinion. None the less the point to be made here is that there is a clear, direct and unbroken line of descent from anti-slavery as an abstract intellectual issue to anti-slavery as the substance of practical politics and reform. It would be quite wrong, then, to imagine that the apparently obscure arguments of eminent philosophers remained the monopoly of an intellectual élite, for, very quickly, those ideas were transmuted into the stuff and argument of everyday political argument.

Montesquieu was especially influential among a new generation of British Enlightenment writers, themselves major contributors to the upsurge of late eighteenth-century reform and anti-slavery. Adam Ferguson, James Beattie, George

Wallace, William Paley and Adam Smith all drew upon Montesquieu's work, incorporating a number of his ideas into their own writing. In their turn, these men proved influential in theological, political and legal debate in late eighteenth-century Britain; never more persuasively or swiftly than on the question of slavery. Of course this British (primarily Scottish) tradition ran parallel to (and was deeply influenced by) the better-known French Enlightenment writers – notably Rousseau, the Encyclopedists, Raynal, Diderot, d'Holbach and Voltaire.[8] We need to recall that educated European society was readily conversant – and linguistically at ease with – contemporary French publications. Indeed French culture of the eighteenth century was of an unsurpassed importance and influence throughout the Western World; a factor which goes some way to explain the seismic influence of revolutionary ideology after 1789. But even before that dramatic impact, French ideas – expressed in their original form and sometimes in translation – had made a major critical impact throughout Europe (and North America). Before the impact of the ideas of the 'Rights of Man', few French ideas had more disruptive and critical an effect than the cumulative pin-pricks against slavery and the slave trade. Furthermore the development of a late eighteenth-century mentality which was increasingly sceptical of long-unquestioned values and institutions was paralleled by transformations in theology.

Scholars have identified two major theological changes in the course of the eighteenth century which served, ultimately, though often indirectly, to challenge acceptance of black slavery. First, the idea of benevolence became progressively more influential, with far-reaching consequences for the promotion of brotherly love. Secondly, the concept of Providence enshrined the idea of progress, an idea which in its turn naturally led to institutional change. Certain changes – progress – were seen 'as the manifestation of a great providential design'.[9] While it may be thought that theologians who addressed themselves to these issues were operating in the inaccessible realms of metaphysics – their hefty and expensive tomes available only to an intellectual élite – via tracts and, especially, sermons, their message percolated down to a wider audience than might initially be expected. One result was the widespread belief in divine retribution for sin and evil. When, late in the century, slavery began to incur moral condemnation it was relatively easy – and certainly convincing – to argue that divine punishment would fall on the heads of slaving peoples and nations. Before the launch of abolitionism it would be wrong to suggest that contemporary religion had begun to turn against slavery. But it is abundantly clear that these theological shifts, long in-train, were transmuted in the changed climate, post-1787, into powerful anti-slavery sentiment.

The roots of abolition can also be traced to the wider literate world where, in a host of literary sources, anti-slavery had begun to make its mark early in the eighteenth century. Again, the genesis of anti-slavery was more directly a concern with contemporary English liberties; a continuation, in 'modernised' form, of the debate about rights and liberties so characteristic of the seventeenth-century revolution and its aftermath. But there was also a widely advertised and supported vogue for secular philanthropy; the operation of charity towards the less fortunate. Indeed it was the accepted obligation of philanthropy which provided the essential lubricant for the workings of eighteenth-century English society. Late in the century, the combined problems of population and urban growth, in conjunction with the dislocations of economic change rapidly rendered traditional philanthropy incapable of maintaining social tranquility. In fact, the inability of philanthropy adequately to cope with the changing problems of want was effectively demonstrated in 1787 when attempts to relieve the black poor collapsed under the sheer weight of the numbers involved. The literary emphasis on philanthropy – on doing good to one's neighbour – was commonly emphasised in eighteenth-century literature. Increasingly, too, there was a literary genre which cast the black in the role of the noble savage; a person deserving of sympathetic and humane consideration and treatment. A number of successful books, poems and plays gave prominence to the primitive, noble black which, at a time of heightened discussion about liberties and humanity, served to illustrate the contrary condition of black slavery. Thus contemporary literary genres served to focus literate attention (itself more widespread and 'popular' than the modern observer might imagine) securely on the problems and conditions of slaves and slavery. And all this was in addition to whatever personal experience existed from contact with blacks in Britain or from working in and around the nation's major slaving ports. There was, quite simply, a growing awareness of the existence, nature and problems of black slavery. Moreover, it seems equally clear that there was little corresponding literary support for slavery, though this was to change dramatically from the 1780s when the onslaught of abolitionists prompted a major literary defence of the slaving system by its supporters and their hired scribes.

It may well be countered that the origins of abolition mentioned so far – in philosophy, theology and literature – belong more appropriately to the realm of intellectual abstractions. In part, this is true. But it is equally clear that at certain crucial junctures, ideas from these particular 'disciplines' spilled over, often in transmuted form, into a wider, more politicised arena. Furthermore there were powerful catalysts at work encouraging the pollination of anti-slavery throughout British (indeed Western) society. Foremost were the Quakers.

The Quakers had, by the mid eighteenth century, evolved into a sizeable – and influential – community on both sides of the Atlantic. Friends – and their abundant theological outpourings – criss-crossed the Atlantic, always sure of a bed and a sympathetic hearing in the expansive network of Friends. From the late seventeenth century onwards, Quakers in the New World had complained about slavery; by the mid eighteenth century this complaint evolved into a major transatlantic onslaught against both slavery and slave-trading, led most notably by John Woolman and Anthony Benezet.[10] Philadelphia, the intellectual heart of the North American colonies, from whence there flowed a stream of articulate, literate and – ultimately – reforming sensibility, was also the centre of Quaker anti-slavery, with notable anti-slavery measures demanded of all Friends in 1755 and 1776. From these purely sectarian beginnings there followed a broader campaign to persuade local (American) legislatures to turn against slave trading. In fact the economic rationale for black slavery in North America was becoming progressively less convincing, and was only to revive, thanks to the cotton revolution, in the early years of the nineteenth century. But it was towards the slave trade that the pioneering American Quaker abolitionists turned their attacks. Anthony Benezet was especially convincing, and his words were sympathetically received in London, no less than Philadelphia.

British Quakers rallied to the cause in the 1760s but the most influential antagonist of the slave trade – the close and influential correspondent of Benezet – was Granville Sharp. Although not a Quaker, Sharp was won over to anti-slavery, as we have seen, by the fortuitous accident of confronting slave problems in London. His subsequent legal researches merely confirmed his initial abhorence. But Sharp was also reassured by Benezet's writing, which Sharp encountered in a bookstall in 1767. The 1770s saw a sympathetic correspondence between the two men and the proliferation of contacts between men of abolitionist sentiment (Quaker and non-Quaker) on both sides of the Atlantic. Thus, on the eve of American Independence, there existed a framework of abolitionist correspondents and friends spanning the English-speaking world; a network readily transformed in later years into the massive political organisation which gave abolition such irresistible strength in the years between 1787 and 1807.

During the American War of Independence, the issues of slavery and the slave trade were partly swamped by the overriding and consuming issues of political representation and, of course, of warfare. But Quakers kept to their self-appointed task of wooing influential and political opinion over to abolition. By the summer of 1783 there had come into being a Quaker committee to supervise abolitionist petitioning of the British Parliament. Backed, too, by extensive reprints of Benezet's tract *The Case of our Fellow-Creatures the Oppressed Africans . . .*, by 1784 the Quakers rapidly built up a national organisation of some 150 sympathisers throughout the country. The embryonic structure was inspired, to a marked degree, by the encouragement and promptings of American Quakers. But it was, equally, bolstered by the increasing prominence given to the slave cases, notably the 1772 Somerset case and the 1783 *Zong* case, both of which were orchestrated by Granville Sharp. Thus there was an important convergence, before and during the American War, of the more abstract (albeit theological) opposition which stemmed from American Quakers, and the uniquely 'domestic' question of slavery in England, Scotland and on board British slave ships. Moreover (and as we have already seen) the question of black society in England was reinforced by the arrival in Britain of substantial numbers of former slaves (loyalists) fleeing from North America. Their plight – and that of the broader black community ('the black poor') – in the years of the mid 1780s, culminating in the 1787 Sierra Leone scheme, served among other things, to give human substance to the humanitarian, philosophical and theological issues already discussed in a broadening community throughout Britain. Thus, the work of Granville Sharp had the incalculably important effect of transforming issues, which had hitherto been over-whelmingly abstract or theoretical, into substantive political, legal and public matters. Slavery and black society in England inevitably raised the question of slave trade and slavery in its broader setting and by the mid 1780s both had been firmly placed on the nation's political agenda.

In the longterm, it was also important that John Wesley had come out publically against slavery. Wesley had first-hand experience of slavery when living in Georgia, and he made a point of baptising blacks in Britain whenever the opportunity arose. But it was the work of Benezet which persuaded him. In February 1772 Wesley recorded in his journal: 'I read a very different book, published by an honest Quaker, on that execrable sum of all villanies, commonly called the Slave Trade. I read nothing like it in the heathen World, whether ancient or modern.'[11] Two years later, Wesley published his own attack, *Thoughts on the Slave Trade* (1774), a tract which had its own importance and influence within the rising tide of abolitionism but which was, more crucially perhaps, instrumental in swinging Methodist organisations (in Britain and America) against the slave trade. In time, with the dramatic growth in Methodism, notably in the expansive urban areas (later among Caribbean slaves), the abolitionism which stemmed from organised Methodism added extraordinarily large numbers – and an insistent ideological objection – to the campaign for black freedom. 'I would do anything [wrote Wesley in March 1790] in my power to the extirpation of that trade, which is a scandal not only to Christianity but to humanity.'[12]

The crucial point here is not so much that Methodists – like the Quakers – came to view black slavery as a wickedly unchristian evil (a fact to be explained by the broader shifts in theological thought) but that they brought their *institutional* strength to bear, on both sides of the Atlantic, as a vocal, highly organised pressure group opposed to the slave trade and, later, slavery itself. Long before the end of slavery, the British

Methodists were to be counted in excess of a third of a million. By comparison, the number of Quakers was minuscule (19,500 in 1800)[13] but their influence was to be counted more in their role as pioneers and in their quite remarkable prominence as a group of secular reformers in these years. Long before organised abolition adopted the motto 'Am I not a man and a brother?', Benezet had asserted the same egalitarian point.[14] This was a principle of fundamental – and ultimately irrefutable – logic and strength, one moreover which was to gain in power by the support it gained from the parallel development of secular rights (of man) after 1789. But it was to acquire a quite unpredictable twist by the early nineteenth century, when the pioneering missionaries (mainly Baptist and Methodist) converted growing numbers of black slaves in the British West Indies. Henceforth the black was not only a brother – a fellow human – but often also a member of the same church. Thus the sufferings and persecutions of the early nineteenth century slaves served to accentuate both the secular and religious outrage felt by the particular religious communities in Britain. And those communities were often to be found at the heart of the changing urban (and sometimes industrial) communities. Thus, the voice of anti-slavery came to be (by the 1820s and 1830s) primarily an *urban* voice. And when the representation of urban Britain was itself changed, anti-slavery was able to secure a more influential niche within Parliament itself.

The crucial years in the transformation of abolition from a minority (however voluble) sentiment, into an organised and public debate were the 1780s. The *Zong* affair, the origins of a bitter tract warfare (planters versus their British opponents) and the protracted argument about the black poor and the Sierra Leone scheme, all cumulatively focussed attention on blacks in Britain and on the ultimate source of their misery – slavery and the slave trade. Throughout, there was an accelerating effort by that small nucleus of abolitionists – as yet unorganised – to bring their viewpoint (and their writings) to the attention of the influential, the prominent and the potentially powerful. For example, Granville Sharp had for a long time persistently pestered Ministers, politicians and clerics with his thoughts on slavery.[15] Concerned clerics denounced black slavery from their pulpits, and pamphleteers begun to seek public attention through their tracts and letters to the London

Press. Magazines and newspapers began to give serious consideration – and space – to the troublesome question of slavery; they also began to give editorial judgements *pro* and *con*.[16] Alarmed at the hostile Press attention given to the slave empires, planters and traders – already well organised for their own economic and political interests – began to defend themselves in print, and by political influence.[17] But it is revealing that the plantocratic lobby in the mid 1780s (like that of 1772) sought to make political capital by pointing to the black community in Britain. Poor, unskilled, dejected and apparently without much individual or collective hope, British blacks provided an object lesson for the planters. Had anyone ever seen (wrote James Tobin, a planter from Nevis)

> a black ploughman, hedger, ditcher, mower, or reaper, in the country or a black porter, or chairman in London? On the contrary, I will be free to affirm, that out of the whole of this number, those who are not in livery are in rags; and such as are not servants, are thieves or mendicants.[18]

This was, of course, an early shot in the plantocratic racist argument that only slavery could be relied upon to keep blacks at their task and without black labour the material benefits of the colonies would simply evaporate. Thus, the problems of black society in Britain were used, by the mid 1780s, by both planters and early humanitarians to illustrate or prove their conflicting and mutually contradictory arguments about slavery and the slave trade. To the one side, British black life illustrated the need, benefits and virtues of maintaining blacks in bondage; to the other it revealed, in local British form, the harm, wickedness and unchristian consequences of the slave system.

Planters and slave traders had long had an effective political organisation – the West India Committee. By the mid 1780s, it was clear to many that the loose federation of friends of the blacks were in even greater need of a comparable organisation. Once more, it was the Quakers who provided the initiative.

Shortly after the three Royal Navy ships left Plymouth, in April 1787, with their 411 blacks from London, bound for Sierra Leone, Granville Sharp met with a group of sympathisers – the bulk of whom were Quakers – and formed the Society for the Abolition of the Slave Trade. In fact the core of this committee had been a Quaker gathering as early as 1783. The new committee was joined by Thomas Clarkson whose tract of 1786 *An Essay on the Slavery and Commerce of the Human Species, particularly the African* had initially been written as a Cambridge prize essay. More important still, the inspiration for that tract had been Benezets' *Historical Account of Guinea*. Clarkson flung himself into the anti-slave trade crusade with a single-minded and indefatigable zeal, becoming what Coleridge described as 'the moral steam engine . . . the giant with one idea'.[19] Like others before him Clarkson begain to pester and badger the famous and the powerful. He turned to William Wilberforce, MP for Yorkshire and close friend of the Prime Minister, William Pitt. Clarkson noted that on their first meeting 'Wilberforce stated frankly that the subject had often employed his thoughts, and that it was near to his heart. He seemed earnest about it, and also very desirous of taking the trouble of inquiring further into it.'[20]

From that day forward, Wilberforce entered the abolitionist campaign, his role primarily that of parliamentary spokesman and pricker of the official (and fashionable) conscience. Wilberforce had been unhappy about the slave trade from his school days. Henceforth his prime role was to be within Parliament where he could help the cause most. In the words of Granville Sharp: 'The respectability of his position as member for the largest county, the great influence of his personal connexions, added to an amiable and unblemished character, secure every advantage to the cause.'[21]

Indeed Wilberforce has come to personify the abolitionist campaign; the one man remembered by millions – black and white – as the prime agent in destroying black slavery in the British empire. It is in no way to diminish Wilberforce's stature or uniqueness to suggest that his importance in abolition was less vaunted (and effective) than is generally imagined, but it is important to stress that the traditional attention paid to Wilberforce in abolition has served to diminish the work of other (sometimes, it might be claimed more influential) activists. More crucial still, the historical fixations with Wilberforce have deflected attention from the broader socio-historical context within which abolitionism thrived and ultimately succeeded. Few serious scholars would now claim that abolition succeeded because of – or even primarily through – Wilberforce. But this is far from claiming that abolition would have taken the same pattern (run the same parliamentary course, for the same duration and with the same consequences) *without* Wilberforce. There is, for instance, a serious case to be made that in the hands of a better parliamentarian, the abolition of the slave trade might have been brought about *sooner*. Yet whatever the qualifications we need to consider, there can be no denying the fact of Wilberforce's association with anti-slavery in the public mind, both in his lifetime and afterwards; it is in certain key respects a classic illustration of the way myth so often transcends reality in the historical memory.

When the initial abolition meetings took place, in 1787–8, the sole ambition was to organise political pressure to end, not slavery, but the slave trade. The early meetings, according to Clarkson, distinguished between slavery and the slave trade.

> Now the question was, which of the two evils the committee should select as that, to which they should direct their attention with a view of the removal of it; or whether with the same view, it should direct its attention to both of them.
>
> It appeared soon to be the sense of the committee, that to aim at the removal of both would be to aim at too much, and that by doing this we might lose all.[22]

The decision to attack the slave trade made logical sense. It was felt, for example, that planters, unable to buy new slaves, 'must treat those better, whom they might then have'. Abolishing the slave trade would lay 'the axe at the very root' and the abolitionists would deflect the criticism 'that they were meddling with the property of the planters'. It was, moreover, an infinitely more manageable, practical and less complex problem. Despite the chorus of abuse from planters and traders, the Abolition Society publically declared that freeing slaves 'never formed any part of the plan of this Society'.[23]

This decision, taken clearly with an eye to the practicalities of contemporary politics, was also influenced by certain preconceptions of the problems of black slavery in the colonies. It seems to have been widely assumed that many of the human outrages witnessed in the West Indies were consequences of the slave trade itself, compounded by the inhumanities of planters who sought to extract the maximum effort from their slaves with no consideration for pain or social justice. There were, however, distinctive problems created by the peculiar demographic structures of slave life which served to confirm (and confuse) contemporary assessments of black slavery. This confusion could only be altered by firm statistical data about the slave population (which abolitionists did not have in 1787–8), but in the short term, the small band of abolitionists sought to persuade Parliament of the justice – and practicality – of their ambition. And to this end it was thought important to tap public antipathy to the slave trade, and direct its flow to Parliament. Not even the most optimistic of abolitionists could have forseen the extent, passion and influence of the public feeling which rapidly expressed itself on the issue of the slave trade.

To rally opinion, the small band of London abolitionists needed contacts with sympathisers throughout the country in order to promote abolitionism in the localities and to direct provincial feeling to the centre of political decision-making in London. Initially, however, they resolved to win support by publishing cheap literature. As we have seen, abolitionist pamphlets (most notably Benezet's) had already proved the remarkable influence of the printed word. In opting for a major publishing venture, the early abolitionists were merely following a well-trodden path. Reformers and radicals of various hues had, since the mid eighteenth century, made effective use of cheap (or free) tract literature. The Wilkes movement, the Yorkshire Association, the Society for Constitutional Information – all in addition to a myriad of less formal, often individual efforts – had strewn their printed arguments across the face of Britain, though concentrating primarily on friends and associates in the major urban areas, especially (and naturally) in London.

Tacts, reprints and abridgements by prominent abolitionists were published in their thousands, a fact which, inevitably, encouraged other individuals to write supporting pieces in newspapers and magazines.[24] Understandably, the West Indies lobby doubled its efforts, thus accentuating the war of words about slavery and the slave trade which had effectively begun during the Somerset case of 1772, but which had substantially increased in the 1780s. Indeed slavery and the trade became something of a literary genre, attracting the most talented (and talentless) of late eighteenth-century poets and novelists.[25] For the next half-century, slavery and all its ramifications, were to generate an unprecedented volume of printed materials; of books, tracts, verses, cartoons, periodicals and newspaper space. It is, naturally enough, virtually impossible to quantify the phenomenon but it is important to stress that in a British society in which literacy was itself becoming more significant and widespread – a society indeed in which literacy was to be a crucial ingredient in contemporary social and economic fortunes – abolitionist literature was produced and consumed on an unprecedented scale. Indeed at certain times and places, it became very difficult to avoid or ignore the abolitionist message, speeches and lectures.

In addition to the abolitionist arguments, purveyed in print, the pioneering abolitionists also needed a national organisation. There already existed a sympathetic network of Quakers throughout Britain. In their turn, they were able to recruit local non-Quaker sympathisers. In London and the provinces men found themselves won over or drawn to abolition; men often (though by no means always) experienced in earlier reforming organisation. Not all reformers were abolitionists, and not all abolitionists were reformers. None the less, enough of them shared a common political ground to enable historians to suggest that abolition was able to appeal to men of a reforming sensibility (despite distinctions between them on the nature of reform). Nonconformists (themselves keen to see their own disabilities removed), men of letters and science (often prominent in local critical enquiries into moral and scientific issues), intellectuals (won over by the rising cerebral objections to slavery), the 'new men' of business, commerce and industry (unsympathetic to the old economic doctrines basic to the survival of the old protected slave system) and others were, by inclination and interest, wooed over to abolition.[26] Such men formed the nucleus for the nationwide proliferation of abolitionist organisations and pressure from 1787 onwards.

To persuade Parliament of the emergent national antipathy towards the slave trade it was decided to petition Parliament. Petitioning Parliament – or Monarch – was an ancient method of expressing grievances or seeking redress and it had been used extensively and with some effect in the reforming campaigns in the earlier part of the 1780s. The suggestion to petition

originated in Manchester where local reformers meeting
Clarkson in May 1788 informed him of 'the spirit which was
then beginning to show itself, among the people of Manchester
and other places, on the subject of the slave trade, and which
would unquestionably manifest itself further by breaking out
into petitions to parliament for its abolition'. Clarkson was
surprised. 'The news, however, as it astonished, so it almost
overpowered me with joy.'[27] Further surprises were in store, for
the decision to call for petitions elicited a quite staggering – and
totally unforeseen – level of abolitionist sentiment. By the end
of May 1788 Parliament had received more than 100 petitions.
The original petition from Manchester attracted an extraordinary
10,639 signatures. That from Bristol – heart of the slaving
empire – 'was signed by a great number', and eventually the
table of the House of Commons 'was loaded with petitions from
every part of the kingdom'.[28] The decision to launch the
petitions was fortuitous, but the abolitionsts' unexpected
strength and success instantly established petitioning as a basic
and standard tactic of abolitionist politics. Like the printed
word, the abolitionist petition was to remain fundamental to
the abolitionist cause for a half a century. It was to remain,
despite the changes in political representation, the best – most
effective, flexible and manageable – means of expressing public
opinion to Parliament. Furthermore the demographic changes,
particularly the concentration of British population in urban
centres, were to make the act of widespread petitioning easier
while swelling the armies of names which were so readily
recruited in vast numbers. More than that, the petitions were,
from the first, politically influential. Their numbers and backing
ensured that Parliament could not ignore them. On the contrary,
the petitions were thought to carry irresistible political clout.
Speaking on the slave trade in 1788, the Prime Minister
remarked that the trade was 'a subject which, it was evident
from the great number and variety of petitions presented to
that House respecting it, had engaged the public attention to a
very considerable extent and *consequently deserved the most serious
notice of that House*'. Burke went even further: 'If that House
neglected the petition from its constituents, that House must be
abolished, and the privy council substituted in its stead.'[29]
   The petitions in the spring of 1788 were to coincide with
parliamentary scrutiny of the slave trade, set in train by Pitt,

himself persuaded by Wilberforce and other abolitionists of the iniquities of the trade. The ensuring Privy Council investigation accumulated a massive body of data on the slave trade, calling witnesses experienced in the trade and from among its opponents. But the Council's proceedings were, naturally enough, detailed, painstaking and lengthy; it did not report until the spring of 1789. It was then decided that further evidence must be heard at the Bar of the Commons, a tactic which delayed until April 1791 a vote on the abolition of the slave trade. The vote was defeated by 163 to 88.[30] The intervening period had been filled with activity; widespread and persistent lobbying and the continuing programme of building up a factual dossier about the slave trade. In this, the lion's share of activity and achievement belonged to Thomas Clarkson whose seven journeys between 1787 and 1794 covered 35,000 miles, yielding (often at great personal cost and hardship) unparalleled data on all aspects of the slave trade (not least important of which was the evidence about the horrific death rates among white sailors). Clarkson also unearthed a series of important witnesses whose testimony before Parliament was to have a decisive impact in establishing beyond partisan doubt the full horrors created by the slave trade.[31] Throughout, the London Committee steadily built up its network of corresponding sympathisers – churches, local abolitionist organisations and individuals – all of whom turned their energies into abolitionist agitations and propaganda in their various localities.[32]

However depressing the Commons' defeat of April 1791, there was no doubt that by that date abolition had been staggeringly successful in accumulating widespread public backing. But it seems, by all accounts – and quite naturally – to have been supported primarily from the propertied nation. In the early 1790s, however, a crucial – and again unforeseen (and to a degree unwelcome) – transformation took place when abolition began to spill beyond the pale of traditional, propertied politics and to embrace 'the people'. This was primarily a result of the French Revolution.

It is tempting to think of the impact of the Revolution in terms of the convulsion of popular and loyalist politics which so bitterly divided Britain after 1792. But in the initial stages of the Revolution, events in France had a muted effect. Initially, few shared Burke's instant and abiding hatred of the Revolution,

preferring instead to view 1789 as the eclipse of a royal
authoritarianism which (so it was felt) the English had dispensed
with a century before. To many (including the Prime Minister)
it seemed that the French were taking a step towards the
constitutional stability achieved by the British. Many, of course,
positively rejoiced in the French changes, few more strenuously
and openly than the small band of reformers – the Society for
Constitutional Information, the Revolution Society (formed to
celebrate 1688) and the early Romantics. And among their
ranks were to be numbered many of the pioneering abolitionists.
But events in France – progressively more extreme, volatile and
ultimately violent – gradually began to alienate propertied
British opinion which had begun to coalesce, informally, around
the standard of opposition raised by Burke in his *Reflections on
the Revolution in France*, published in November 1790. On the
other side of the ideological fence, men who had been active in
the SCI and anti-slavery came together to form local
reforming organisations (often named 'Constitutional Societies').
Meanwhile Burke's old associate and erstwhile friend Tom
Paine, back in England after his influential sojourn in America
(where he had taken an abolitionist stance in the constitutional
arguments which heralded American Independence), published
his epochal answer to Burke. *The Rights of Man* proved to be one
of the major landmarks in modern radical politics and thought.
The book gave a remarkable boost to flagging radical fortunes,
aided late in 1791 by a downturn in the economy.

Paine's book derived much of its ideological inspiration from
the fundamental rights already asserted by the Revolutions of
1776 and 1789. Men began to talk about their 'natural rights'.
A Cambridge group argued 'Every individual of mankind is
born with a natural right to life, liberty and property.'[33] Like
the Declaration of Rights of Man in France, so bold an assertion
could not, by definition, be hedged in by qualifications. It must
of necessity apply to all; young and old, male and female, black
and white. In the words of that doughty female enemy of
radicalism, Hannah More:

> It follows, according to the actual progression of human
> beings, that the next influx of that irradiation which our
> enlighteners are pouring on us, will illuminate the world with

the grave descants on the rights of youth, the rights of children, the rights of babies.[34]

No less important, these rights were clearly applicable to non-white people. Thomas Hardy, the Scottish shoemaker who lived in Piccadilly and who founded the working mens' London Corresponding Society in 1792, expressed the point simply: 'The rights of man are not confined to this small island but are extended to the whole human race, black and white, high or low, rich or poor.'[35] Trying to build up contacts with reformers in the provinces, Hardy was told of an abolitionist, the Reverend Bryant, in Sheffield and 'inferred from that that you was [sic] a friend of freedom on the broad basis of the Rights of Man'.[36] The links were, as we have seen, much more complex than Hardy imagined. In the short term, however, there is no doubt that the popular societies led by the London Corresponding Society, which proliferated throughout Britain in 1792 and which consisted overwhelmingly of working men, inspired by Paine and seeking political reform, were abolitionist. There was a universal identification between men who viewed themselves as dispossessed – the victims of an unrepresentative and oppressive system – and black slaves, stripped of all their rights and consigned to inhuman bondage – by the same political and economic system. Indeed from 1792 through to the 1840s, the language and imagery of slavery were infused into British radical and working-class politics (not always fairly, it has to be said); it strengthened an argument to compare the problems of Britons with those of contemporary slaves.

The most powerful provincial radical society was the Sheffield Constitutional Society, rooted among the artisans in the local cutlery trades. At their largest public meeting (in 1794) they resolved, among other issues, to end the slave trade; 'Wishing to be rid of the weight of oppression under which we groan, we are induced to compassionate those who groan also.' But they went much further, arguing that 'no compromise can be made between Freedom and Tyranny' and, accordingly, there should be a 'total Emancipation of the Negro Slaves'.[37] This was well in advance of formal abolition which, although embracing some individuals committed to emancipation, had specifically limited their collective ambition to ending the slave trade.

More important perhaps than the keen attachment to

abolition shown by plebeian radicals in the early 1790s was the
fact that their national network of links and organisations lent
the strength of their unprecedented numbers to the campaign
for abolition. When, in 1792, the abolitionists called for renewed
petitioning, the corresponding societies were able to assist. In
the spring of that year abolitionist petitions rained on Parliament
in unparalleled numbers; eventually there was a total of 519.[38]
The following parliamentary debate was, again, unsuccessful
but the balance between the two sides was very fine indeed;
Wilberforce had wooed over more MPs to his side and the
outcome of parliamentary votes had clearly become haphazard
and unpredictable. Illness, absence, laziness – or poor
parliamentary management – could tip the vote on the slave
trade one way or the other.[39] Furthermore, Wilberforce's dogged
insistence on total (as opposed to gradual) abolition alienated
parliamentary wavers. Had he moderated his position, the slave
trade could quite easily have been voted into extinction as early
as 1793.[40] The simple truth of the matter was that by early 1792
abolition had firmly lodged itself within Parliament. This was
due primarily to the massive public campaign of recent years
and to Wilberforce's single-minded nagging of Ministers and
MPs at Westminster.

In a sense, abolition no longer needed the public pressure,
save only to complement parliamentary debates. But what *was*
needed, by 1792, was astute parliamentary management (never
a possibility under the unpredictable leadership of Wilberforce)
or a major change in governing circles. Pitt, for all his sympathy,
could not commit his Cabinet to abolition as a government
measure. Moreover, by 1792 a number of factors had begun to
alienate ministers and MPs from the abolitionist cause. Firstly,
the success of the corresponding societies alarmed men of
property who, siding with Burke, sought to distance themselves
from popular pressure and from any associated hint of reform
(of Parliament or the slave trade). Secondly, events in France
veered further and further towards violence, extremism and,
eventually, republicanism (though this did not, initially at least,
repel the corresponding societies who continued to look to
France for ideological leadership). But the most cataclysmic
repercussion of the Revolution was in the French colony of St
Domingue (Haiti) where the initial political skirmishing (on
the model of 1789) was, within a few years, to herald communal

racial violence, full-scale war (including the destruction of a British army), the eventual end of local slavery and the collapse of the prospering economy of the island. Haiti was to be a fearful example used by all sides in contemporary and subsequent debates about abolition and emancipation.

The slave lobby viewed the Haitian revolt as proof of the folly of tampering with so volatile a substance as slavery; the abolitionists regarded Haiti as an appalling illustration of what happens when no effort is made to ameliorate the conditions of slavery. Among slave holders throughout the Americas, Haiti was a nightmare; an example of slave vengeance and the dormant potential, in all slave communities, for savage revolt. It is now possible to see the Haitian revolution as unique; a distinct set of conditions unrepeatable in their form anywhere else. At the time, however, Haiti inspired a fear of the uncontrollable contagion of black revolt. Reports from the British islands suggested that the slaves had formed their own (dangerous) conclusions about the events in Haiti. A letter of November 1791 to the Colonial Office remarked, of Jamaican slaves, 'I am convinced the ideas of liberty have sunk so deep in the minds of *all* Negroes, that wherever the greatest precautions are not taken they will rise.'[41]

Moreover there was clear evidence to show that British abolition – no less than the more immediate lessons from Haiti – had begun to affect British slaves. It was reported in November 1791 that large crowds of slaves had gathered in western Jamaica to celebrate the birthday of Wilberforce. In all this, however, we need to remind ourselves of the apprehension – at times the simple terror – of whites in the islands, where traditional nightmares of slave insurrection had been amply fulfilled on a scale which even the planters had scarcely imagined. In the words of the cartoonist, George Cruikshank, in a caricature of plantocratic life:

> The planter's dream doth plainly seem
> To point a moral deep
> If you choose to whack a nigger's back
> You should never go to sleep[42]

By 1792 it was quite impossible to disentangle the story of Haiti from the British arguments about the slave trade.

The Haitian revolt compounded the doubts – first sown by events in France – about the wisdom of conceding change in times of unpredictable international upheavals. Thus, those men who agitated for political reforms – notably abolition of the slave trade and the reform of Parliament – came to be lumped together; to be condemned as different forms of the same subversive group. Reformers and abolitionists came to be labelled 'Jacobins', a process given greater political strength, after the outbreak of war between France and Britain in February 1793. A few months later, the Earl of Abingdon remarked in Parliament:

> The idea of abolishing the slave trade is connected with the levelling system and the rights of man; his lordship asked who would controvert such a proposition? For the very definition of the terms themselves, as descriptive of the thing, what does the abolition of the slave trade mean more or less, than liberty and equality? What more or less than the rights of man? And what are the rights of man, but the foolish principles of this new philsophy. If proofs are wanting, look at the colony of St Domingue and see what the rights of man have done here.[43]

As if to prove Abingdon's point, within the month the corresponding societies – now pursuing the abolitionists tactics – inundated Parliament with their reform petitions. Indeed it was noted that Parliament had been elected by *fewer* people than had signed the petitions.[44] The petitions revealed the remarkable demand for reform; they came from throughout urban Britain and attracted tens of thousands of names. The one from Sheffield had 8000 names (compared to a mere 800 in 1789),[45] 3700 names came from Norwich while that from Edinburgh stretched 'the whole length of the floor of the House'. The petition from the London Corresponding Society took half an hour to read; some 10,000 names were attached to it.[46] This manifestation of unprecedented popular radicalism – closely monitored from its inception by the intrusion of government spies – was but one reason for increasing government alarm about the state of internal security and peacefulness. Faced by a hostile revolutionary France across the Channel and by a thriving radical movement in British cities (which also openly expressed sympathy for France and its continuing changes), men of property inside Government and out, began to spurn the ideals of reform. Even those men (including Pitt) who had once favoured a variety of reforms began to renounce their former sympathies and to resist demands from those outside the political fold. There was indeed a generalised dismissal of all forms of reform, whether parliamentary change or abolition of the slave trade. There was, quite simply, a growing fear that concessions would encourage the political upheavals which had inundated France since 1789. Pitt and the Home Secretary began to plan how best to curb the rising passion of public mass politics.[47]

It was ironic that at the very moment abolition had become unprecedentedly popular, the basis for its popularity came under political attack. According to Wilberforce: 'People connect democratical principles with the Abolition of the Slave Trade and will not hear mention of it.'[48] Absurd – but none the less damaging – accusations were levelled in print against 'the JACOBINS OF ENGLAND, the Wilberforces, the Coopers, the Paines and the Clarksons'.[49] One man complained to Wilberforce, 'I do not imagine that we could meet with 20 persons in Hull at present who would sign a petition, that are not republicans.'[50] Parliamentary abolitionists and their public enemies agreed that there was a growing popular confusion of abolition with French principles. 'I am justified [wrote one hostile critic] in classing the promoters of Abolition and Republicans together.'[51] Such an accusation was politically effective, especially when a British army was, at that precise moment, being sucked into a fatal conflict in Haiti.[52] But the key question is, how valid is the accusation? There is no doubt that many of the prominent popular radicals were abolitionists and some were openly sympathetic to the revolution in France. John Thelwall, the most prominent lecturer within the London Corresponding Society between 1793 and 1795, proclaimed himself 'the only avowed *sans culottes* in the metropolis', 'in plain truth I am a Republican, a downright sans culottes'.[53] Thelwall also spoke out against the slave trade and slavery (though unhappy at the way the slave trade had, by the mid 1790s, come to monopolise the national conscience). For Thelwall and his fellow radicals, the political sway exercised by the West Indian lobby in London was further proof of the corruption of slavery. Ending

slavery would have the added political advantage of overthrowing
West Indian political power in London. Conversely, a reform of
Parliament would destroy the West Indians' metropolitan power
base, a base they clearly needed for a successful defence of their
slaving interests.

While Thelwall became the popular radicals' most prominent
spokesman, their most effective organiser (and, in effect,
founder) was Thomas Hardy, the shoemaker. His house guest in
Piccadilly was Olaudah Equiano, the African and ex-slave who
became the accepted leader of London's black community and
whose autobiography was revised in Hardy's home. Equiano
also joined the London Corresponding Society and provided
Hardy with useful correspondents in the provinces (people
Equiano had already met as abolitionists).[54] One provincial
corresponding society, in Melbourne, Derbyshire, adopted as
its motif a picture of Africans being enslaved.[55] And whenever
corresponding societies asserted their principles, they often
paralleled demands for parliamentary reform with an insistence
on abolition. The popular radicals were openly in favour of
abolition and even (more fundamentally) of black equality, and
it was perfectly correct for opponents of abolition to suggest
that there was a close association between the two issues. It
was, however, quite wrong to impute to reformers (and
abolitionists in general) the principles of French Jacobinism.
British radicals were steeped in the traditions and vocabulary
of British reform, but their ideals were transmuted, by the
lengthening shadows from France, into Jacobinism, at least in
the eyes of their opponents.

Wilberforce himself came to denounce them, his anger
doubtless sharpened by the apparent damage caused by the
association between radicalism and abolition. He claimed that
radicals had created

> a contempt for the British Constitution and an attachment to
> those false principles of liberty which had produced such
> extensive mischief in a neighbouring country; nor was it only
> French politics which they imported into this country, but
> French philosophy also; in the numerous publications by
> which their opinions were disseminated, there was a marked
> contempt for everything sacred, an avowed opposition to the
> religion, as well as the constitution of Great Britain.[56]

By the time of the Two Acts, late in 1795, banning most aspects of the popular radical movement, the radicals had come to be denounced even by those whose own principles the radicals supported. Propertied reformers had shied away from them and abolitionists disliked them. Yet in a sense it did not matter because, by then, Wilberforce and friends had built up a sufficiently solid parliamentary base to promote abolition within Parliament itself. The popularity of abolition had been instrumental in lodging the cause firmly in Parliament. By the mid 1790s, parliamentary abolitionists no longer needed such extra-parliamentary pressure (indeed, in the changed political climate their cause could actually be damaged by popular backing). What was needed henceforth was astute parliamentary management, and ministerial help (or changes) to transmute public support into tangible votes of change. Henceforth abolition was prone to the capricious circumstances of parliamentary life and exposed to the unpredictable lobbying of Wilberforce in Parliament.

The campaign for the abolition of the slave trade had been able to demonstrate its remarkable national support by using distinctive and effective political tactics. In 1795, however, the foundations of public agitation were, at a stroke, demolished by the Two Acts which, though aimed primarily at the corresponding societies, were equally destructive to other forms of open and public agitation. It was a process completed by further repressive legislation in 1799. Thereafter, popular and public politics was under the ban; with savage punishments for those desperate enough to continue with the long-established traditions of popular campaigns. For popular radicalism, the Acts of 1795 and 1799 were a death blow, driving most activists into a truculent and begrudging silence, others – a small minority – into desperate and sometimes violent insurrectionism.

The ban was less serious for abolition. The campaign to abolish the slave trade was, henceforth, essentially a parliamentary struggle, focussed on the motion, periodically moved by Wilberforce, for immediate abolition. In the decade between the Two Acts and the passing of abolition, the arguments about abolition remained fundamentally the same; a recitation of the *pros* and *cons* well rehearsed since 1788. But, for once, it was without that descant of public opposition which had been the hallmark of abolition up to the mid 1790s. The

Parliament returned in 1796 was, as a body, collectively influenced by the fear of 'French principles', and abolitionist motions failed in 1797, 1798, 1799 and 1802, though sometimes by the narrowest of margins.[57] Throughout, the powerful West Indian lobby of MPs waged an effective defence of the slave trade, though a small number began, in the late 1790s, seriously to consider concessions to the abolitionists, particularly by offering appropriate amelioration among the slaves themselves. Equally, the parliamentary abolitionists were able to steer through Parliament a number of revisionary Bills which served to modify (and improve) conditions for slaves on the middle passage.[58] But new conquests in the Caribbean, notably Trinidad, apparently compounded the abolitionist difficulties by offering new and relatively untapped land for further exploitation by slave labour. By a strange twist of fate, the new possessions were to prove grist to the abolitionist mill. With the possession of Trinidad confirmed by the Peace of Amiens, abolitionists were, ironically, presented with the major chance of a breakthrough for their ambitions. Pitt was now out of office; his successor, Addington, quickly subjected to Wilberforce's personal pressures. But it was the motion of Canning in 1802, seeking to prevent further slave importations into Trinidad, which obliged Addington's Government to pledge caution (and parliamentary approval) on the future development of that island. Furthermore, the continuing recalcitrance of the West Indian planters had, by the turn of the century, begun to alienate more and more MPs.[59] It was paradoxical that with anti-slavery firmly wedged in Parliament, the British slaving system was enjoying unparalleled success. The slave populations of the British islands were more buoyant than ever before; they greatly outnumbered their nearest rivals, the greatest of which, Haiti, now lay in feuding ruins. Moreover, the economic strength of the British Caribbean remained undiminished, its tropical staples being consumed in increasing volume by metropolitan society.[60] Furthermore its expansive economic and geographic frontiers (in Jamaica, Guiana and Trinidad) provided little but continuing growth and its associated prosperity. The military victories in the wars of the 1790s and the territorial acquisitions – none of which could have been predicted (indeed the British disaster in Haiti provided a cautionary tale of a possible alternative military scenario) – had given an unexpected fillip to the British slave trade and slavery. The result, by the end of the century, was a revitalised British slave trade, pouring ever more Africans into the Caribbean and threatening to overwhelm all the earlier successes of metropolitan abolitionists by the sheer momentum of the slaving interests. Indeed the slaving interests were bigger and stronger at the dawn of the nineteenth century than they had been when abolitionism had been launched in 1787. Yet within a few years, the slave trade had been ended.

The key lay in the realisation (initially by James Stephen, Wilberforce's most effective ally) that an embargo on *foreign* slave trading would cripple a substantial part of the slaving system.[61] Submitted in 1806, in the early months of a new administration, the Foreign Slave Bill provoked little of the fierce opposition and controversy which had overshadowed earlier abolitionist measures. Few *pro*-slave parliamentarians seemed to have realised that the Bill, though far from the old demand for general and immediate abolition, would in fact destroy between three-quarters and two-thirds of the British slave trade.[62] By the early summer of 1806 Parliament had abolished the great bulk of the British slave trade, and abolitionists immediately began to plan to complete the attack. The Foreign Act also wore down opposition, for it had the effect of convincing large numbers of people that abolition was effectively in operation; there seemed little reason to fight the inevitable completion of the process. The initial Act had been promoted in the national economic interest – a blow against real and potential competitors of slave-grown produce. Thereafter it was possible to appeal, once more, to the familiar themes of humanity and justice.[63] When the Abolition Bill was debated in February–March 1807, it made remarkable and successful progress, and received Royal Assent on 25 March. In the short term, it was the result of astute lobbying and open pressure from the new Prime Minister, Grenville. Canning remarked that 'the decision of the slave trade shows what a Government *can* do if it pleases'.[64] Both Acts, of 1806 and 1807, were functions overwhelmingly of parliamentary tactics and ploys. The pressures and arguments, the deals and threats, the rhetoric and the evidence, took place, not in public but within Parliament, Government and within the close circle of the politically influential who were the brokers and dealers of the main political activists. When abolition succeeded it was widely *assumed* that it had public support and that it was, indeed, a victory both for morality and outraged public feeling. Yet, for the past decade public feeling had not been permitted to express itself on this or other matters. In retrospect, however, it is possible to see that it was not needed. Public support for abolition had, however, been crucial in the broader abolitionist campaign for it had been the agency which had transmuted the intellectual and religious criticisms of slavery (by definition a minority preoccupation) into the substance of mass politics. And the tactics and arguments of popular abolition had served to lodge the issue securely with Parliament itself. When fear of 'French principles' persuaded the Government to undermine popular politics (including abolition) the parliamentary base for abolition was secure. Thereafter the fight was essentially parliamentarian. The *Edinburgh Review* remarked: 'This is not, we apprehend, one of the cases where the wisdom of government has gone before the voice of the people. . . . The sense of the nation has pressed abolition upon our rulers.'[65] The Abolition Acts of 1806 and 1807 were substantially aided by contingent and fortuitous circumstances, though this does not diminish the abolitionists' tactical achievements which lay behind them. The public abolitionist voice had long been silenced, but this should not deceive us into minimising its earlier influence. And yet, for all the unquestionable significance of abolition, there remained hundreds of thousands of black slaves in the British Caribbean. The logic of abolitionism was to embark on a new crusade; to bring freedom to Britain's enslaved Caribbean people.

6 Outraging Opinion: Slavery in the Aftermath of Abolition

Ending the British slave trade was an undeniable, major political achievement. But it remained unclear what the consequences would be. There were, after all, many other European nations with an interest in feeding the voracious economies of the Americas and however strong and ascendant the Royal Navy, it could scarcely hope successfully to patrol the whole of the African coastline and the Atlantic shipping lanes against slave traders. However effective this Royal Naval presence and, later, notwithstanding the effectiveness of the Foreign Office treaties seeking to outlaw slaving and maritime slave trade, total enforcement of anti-slave trade was obviously impossible. Indeed the subsequent economic boom in a number of slave societies in the Americas (notably Cuba and Brazil) encouraged massive importations of Africans long after the British abolition of 1807. An estimated two million slaves crossed the Atlantic between 1811 and 1860.[1] Although the buoyant US cotton economy similarly needed slaves, its indigenous black population was sufficiently fertile and self-producing as to eliminate any further dependence on African imports.

In 1807 – just as in 1788 – the architects of abolition could not, of course, predict these events. But it is important to recall that their determination to end the slave trade was designed to transform slavery itself. It was assumed that ending the supply of Africans would oblige slave owners – the planters – to improve their slaves' conditions. Such amelioration would, in an unspecified way, lead to the gradual withering and decay of slavery itself. This was an argument repeated by Wilberforce in 1807 when reflecting on abolition:

All ideas of supply from without, being utterly cut off, it would immediately become the grand, constant and incessant concern of every prudent man, both proprietor and manager, to attend, in the first instance, to the preservation and increase of his Negroes. . . . The abolition would give the death-blow to this system. The opposite system, with all its charities, would force itself on the dullest intellects, on the most contracted and unfeeling heart.

This was, however, a gradual process. After their victory of 1807, as before, abolitionists went out of their way to deny that they sought immediate black freedom. Wilberforce rejected the claim that they sought 'the design of immediately emancipating the Slaves. Can it be necessary to declare, that the Abolitionists are full as much as any other man convinced, that insanity alone would dictate such a project.'[2] Not until the mid 1820s did abolitionist patience run out and powerful sections in their midst begin to demand immediate black freedom.[3]

One central problem facing abolitionists in 1807 was to know precisely what were the human and demographic consequences of abolition. And related to this more general proposition was the need to know whether (and how) the planters were able to circumvent the provisions of abolition. In order to curtail slave trading by other nations (who might of course illicitly supply British planters), the humanitarians launched an attack, through diplomatic channels, on international slave trading. One month after abolition, 'The African Institution' was formed to promote 'such measures as were best conducive to promote . . . [the] civilization and happiness' of Africans and 'to promote the abolition of the African Slave Trade by Foreign powers'.[4] With powerful political – and royal – patronage the officers of the Institution – notably Thomas Clarkson – were guaranteed an immediate audience with Ministers. Moreover the abolitionists determined to press for international abolition in the Congress system, inaugurated in 1814, and had the ear, sympathy and invaluable practical help of the senior British statesmen involved. Clarkson was indefatigable in lobbying the high and mighty throughout European political circles, and was even granted the remarkable facility of using the diplomatic bags (by Wellington).[5] Clarkson scurried between appointments with Ministers and royalty in the major European capitals, pressing on them the need to outlaw the slave trade. Indeed, Thomas Clarkson was granted direct and privileged access to the most rarified of European circles; his letters, publications and promptings (later still his own person) swiftly ushered into the offices of Kings and senior ministers assembling to negotiate the reorganisation of post-war Europe.[6] There were, however, powerful countervailing pressures, notably the French determination to assert their own best economic interests. When, at the Vienna meetings, it seemed likely that the French slave trade would receive formal sanction rather than prohibition,[7] British abolitionists turned from high politics to the activities which had given them such political strength – and credibility – in the first place: the power of public support. A small band of prominent abolitionists had come together as early as 1813 to plan new tactics; to discover precisely what were the consequences of the abolition of the slave trade on the slave populations of the islands. They were especially concerned lest planters had been able to smuggle new slaves into the Caribbean.[8] But the diplomatic threats of 1814 brought a swift abolitionist response, a revival of the main metropolitan abolitionists committees and a flurry of correspondence to revive old contacts and committees throughout the whole kingdom. A prototype petition was swiftly dispatched to provincial sympathisers who were goaded into action in their localities.[9]

In the summer of 1814, the protracted French wars apparently drawing to a close, popular politics re-emeged from its enforced wartime hibernation. News of the possible revival of the French slave trade galvanised the old band of abolitionists, though now joined by a remarkably wide circle of radicals, reformers, Whigs and others, united to revive popular abolitionism. An anonymous correspondent to *The Times* (using the pseudonym 'Alfred', the most popular radical camouflage of the 1790s) intoned: 'My countrymen! Let us arise as one man throughout the kingdom, and at once cry NO to the further continuance of this detestable crime. . . . Let the voice of the British nation once declare itself and the African Slave Trade must universally cease.'[10]

Naturally enough, the task was to prove more difficult and protracted than he imagined. But the public cry of outrage was loud and remarkable. The public meetings called to protest were often the first major political gathering in the localities for twenty years,[11] a fact which may explain the extraordinary support they received. These meetings organised petitions, in a reprise of the tactics of 1787–95. In the words of Samuel Romilly, 'The example was followed in most of the great towns in England; and more than 800 petitions were, in little more than a month from this time, presented to Parliament against the slave trade, signed by 700,000 persons.'[12]

From a population of perhaps 12 millions, 1.5 million put their name to abolitionist petitions.[13] Samuel Whitbread's fitting remark was that 'The country never has, and I fear never will, express a feeling so general as they have done about the slave trade.'[14] More than 800 abolitionist petitions showered on Parliament, and reports of petitioning were a daily item in *The Times*.[15] The Ambassador to Spain noted 'the nation is bent on the subject. I believe there is hardly a village that has not met and petitioned upon it: both Houses of Parliament are pledged to press it; and the ministers must make it the basis of their policy.'[16] Clarkson for one was in no doubt that the public pressure of 1814 had forced the Government's hand. 'No other reason can be given why Administration was so apparently indifferent to the Subject when the Treaty was made, and why so interesting since.'[17] Clarkson's private letters to his wife Catherine confirmed his public assessments; that petitioning was politically persuasive. 'We must however go on and persevere in Petitions to show the Voice of England, and to strengthen Ministers thereby.' He was in no doubt of the extent of support; 'People seem but of one mind on our Subject.'[18] No less a figure than Talleyrand felt the same way; abolition had 'become for the English people a passion carried to fanaticism, and one which the Ministry is no longer at liberty to check'.[19]

The abolitionist response, in the summer of 1814, was universal, dramatic and quite unexpected. It was, however, ultimately to little avail because the cause of international abolition was merely shunted around the diplomatic circuits of the Congress system. Prominent abolitionists gradually realised that the initial enthusiasm they had encountered in 1814 was slowly dissipated by the cynical diplomatic manoevrings for national advantage. The French in particular proved impossibly resistant to the idea of international abolition (doubtless cynical about the altruism of the campaigning British). By 1822 a shocked Thomas Babington wrote, from Paris, 'No member of the Ministry cares a fig for the abolition of the Slave Carrying Trade, and many are really interested in its continuance.'[20]

However unsuccessful the diplomatic outcome, and quite to their surprise, the abolitionists had shown the speed, power and ubiquity of their political reflexes. After almost four decades, the cause of abolition had shown, at the end of a long and ennervating war, that it would elicit a remarkable response from the British people. The problem remained how to transmute the undoubted national antipathy to the slave trade and slavery into specific acts of political change.

The campaign against the slave trade had carried such conviction largely because of the irrefutable evidence it accumulated and displayed to the public about the bestialities of the trade. Clarkson's researches and the testimonies of sailors, traders and by-standers provided an accumulating dossier of horror stories which served to outrage public and political opinion and to steer it towards abolition. How to uncover evidence about the lives of the slaves in the colonies was more troublesome and indirect. Clarkson was particularly keen to hear of people who had spent time in the West Indies and whose personal testimonies he might use. But a more systematic source was needed. It came initially in the form of an Order in Council of 1812 ordering all slave-owners in Trinidad to register their slaves by a certain date. This attempt to form a slave census, designed primarily to prevent illegal importations, had little practical effect in the teeth of local plantocratic opposition and political indifference.[21] Registration did, however, offer a step towards the kind of regulation and control which abolitionists wanted to see as a barrier between planters and slaves. Proposed as a general principle in 1812 by James Stephen, Wilberforce agreed in Parliament in 1815 that there should be a universal registration in all the slave colonies.[22] Registration was, in effect, a step towards amelioration of slave conditions, without which emancipation itself could not be contemplated. It was later claimed that, at the time of the registration campaign, only Zachary Macaulay wanted emancipation sooner rather than later; 'actual emancipation was a grand concession to humanity which I firmly believe that the most sanguine abolitionists never contemplated in 1813 . . . they deemed it visionary, and many distrusted its practicability with safety'.[23] Registration was, eventually, to yield the data which pushed men towards black freedom; by the mid 1820s powerful groupings began to demand immediate black freedom.

Abolitionists were unsure of exactly how registration would improve the slaves' conditions, though it was felt that public scrutiny of the subsequent demographic data would itself persuade planters of the need for a more benign policy towards their slaves. Clarkson for one felt that if

> the owners of slaves, and the Colonial Legislatures, are deaf to Reason, they must be *compelled to obey it*. They must be *overawed by the public voice*. The British public must never cease to complain, till the poor Negroes are treated something more like British Subjects than they are at present.[24]

It is revealing that, throughout, Clarkson assumed that 'the public voice' was an irresistible force, to be unleashed on the heads of the unbending slave lobby, if they refused to see reason. In fact, the threats of registration brought an outcry from the planters throughout the islands. Their claims that a general Registration Bill violated key constitutional rights persuaded Wilberforce to drop the idea. Instead, the various islands were encouraged to establish their own local registrations. The subsequent Acts provided demographic data – all lodged in a central Registry in London – of the richest and most detailed kind. Contemporaries (and modern historians) were henceforth able to analyse the short-term fluctuations and long-term trends in the population structures of British West Indian slaves.[25] Abolitionists now turned to the London Registry for the factual evidence needed to advance their case against slavery itself.[26] Henceforth, throughout the 1820s and 1830s, arguments about slavery, its *pros* and *cons*, shifted to a qualitatively different level; the impressionistic (and to a degree emotional) quality of the attacks on slavery was superceded by carefully documented and substantiated argument. Registration, for all its imperfections, provided an entrée into the reality of slavery. It afforded a qualitatively new approach to the study (and denunciation) of slavery, comparable in its importance to the evidence Clarkson had amassed in the earlier campaign against the slave trade.

West Indian planters, and their spokesmen in London,

bitterly denounced the 'intereference' in the relations between themselves and their slaves; it was, they claimed, unnecessary and potentially disastrous. The memories of the Haitian revolt had, after all, scarcely begun to fade. The Barbadian Assembly denounced 'those deluded Philanthropists' demanding registration which would, instead of improving things, merely excite 'ill-defined expectations that cannot be gratified' and encourage 'an Insubordination'.[27] As if to prove their point, within the year a major slave rebellion had rocked that apparently secure and stable slave society. Barbados, the pioneering British slave island which had witnessed the important transition to plantation sugar in the seventeenth century, was a compact geographical settlement, housing 77,000 slaves, some 93 per cent of whom were Creole (rather than African) in 1816. But like all the slave islands it was replete with its own distinctive problems and discontents between and among the various social – and racial – groupings. The planters denounced the Registration Bill 'as a plan for the emancipation of the slaves'.[28] Not for the first or last time, the plantocratic outrage expressed in often splenetic outbursts in the local Press, and – most influentially – in casual (often careless) conversations in public or over the dinner table, inevitably caught the attention of local slaves. Overheard conversation and garbled snippets of information served to convince some Barbadian slaves that their friends in England had secured their freedom just as they had ended the miseries of the slave trade. The slave revolt of April 1816 had complex (short- and long-term) causes and was suppressed with the killing of 120 slaves, with a further 144 executed and 132 deported.[29] Its successful suppression did nothing to soften the planters' anxieties, or to minimise the slaves' grievances. The Speaker of the Barbadian Assembly remarked sourly that 'the spirit is not subdued, nor will it ever be subdued whilst these dangerous doctrines which have been spread abroad continue to be propagated among the Slaves'.[30] Henceforth, white West Indian society (not by any means uniquely plantocratic) developed a mounting suspicion of metropolitan humanitarians, assuming that the arguments about slave society – about amelioration, registration, Christianisation and, later, black freedom – formed a subversive and potentially insurrectionary influence among the slaves.

After a fashion, West Indian whites were correct to fear the transatlantic contagion of the ideals generated by revived British humanitarianism. Slaves clearly (and demonstrably) *were* influenced by news from Britain, and much of that news was garbled and distorted (often, however, by the whites themselves). Caribbean whites needed no reminding that the disaster of the Haitian rebellion was initiated by the ideological debate, begun in Paris in 1789 and wafting its socially (and racially) disruptive ideas westward into the slave colonies. Of course, it is perfectly true that the history of the slave islands had, from the early days of black demographic predominance, been characterised by an unshifting nightmare about the precariousness of sound control and the perennial fear of black plebeian insurrection. No white minority could rest tranquil in the face of an oppressed and perpetually discontented and enslaved black labouring force. The difficulties of managing and controlling the enslaved populations were basic to the system, particularly up to 1807 when the demographic dependence on the African slave trade ensured regular infusions of fresh batches of Africans into the slave quarters. Controlling the slave societies was an unceasing problem, though the nature of the problem varied between the islands and differed from time to time. None the less, whether it was an island-wide problem, notably a problem of governance, or the specific difficulties of controlling and managing small coffles of slaves on particular plantations, the governing and propertied élites of the British Caribbean faced a continuing and apparently insoluble headache. Furthermore, throughout the history of black slavery it was a regular and familiar response for whites to blame their troubles, to blame their slaves' discontents and resistance, on outside forces and people. Maladroit royal governors, meddling policies from London, barbaric peoples and customs from Africa or, by the late eighteenth century, the unwelcome attention and activities of British missionaries and humanitarians were all proffered as explanations for the continuing unrest and the periodic upheavals among the slaves.

Sometimes, it is true, these were indeed the spark which lit combustible materials. But they were, invariably, the occasion rather than the cause for the slave outburst. The real cause of slave discontent and unrest lay in the nature of their bondage and in the structure of local economic life which had transmuted them (and their heirs and successors) into inanimate beasts of burden for the material betterment of their masters and others. It was scarcely surprising that slaves, by the early nineteenth century, began to adopt British abolitionists as their mythical or potential heroes. As early as 1816, a slave song from western Jamaica captured the point:

> Oh me good friend, Mr. Wilberforce, make we free!
> God Almighty thank ye! God Almighty thank ye!
> God Almighty make me free!
> Buckra in this country no make we free!
> What negro for to do? What negro for to do?
> Take force with force! Take force with force![31]

However mythical a figure, Wilberforce was clearly known among the slaves. Furthermore, it was a two-way process, for the forces which fed news from the metropolis into the colonies were also at work disseminating information in Britain about Caribbean slave society. Few were to have more abiding and influential results than the British missionaries whose work among the slaves, from the late eighteenth century onwards, provided a rich source of evidence which was fed into the communities and congregations of their own followers in Britain. We have already seen that the established Church had displayed a marked ambivalence about slavery and had shown scant regard for the spiritual needs of the slaves. This had begun to change in the late eighteenth century, notably at the prompting of Bishop Porteus.[32] But it was still the case, by the turn of the century, that the only effective attempts to convert (and 'civilise') the slaves came at the hands of various Nonconformist sects.

The pioneer missionaries were the German Moravians in the mid-eighteenth century. Baptists from North America had begun to preach in Jamaica in the mid 1780s. In 1789 the first Weslyan preacher began to work in Kingston, Jamaica, and in the following decade a spate of missionary societies was formed in Britain. Before the new century had dawned their enthusiastic representatives had begun their missions to the slaves.[33] To their plantocratic opponents, it was no mere coincidence that the decade of revolution should also usher in the first major attempts (by outside agents) to bring Christianity to the slaves. Many of the missionaries – and their metropolitan supporters –

abhorred slavery, but in their work in the West Indies they had
to accept the institution as it existed and to divorce themselves
from formal abolition. Baptist missionaries were warned, 'Do
not meddle with politics. . . . Remember that the object is not
to teach the principles and the laws of an earthly kingdom . . .
but the principles and laws of the Kingdom of Christ.'[34] Such
claims were hardly likely to soothe the doubting planters (more
so when they knew leading abolitionists to be in favour of black
conversions). From the planters' viewpoint, most worrying of
all was the effectiveness of black Baptist preachers and their
ability to attract and lead substantial black congregations by
the early years of the nineteenth century. Planters were correct
to imagine that the coming of black Christianity, more especially
the development of independent black congregations with their
own powerful, often charismatic, black preachers, had formed a
rod for the plantocratic back. It was symptomatic that
missionaries' chapels were attacked by local whites whenever
local slave unrest seemed to confirm the endemic plantocratic
fear that missionaries were agents of social and racial discord.
In 1807, missionaries to Jamaica were denounced as 'the
instruments of Fanatics and Enthusiasts in Great Britain for
the purpose of effecting political mischief, and with it the
destruction of life and property to His Majesty's white subjects
in this island'.[35] Of course it is also true that new dissent,
notably Methodism and its various offshoots, was no less
disliked among men of substance in Britain in the same
years. Indeed throughout the years of revolution, Methodist
congregations took great pains to deny allegations of subversion
and to declare their loyalty to 'King and Constitution'.
Prominent abolitionists were among the most bitter critics of
Methodism. Zachary Macaulay felt that 'Methodism has so
direct a tendency to exalt animal feelings to an undue empire
over the judgement, that with people of weak judgement and of
little or no knowledge, it may expected in most cases to produce
enthusiasms.'[36]

Wilberforce, despite a juvenile flirtation with Methodism,
wrote of a 'bigoted, despised Methodist'.[37] Anglican abolitionists
were, however, in a quandary, for however much they might
dislike Methodism and its successful encroachment into wide
areas of British life, among the slaves it provided, along with
other sects, the very process of 'civilisation' which the

humanitarians desired. Thus, the missionary impulse (not merely among the slaves, but also among all those peoples of the world unfortunate enough not to have been born into Christian life) was but one aspect of varied humanitarianism; to win over to British civilisation the deprived and benighted peoples of the world.

The absence of Christianity among the slaves (conversely, their natural or indigenous paganisms and heathenisms) had long been viewed as an obstacle to black freedom. With the development of a revived Christian conscience from the mid eighteenth century onwards – of which humanitarianism was a sub-species – growing numbers of Britons came to see, in the apparent irreligion of the slaves, one of the fundamental objections to slavery itself. The slave lobby might argue that enslavement and slavery plucked successive generations of Africans from indigenous heathenism, or, if prisoners of war, from death, but there was precious little evidence of their endeavouring to use the opportunity to convert their new wards into black Christians. Indeed, with a few isolated exceptions, the story of slavery in the British Caribbean was marked by a plantocratic resistance to the conversion of slaves. And so it continued until the end of slavery itself. From the late eighteenth century onwards, however, although the planters themselves remained fiercely resistant, the slaves were won over, in growing numbers, to an emergent and assertive nonconformity which, despite remarkable and persistent obstructions, succeeded in gnawing away at the 'irreligion' of the slaves. The missionaries' efforts – and the influence of converted black preachers – were to have a fundamental effect on the whole of slave society. Black Christianity was to prove (along with the abolition of the slave trade itself) a most corrosive agent serving to loosen the very structure of slavery itself.

Conversion was welcomed, at many levels of British society, as an indispensable improvement in slave society. Burke, in his 'Sketch of a Negro Code' (1792), made specific provision for the widespread conversion and education of the slaves.[38] Abolitionists assumed that conversion would make emancipation a more realistic ambition for, in the words of George Stephen, they were aware that the slaves were 'unacquainted with the language, unskilled even in the humblest arts of labour, strangers to religion, and destitute of all ideas of civil rights or social duties'.[39] Once provided with these various social (and personal) qualities, the slaves would become progressively more 'civilised' and the arguments for their continuing enslavement consequently weakened. What no one could fully appreciate at the beginning of the campaign to convert the slaves was the powerful political allies this would win over to black freedom among the congregations of the same sects in Britain. The massive growth of British nonconformity, notably at the lower reaches of society (among economically depressed, skilled and out-workers and among certain working groups in new industrial processes) served to create unprecedentedly large constituencies which not only (and naturally) supported their missions to the slaves, but which were also unanimously outraged at the injustices doled out to their enslaved co-religionists. Ill-treatment of slaves was bad enough, ill-treatment of black Methodists (for example) was thought to be unacceptable.

The central and determining importance of the growth of black nonconformity among the slaves was that it was paralleled (and, indeed, sustained) by a remarkable growth in British nonconformity. When the campaign against the slave trade was launched in the late 1780s, the newly formed Methodists numbered 46,559. By the time the revived campaign was directed against slavery itself in the 1820s, the Methodists' numbers were more than a quarter of a million. By the time British slavery was in its last years, the numbers had grown to more than one-third of a million.[40] The Baptists, though nothing like so numerous, similarly registered sharp increases in their British membership, growing from *c.* 10,000 in 1750 to almost 100,000 in 1838. Dissenting places of worship speckled the country, their numbers and density increasing markedly by the late eighteenth century. Whereas there were 2810 dissenting places of worship in the 1780s, by the 1830s this had increased to 14,648.[41] Of course, these were the years of extraordinary population growth and the gradual shift of the population to an urban habitat. As the British people became more numerous, they became more urban; by 1850 the majority of the nation were town-dwellers. And it was to serve their spiritual (and to a degree material) needs that the new churches and chapels were constructed in the new centres of population. In this process, the established Anglican church was left far behind. Indeed, the rise and successes of the Nonconformists were, to a marked degree, a measure of the Church of England's failure, notably its inability to keep pace with the geographical switch of population. The Anglican Church's pre-modern structure was designed to minister primarily to the south, the south-midlands and the south-east, with much of its parochial efforts being devoted to rural life. But as the population changed, it found itself increasingly remote – in spirit and distance – from the new concentrations of the British population.

In the years of the campaign against the slave trade and slavery, the Church of England registered little growth in its manpower and little adjustment of its parishes to accommodate the shifts and growth in population. Nonconformity was at its strongest where Anglicanism was weakest. The centres of Nonconformist strength lay in many of the new industrial areas; the coal and iron communities in the north-east, the textile districts of Yorkshire and Lancashire, Derbyshire and Nottinghamshire and the potteries of Staffordshire. From these, and similar early industrial and urban communities, there flourished a remarkable network of nonconformity which was to have far-reaching consequences on the development of British life. For the purposes of this study, however, it is important to note that this Nonconformist network, linking the urban and industrial areas, could summon forth growing numbers of people to its various campaigns. Most of these, naturally enough, concerned their own sectarian or congregational interests. But, when placed at the service of anti-slavery, the dissenting chapels, preachers and congregations could rally an unusually national, vocal and powerful support. British Nonconformists could be rallied to the side of black conformists often, and most effectively, by preachers from their own denomination who had spent time as missionaries among the slaves. When the time came, from the mid-1820s onwards, for a concerted onslaught on slavery, British Nonconformity offered a unique organisation, an unparalleled strength of numbers and an unmatched sympathy. In the public attack on slavery, dissent was to deliver some of the most crippling blows.

The British society which emerged in 1815 from a generation of warfare was, then, markedly different from the one which had stumbled into the war in 1793. But so too were the slave islands. When the war began (and it was a war which saw a great deal of military activity in the Caribbean, as the contending sides fought over the highly prized slave islands), the slave empire was in an economically buoyant phase, its tropical produce highly valued in the metropolis and in Europe. But, as we have seen, there were already serious problems in view. Social stability could never be guaranteed, a difficulty accentuated during and after the Haitian revolt, and apparently worsened by the encroachment of the new missionaries and news about the progress of abolition from London. But the greatest force for change was abolition itself. Until the ending of the slave trade there had been infusions of batches of Africans into most of the slave islands, to make good the regular shortfall in slaves (itself a function primarily of a sexual imbalance within the slave communities). There were exceptions to this general rule, notably the relatively balanced (and increasingly Creolised) island of Barbados. But in the newly acquired (and relatively sparsely developed) colonies of Trinidad and Guiana, and in Jamaica with its fertile and under-populated interior, the ending of the slave trade had serious economic consequences. The demand for ever more African labour by frontier or 'imbalanced' slave societies had traditionally been the engine behind the transatlantic slave trade. What were the employers of slave labour to do, now that they could no longer replenish their depleted labour forces with new coffles of Africans?

The immediate consequence of abolition was a decrease in the slave population. This led to greater impositions on the existing slave populations.[42] Planters were widely agreed, from the mid eighteenth century, that it was cheaper to buy rather than breed slaves, their preference being for healthy young males. After 1807 they did not have the option. Instead, they were faced with a diminishing labour force, and/or they needed to support a growing proportion of women and children.[43] Many began to reorganise their labour forces, often rationalising the slave gangs in ways which upset the well-tested regime of management and discipline. Removing slaves from small (uneconomic) properties to bolster the labour force on more viable concerns, using female and child labour for demanding tasks previously the preserve of young men, relegating privileged or skilled slaves from élite, artisan or privileged work to the more physical and onerous field tasks which were traditionally allocated to Africans were changes which provided planters with the means of coming to terms with the ending of the slave trade. All were features of the planters' determination to exploit their slaves' labours as efficiently as possible and to prolong the profitability of the slave economies.[44] In fact, the structure, management and discipline of the slave labour force had developed over two centuries to a remarkable degree of agronomic sophistication (notwithstanding its undeniable inhumanities and brutalities). The divisions of labour, of sexes, of ages, of colours and of skills were carefully drawn up to secure the best physical returns from the slaves and the best yield from the lands. Like all labour systems, the disciplines of the plantations functioned not merely via physical intimidation, through the physical dominance and power of the governing (white) élites, but also required the acceptance (albeit grudging) of the code of labour discipline by the labour force. Clearly, this is not to claim that the slaves were merely compliant labouring tools in the hands of their owners and employers. But without the development and acceptance of a labouring discipline among the slaves (normally in return for a few miserable crumbs thrown from the plantocratic table), the plantations could never have functioned, still less functioned profitably.

The slaves' labour discipline required, in return, that planters make certain material concessions and accept certain established codes of management and conduct.[45] In large measure, these may seem merely to have been plantocratic self-interest (to employ the old or disabled at gentler tasks, to moderate the work for the young, to set aside 'privileged' – notably domestic – labour for 'coloured' slaves). In time, however, they came to be accepted by the slaves, and even prized by the beneficiaries.[46] A slave of colour, for example, could reasonably expect not to have to undertake the most daunting of field work. But all this was to change – for the worse – when the abolition of the slave trade produced changes in the slave population of the islands,[47] and as planters had to respond to those changes by revising the conventions of slave management.

After abolition, more and more women found themselves working in the heavier field occupations. Similarly, planters were obliged to put growing numbers of 'coloured' slaves into the fields. This ran counter to the planters' fundamentally racist perception that the lighter the skin colour, the weaker the slave, while clearly offending those slaves' expectations of less onerous work on other parts of the plantation. In essence, this created a basic malaise, a fundamental discontent, in the slave quarters (compounding, of course, a host of other, long-standing grievances). The fair-skinned slave children could no longer expect preferential treatment by being allocated to less difficult work. Furthermore, planters were unable to report that, as the slave population became more Creole (i.e. less African), it became more docile and less truculent. Throughout much of the eighteenth century, slave discontents, notably slave violence, resistance and running away, had been primarily African 'vices'. Local-born slaves, by contrast, had traditionally been more amenable (though rarely trustworthy). Indeed the most violent and powerful forms of slave resistance up to the late eighteenth century were African. This is, after a fashion, perfectly understandable; Africans unlike the Creoles had, after all, known a different life and had endured the traumas of enslavement and the middle passage. It was also natural that, as the Africans died out after 1807, and as slave society became more Creole, the slave owners could legitimately expect a more peaceable body of slaves. In the event, this did not materialise. Indeed, it was a cause of acute distress to slave owners throughout the British West Indies that, as the slave communities became progressively less African, the problems of slave unrest and resistance seemed to multiply.[48] It was a simple reflex for planters to seek the explanation in the work of outside (i.e. subversive) agencies and organisations. In a sense the planters had some strength to their fears. The abolition of the slave trade, the prime cause of increasing slave unrest, had, after all, been forced on the planters by the imperial Parliament. Equally, the proliferation of missionaries and black Christianity took place in the teeth of fierce plantocratic opposition (and often violence). It was also true that the rising tide of British humanitarianism (news of which inevitably filtered back, as we have seen, in distorted form, into the slave quarters) also developed despite the fierce resistance of the planters and their metropolitan spokesmen. There was, then, little evidence to suggest that Creolisation was making the slaves 'well disposed'. In fact, slave resistance seemed to become progressively more violent.

There were, naturally enough, a multitude of ways in which slaves could resist. Most spectacular of all was open rebellion,

variants of which had periodically wracked the islands, notably
Jamaica, throughout the eighteenth century.[49] Only nine years
after abolition, Barbados was, as we have seen, thrown into the
turmoil of 'Bussa's Rebellion'. Seven years later, in 1823, it was
the turn of Demerara. The 1823 revolt was much less surprising
than in 1816. This new colony had attracted a new breed of
rapacious investor (including W. E. Gladstone's father), whose
more exploitative systems of management were in sharp contrast
to the rising tone of humane concern in Britain. Shorn, like the
other British colonies, of fresh African imports, Demerara's
planters reorganised and pressed their labour force more
aggressively than most. John Smith, the preacher from the
London Missionary Society, noted tersely

> A most immoderate quantity of work has, very generally,
> been expected of them, not excepting women far advanced in
> pregnancy. . . . When sick they have been commonly
> neglected, ill-treated, or half-starved. Their punishments have
> been frequent and severe. Redress they have been so seldom
> able to obtain, that many of them have long discontinued to
> seek it, even when they have been notoriously wronged.[50]

In a sense, exploitation of this order had been common in the
early pioneering days in all the slave colonies; in Barbados in
the early seventeenth century, Jamaica in the late seventeenth
century and in St Domingue from the mid eighteenth century.
By the early nineteenth century, however, it ran counter to a
rising contemporary sensibility which found offence and moral
outrage (to say nothing of unchristian vice) in a growing
number of 'inhuman' institutions. Indeed, the very concept of
inhumanity was a function of this same sensibility and was to
bear political fruits against a host of practices and customs
which had gone unchallenged since time immemorial. The
treatment of the Demerara slaves would have raised few
eyebrows a century earlier. By the early nineteenth century, it
was utterly out-of-kelter and an undeniable offence to a growing
body of British opinion. Moreover, British opinion was primed
by the missionaries with news of life on that new South
American frontier.

Demerara had a recent history of servile revolt and suffered a
persistent drain of slaves escaping from the coastal settlements,

up the rivers and into the security of the river systems and the jungle. It was also a colony with a record of barbaric punishment and reprisal against rebellious slaves, reprisals the callous sadism of which shocked even late eighteenth-century conscience.[51] Into this brutal colony the London Missionary Society dispatched its missionary, John Smith, in 1817. Like his fellows elsewhere, Smith faced painful plantocratic (and colonial) opposition, but his efforts were rewarded by swelling black congregations. It was from among these black chapel-goers that there developed a major black insurrection in 1823, faced by that motley federation of armed forces and armed planters hastily gathered to resist. Again, the slave casualties were out of all proportion to the damage they had inflicted on property or on whites. Protracted trials were followed by public executions, and mutilations of a kind more suited to the seventeenth than nineteenth century. About 250 slaves died, in response to the killing of three whites. More telling than this fatal litany, however, was the subsequent trial of the Reverend Smith, a proceedings of 28 days, whose human drama was highlighted by the accused's chronic consumption. Smith was found guilty of complicity in the rebellion, the royal pardon coming too late, and he died in jail in February 1824.[52] As outrageous and malicious as Smith's prosecution undoubtedly was, the British outcry against his death was little less than an insult to the hundreds of dead slaves whose fate was the true indication of plantocratic and colonial viciousness. But Smith's death provided the symbolic martyrdom which was to be used to great political effect by the subsequent emancipist agitation. It also created a political furore in London, obliging ministers and politicians of all shades seriously to consider the role and future of the West Indian colonies.

Humanitarians and the mission societies naturally made great capital from the event – even before Smith's death. By late 1823 it was widely assumed – and argued – that the revolt merely pointed to the need for emancipation,[53] though when news of the revolt first broke, abolitionists tended to be blamed for causing the unrest.[54] In the other slave colonies, the revolt sent the usual tremors through the plantocratic society, while persuading the local missionaries to tread more warily – for the moment at least. There is no doubt that, viewed in the long term, Smith's death gave the humanitarians an important weapon with which to batter slavery and colonial Government. Government ministers were mercilessly taunted in Parliament for permitting the legal chicanery which had characterised Smith's trial (which had in fact been a court martial). The whole of West Indian life and society came in for withering criticism from leading humanitarian writers and speakers. Indeed, it was the occasion for the first public speech by Thomas Babington Macaulay, in which he dismissed the slave islands thus: 'In these wretched islands we see a press more hostile to truth than any censor, and juries more insensible to justice than any Star Chamber. . . . I by no means presume to set any limits to the possible injustice of a West Indian judicature.'[55] In the development of anti-slavery sentiment, the Smith affair formed an important turning point, persuading more and more people inside and outside the abolitionist movement that the institution which succoured such outrages, against black and white, was an unpalatable wickedness worthy only of swift and complete destruction. Precisely how to bring that about was to preoccupy the campaign for a further decade. But, for the time being, perhaps the most poignant epitaph to the Smith affair were some words written by Smith on a bill drawn on the London Missionary Society to pay for his trial. Smith wrote on the bill, '2 Corinthians, iv, 8, 9', his last clandestine message to his friends, and a statement which applied no less to the thousands of slaves whose sufferings and daily tribulations had been overshadowed by his own misfortune: 'We are troubled on every side, yet not distressed, we are perplexed, but not in despair. Persecuted but not forsaken; cast down, but not destroyed.'[56]

In the 16 years since the abolition of the slave trade, news from the Caribbean had given British abolitionists few signs that slavery was withering. Scrutiny of the slave registration returns showed that the enslaved populations were in decline (which is what the planters had always claimed would happen). In its turn this had forced planters to tighten their regime of management and discipline in a fashion which often accentuated slaves' problems. Slaves were more prone than ever to arbitrary removal from family, to be plucked from one property and set to work elsewhere, to be given more onerous work or to lose the perks and privileges which had been the lot of their ancestors. The initial attempts to 'civilise' the slaves via conversion to various Nonconformist sects had certainly made effective inroads among the slaves, and had encouraged the development of black chapels, where local black preachers emerged as prominent local figures exercising considerable sway over the local community. The plantocracy remained fiercely resistant to the spread of black Christianity and obstructed its development in every way possible, including violence and destruction of the chapels. Missionaries and their converts were persecuted by local whites in a fashion which was, ultimately, counter-productive. Nothing was to prove more offensive to the growing armies of Nonconformists in Britain than to read and hear of their co-religionists, black and white, assailed and obstructed in the simple and peaceable pursuit of their beliefs. At a time when the British were rapidly removing a range of religious disabilities at home (notably by removing restrictions on dissenters and Roman Catholics), it was doubly offensive to see religious liberties retarded and prevented in the slave colonies. Furthermore, whatever progress had been made in the ill-defined direction of 'amelioration', slave society continued to remain highly volatile; slave communities readily exploded in acts of small-scale or major violence. But even worse, when viewed from Britain, was the excessive violence of colonial whites in avenging themselves against rebellious slaves.

Whatever progress had been made in 'civilising' the slaves, the task of reforming the plantocracy seemed hopeless. In Barbados in 1816 and Demerara in 1823, British observers were shocked to see the endemic violence of the slave system – black violence to secure basic liberties, white violence to repress black demands. Moreover, the British government seemed powerless to insist on less barbaric governance in the islands, if only because colonial officials were so often of poor calibre and were, in any case, beholden to local white society to a degree which curtailed their political effectiveness. There was, then, no immediate prospect of improvement, no sign that slavery would die a natural death or that slave owners could be relied upon to mitigate the worst features of slavery. Indeed, during and after the Demerara revolt, there was every reason to believe that life in the slave colonies would get worse; that slaves would be worked harder, in a more exploitative fashion and could expect to face nothing but unflinching plantocratic hostility to whatever social improvements they might pursue. This, again, flew in the face of contemporary British ideals which saw boundless material and personal improvement in the transforming conditions of the early nineteenth century. The material progress already yielded by economic change (and notwithstanding the appalling conditions endured by legions of working people) unleashed an optimism which saw a future prosperity of almost limitless and universal nature. Yet in the slave colonies, however economically buoyant, there was little sign of a related commitment to progress. Indeed, the slave islands seemed, in every respect, a survival of a lost age, an economic and social structure whose economic rationale had been shaped long in the past, whose inhumanities were an affront to newly emergent European sensibilities and whose dogged resistance to black Christianity posed a curious challenge to the assertive (and to a degree aggressive) British missionary instinct. By the death of the Reverend Smith, all optimism that the slave colonies could improve themselves had evaporated. The humanitarian concentration on outlawing the international slave trade had run into the quagmire of international diplomacy, where principle was relegated to national self-interest. It was clear, to ever more people, that only a direct assault on slavery could produce those improvements and changes for the slaves which an earlier generation had expected to derive from abolishing the slave trade. Moreover, it was clear, by the early 1820s, that the potential existed in Britain for the rapid and effective mobilisation of a major public campaign. The structure of the abolitionist organisation survived; the nationwide and expanding network of Nonconformist chapels was, by 1823 (and thanks largely to the outrage felt at the treatment of black Christians), already itching to involve itself against slavery. And older abolitionists had shown the way to tap and direct public feeling. What was needed was an impetus to renewed and revitalised action.

7 Confronting Slavery: Pressing for Black Freedom

When describing the efforts to secure the emancipation of the slaves, Thomas Clarkson wrote:

> In the beginning of the year 1822, the eyes of the friends of Africa began to be turned to another subject. They had formerly been considering how they should lay prostrate the *Slave Trade*. They now directed their attention to the *Slavery in the British Colonies*, as the *next evil to be subdued*.[1]

In the early months of 1822, James Cropper, a Quaker with East Indian business interests, began to badger other humanitarians with the idea of attacking slavery by ending the sugar duties. The ending of the war in 1815 had encouraged enterprising capitalists and shippers to look to the wider world for new economic opportunities, and it was clear that certain tropical produce (notably cotton and sugar) could be bought more cheaply in the East. But the powerful West Indian interest, whose sugar was comparatively costly, had been able to persuade British governments to levy sugar duties that raised the price of East India sugar to the level of its slave-grown Caribbean competitor. Thus, the British consumer was prevented from buying sugar at its natural, 'market' price; instead, the duties paid on sugar formed, in effect, a subsidy to slave-grown sugar. In a completely open market, the slave sugars (grown, by and large, on long-established lands which were therefore not as fruitful or profitable as newly converted sugar-lands) could not compete. Conversely, a number of people began to realise that removal of the sugar duties would expose slavery to a competition it could not withstand. It was felt that free (or freer) trade in sugar would fatally damage the slave economy. And it was no accident that this was first realised by men with East Indian interests. It was a case not so much of economic self-interest masquerading as morality but of economic involvement revealing a fatal weakness in the flanks of the slave economy. In the earlier arguments against the slave trade, economic criticisms had played only a minor, almost incidental role. From 1822 onwards, an economic critique was to become enmeshed in a wider onslaught on slavery; morality and economic self-interest proved (not for the last time) to be a potent combination.

James Cropper provided the crucial initiative, privately pointing out that the sugar duties were the key to a new attack on slavery. West Indian planters knew, he claimed, that the 'free introduction (of East Indian sugar) will destroy their System of Cultivation'. Good Quaker that he was, Cropper felt that this 'West Indian Sugar Question' was 'the means which an all wise Creator has in the nature of things appointed for the destruction of the abominable system whether of the slave trade or slave cultivation'.[2]

Within a few years, this assessment had been transformed from a highly perceptive and original insight into a loudly proclaimed assumption throughout the anti-slavery campaign and in the Press. The *Edinburgh Review* declared (in 1827): 'There is, in fact, but one way to put down West Indian slavery, and this is by allowing the produce raised by comparatively cheap labour to come into competition with that raised by slaves.'[3]

Cropper set out to accumulate evidence – much of it via overseas correspondence – which proved his major point; that free labour was cheaper than slave labour. Armed with such material, he began to press, early in 1822, for the formation of a society which would agitate for gradual emancipation. But it was also vital to build up public backing; to 'feed the public through the medium of the Papers'.[4] Cropper, like the other traders and pioneers, was cautious about his goals; 'we have no wild schemes of emancipation', but rather sought gradual black freedom. But, from the first, he was acutely conscious of the need for public backing

I am more than ever convinced that we cannot have the

public voice unless we do openly attack the System of Slavery
... we should only lose ground with the public if we do not
come forward boldly, but though it must be boldly and
unreservedly yet it ought to be wisely and prudently.[5]

The memories of the early campaign against the slave trade
provided clear proof of the seminal role played by public
pressure. Now, in the incubation of a new campaign, thoughts
inevitably turned to harvesting the same political force: 'Public
opinion is necessary to some extent to the successful prosecution
of our enquiries.'[6] Thus prompted, a small group of
humanitarians contacted friends and associates from the old
campaign, seeking the obvious points of entry to local support
throughout the length and breadth of the nation, discussing the
best tactics to whip up feeling, pressurise Parliament and – ever
mindful of the central and determining feature of their proposed
agitation – 'to rouse the public mind'.[7]

Late in 1822, the proposal was in place to form a 'Society for
the Amelioration and Gradual Abolition of Slavery' with a
clear statement of principles:

> The slave-trade being abolished, because repugnant to the
> principles of justice and humanity, the holding of slaves must
> be depreciated upon the same principle ... it is quite
> inconsistent to condemn the slave-trade, and to perpetuate
> the slavery of its victims, through generations yet unborn.[8]

Initially, the Society remained small, its members meeting in
secret because they feared that their opponents, the West India
lobby, were stronger and better-organised than ever. Finally,
on 31 January 1823, the Society was launched in public,[9] its
first task to re-establish a nationwide network of supporting
committees, some old, many new. And with that end in view,
Thomas Clarkson embarked on yet another national tour,
visiting friends, contacting sympathisers, encouraging the
doubtful. Largely at Clarkson's initiative, some 250 local anti-
slavery committees had come into being within a little over a
year.[10] Wherever he went, Clarkson breathed fresh life and
energy into men who had long been absent from the cause; 'the
visit of our friend, Clarkson, was the means of re-animating my
zeal, and of leading me to take a fresh survey of the principles

in which the Abolitionists are proceeding.[11] Henceforth, these local committees (which proliferated in even greater numbers at the subsequent peaks of anti-slavery) were to prove the driving and organising force, generating, marshalling and directing each successive wave of public pressure. In the words of Clarkson:

> Each committee enlightened those in its own County and neighbourhoods and continued to enlighten them, till almost all within its district *high and low*, had gained a knowledge of the evil. Hence, petitions founded on *knowledge* were sent in unexampled numbers to Parliament.[12]

Here, in essence, lay the essential features of anti-slavery as it operated from 1823 until the final demise of British slavery in 1838. A central London committee had agents travelling to provincial allies, the nation was divided into local units able to drum up unprecedented support and express it through petitions, and was all held together by a quite remarkable plethora of national and local publications, and by the activities of local delegates dispatched at regular intervals from the localities to the metropolitan nerve centre. It was an organisational structure ideally suited to generating and channelling public feeling. And it was able to do this, in large part, because of the changing nature of British society. The initial phase of urban growth brought ever more people readily and accessibly within the reach of political organisations. The development of literate habits (themselves greatly encouraged by the nature of urban life) exposed growing numbers of people to the persuasion of the abolitionist printed word. The new institutions of urban life – notably the churches and chapels – provided seminal meeting places, centres of activity and seedbeds of information and ideas for the broader abolitionist movement. Thus, the major institutional and human transformations of early nineteenth-century life – quite apart from the equally important changes in outlook and mentality which paralleled the more obvious, physical changes – provided a fertile ground for revived anti-slavery.

It is also true that there were key intellectual changes – in the broad political and social values of contemporary life – which were no less supportive of anti-slavery and hostile to slavery and a slave economy. The emergence, for instance, of a broadening commitment to free trade, to *laissez-faire*, however limited its impact and influence, was none the less congruent with the growing chorus of economic abuse levelled at the slave economy. Indeed, the rise of the new campaign against slavery from 1823 coincided with and was in some degree a function of demands for freer trade in a broad economic–political front. Government policies in the 1820s, and the demands of new pressure groups (of which anti-slavery was but one) were broadly agreed on the desirability of free trade. Furthermore, the material benefits which appeared to be accruing to the nation, thanks to the economic changes associated with early industrialisation (although not spreading evenly or equitably among the people) seemed to many to be proof and testimony to new economic thought as much as to new machines and mechanical processes. It was no coincidence that abolitionists began to quote the classic free-trade writers. Clarkson commented (of Adam Smith): 'in his *Wealth of Nations* he showed in a forcible manner (for he appealed to the interests of those concerned) the dearness of African labour and the impolicy of employing slaves'.[13] Thirty years later, Buxton asked in a parliamentary debate: 'What, in the case of emancipation, was to make the negroes work? He would ask what made other people work? and he would say wages and free labour.'[14]

Slavery and slave-grown products were, as Cropper first pointed out, not only survivors of an archaic economic system (a mercantalist system, appropriate perhaps in the seventeenth and eighteenth centuries) but were able to survive thanks only to artificial governmental fiscal intervention which offended the new commitment to free trade and which penalised the British taxpayer. Thus, at one level, the emergence of a free-trade mentality made the task of abolition much easier; slavery could be damned as a drain on the hard-pressed British taxpayer and as a brake on the broad economic progress in which so many contemporaries took pride. But this is not to claim that economic utility pushed aside or dominated the issues of morality or Christian conscience. In the swift re-establishment of abolition sentiment as a major national political force after 1822, morality, religion and economics proved perfectly compatible objections. Indeed, it was quite a simple matter for abolitionists to assert that slavery was an immoral and uneconomic affront to the Christian conscience. The West India lobby, on the other hand – and notwithstanding their strength, money and political influence – were, from the first, confronted by a daunting task in trying to defend and justify their interests to the British people, and in Parliament. If the abolitionists, from 1822, were able to utilise the physical and intellectual changes in contemporary Britain to their advantage, these same transformations proved to be major obstacles to the West India lobby. Their political/economic ideology was out-of-kilter with ascendant values; their natural political constituency lay in unreformed, rural (and in large part 'corrupt') political life; and their hostility to black Christianity offended the swelling ranks of British nonconformity. But what ultimately doomed the planters' case was the ubiquity and strength of anti-slavery. To quote Thomas Clarkson again, even Ministers were obliged to give way because abolition 'spoke the national voice'.[15] The story of abolition between 1822 and 1838 is, substantially, the history of that 'national voice', and one, furthermore, which did not face the political restraints which so effectively silenced public abolition after 1795.

Abolitionists were not alone in promoting the slaves' interests. The Government – notably the Colonial Office – had itself begun to exercise a more interventionist role to secure slave amelioration. When, early in 1823, the Commons resolved to seek gradual emancipation (an early victory for the new abolitionist cause), the Colonial Secretary informed his various colonial officials of the need to establish specific improvements in the treatment of slaves.[16] Planters were henceforth confronted not only by mounting public pressure, but by successive governments (and their colonial officials) committed in principle to securing amelioration and then black freedom. Of course, it is also true that Ministers were themselves wooed over to this stance by the efforts of the abolitionists, inside and outside Parliament. As in 1814, contemporaries were in no doubt that public support had forced the ministerial hand. According to Clarkson, by 1823 public abolition had become 'so imposing that the Ministers themselves were obliged to give way'.[17]

Ministers were to be hemmed into an abolitionist corner by the sheer pressure of opinion expressed through petitions.

Will not an uninterrupted chain of petitions coming on

during the whole of the present session *show* Ministers that they will not be forsaken . . . will not the voice of the Nation, thus displayed, show the Planters the impossibility of a successful resistance, and will they not therefore be more inclined to submit?[18]

Petitions had been the main pressure applied by the abolitionists in their earlier campaigns against the slave trade. In the changed social circumstances of the 1820s and 1830s, they were to be more numerous, more popular and more influential than ever before. Wherever Clarkson travelled, he urged his contacts to draft an abolitionist petition, asking them to persuade other neighbouring sympathisers to do the same.[19] He was particularly keen to recruit the services and support of local government officers. But he was even happier to draw support from all sectors of contemporary political life, for the abolitionists sought to present their case as a *supra* Party issue, unalloyed by considerations of faction or party commitment.

Yesterday I waited upon ten Persons at Ipswich, Magistrates, Clergy, and persons of large fortune, all Government men. Every man signed the Petition. . . . The names of these having been obtained, all the list of the Inhabitants will follow, for there are Whigs, and friends to Liberty, in every reasonable Shape. Thus, you will have a Petition from Ipswich, signed by Whigs and Tories, an event which has not taken Place for the last 35 years. The Petition will include the Names of almost all the Property in the Town.[20]

Such all-Party support was a crucial factor in presenting abolition as a *national* issue. Indeed, it was a conscious (and astute) ploy of the abolitionist movement in the ten years to emancipation to recruit support from every conceivable social and political quarter, and to persuade Parliament and Government that abolition was supported by a unique and unprecedented mosaic of groups and interests. And, from 1823 onwards, abolitionists expected their supporters to be able, quickly and efficiently, to organise a petition.[21] The churches offered a ready-made national network of potential sympathisers and petition-organisers, and Clarkson was quick to establish links with the Church of Scotland, the Methodists and the

Church of England. The latter was particularly important. 'The more the clergy of the Church of England interest themselves (in our cause), the better our Petition will stand in the Eye of Parliament, and of our Ministry too.'[22]

The relaunching of abolition was done in a systematic and calculated fashion. Each county was analysed for supporters and friends, and the consequent social geography of support provided the initial outline of a new mass movement.[23] Even before he set off on his tour (in 1823), Clarkson had drawn up a list of 597 names he hoped to use as the foundation for a rapid and national build-up of abolitionist organisation and activity.[24] Wherever he went, Clarkson gave a standard speech, suitably amended in each locality, designed to inspire the audience to embark on the new crusade and to provide a blueprint for action. Clarkson's speech provides as clear a statement as there is of the Abolition Society's principle aims

> To improve, gradually, both the moral and temporal condition of the Slaves in our colonies; that is to change the present cruel manner of their labour, to put them more under the protection of the law, to institute marriage among them, and to secure it from violations; to give them religious instruction and after all this has been done, to confer upon them one civil privilege after another, as they shall be found capable of bearing it, till at length they shall rise insensibly to the rank of free peasantry.

They did *not* seek immediate emancipation; 'Be assured that nothing so insane could have entered into our heads.' Conscious of the criticisms which had already been flung at the abolitionists, more especially that their words had been responsible for slave unrest, Clarkson couched their ambitions in the most cautious of terms 'To civilise them, to Christianise them, to make them more useful to themselves and families than before, to make them better servants to their masters, and to make them more useful members of the community at large.'[25]

Here was black freedom portrayed as an eminently reasonable, peaceable, and unexceptional ambition; the transmutation of bonded people (whose slavery would, Clarkson argued, forever stimulate violent insurrection) from brutalised and reluctant slaves into a co-operative and satisfied peasantry. Such a vision suffered from a surfeit of romantic and inflated optimism. Yet these were important political qualities when contrasted against the barbarities and despair of slavery itself. Moreover, the ambition to recreate black slaves in this image had a powerful appeal to a generation deeply influenced by the commitment to human progress (and even to perfectibility) and not yet inured or hardened to a more cynical outlook. But, as we shall see, it was this inflated and (to modern eyes) unrealistic expectation of what black freedom might achieve which was to lay the basis for subsequent disillusionment and despair when, after 1838, the former slaves failed to reach the exalted status expected of them by their erstwhile friends. It may seem paradoxical, but from the inflated aspirations of abolitionism, there was created the germs of early Victorian racism.

Clarkson told his audiences, in 1823, that abolition would be advanced by enlightenment; the more people knew about slavery, the more powerful would be their outcry. 'In circulating light and information on the subject of Negro Slavery, throughout the Kingdom, so that, as few as possible should be ignorant of the case, and this with a view that more petitions might be sent to Parliament.' An 'unexampled number of Petitions' flooding Parliament would express the national opinion, and fortify the Government. Petitions, argued Clarkson,

> are necessary to encourage and support Government in the arduous contest which is coming on in the next Session of Parliament. There can be no doubt that Petitions, if sent to Parliament, to a universal extent would have the effect of fortifying Government against yielding too easily, or more than they would wish to the clamours and misrepresentations of the West India opposition.

Government steps towards amelioration and gradual emancipation would be helped by public support 'they will be supported by the Voice of the People. By the Voice of the People, I do not mean the Rabble, but of the respectable part of that community.'[26]

Of course, it may be felt that such a comment points to a very restricted potential constituency for abolition. In fact, the ultimate backing for abolition was to prove much broader than anyone could have envisaged in 1823. Moreover, it was to be drawn from a much broader base – including women – than Clarkson and his friends planned. But it remained, throughout, 'respectable', rational and articulate, even when plebeian. The fear of the 'rabble' was not so much an anxiety about the non-propertied *tout court* but a fear of that undisciplined (primarily, though not uniquely, urban) mob whose violence – in London in 1780, in France in 1789 – had left an indelible scar on the memories of men of property. Abolitionists – no less than contemporary reformers of various persuasions – were anxious to deflect the obvious and oft-repeated accusation that their words and actions formed an incitement for those elements which forever threatened the peace and stability of contemporary life. This accusation was especially poignant in the post-war years. Not only had abolitionists and their ideals allegedly proved disruptive in the slave communities of the Caribbean (notably in the slave revolts in Barbados and Demerara), but Britain itself had only just passed through an unsettled period. The post-war dislocation – of demobilisation, economic contraction, the revival of radical and industrial organisation, and widespread social unrest – left no one in any doubt of the volatility of British life. And this was, by the 1820s, more especially a problem with the development of major urban (and industrial) areas in the Midlands and North. The traditional difficulties of governing London were now replicated throughout provincial urban life and were not to be brought to heel until the coming of local police forces from the 1830s onwards.

Thus the abolitionists, embarking in 1823 on a new attempt to whip up popular opposition to slavery, were sensitive (like many others) about the effect their actions might have in the more unstable corners of the nation and hence upon propertied apprehensions. They could ill afford a reprise of 1793–5 when fear of 'the rabble', however wrong-headed or hysterical, undermined the strength and momentum of popular abolition. In the event, it was the massive backing for abolition which was to prove the most seminal force in securing black freedom.

Some indication of the progress made by abolition can be gauged by the membership of the 'Society for the Mitigation and Gradual Abolition of Slavery throughout the British Dominians'. Founded in January 1823, its president was a Duke, it had five peers as vice-presidents, and fourteen MPs on its committee. Many more members were of similarly elevated station. The Society of 1787 had a founding committee of twelve, nine of whom were Quakers. Now, 36 years later, abolition had come to dominate the high ground of British politics and could appeal to a wide constituency of interests. It was no longer the preserve of small bands of Quakers, intellectuals, and men of sensibility. Moreover, abolition could henceforth openly advertise itself as a Christian crusade; an attempt to purge the nation of a major affront to the collective Christian conscience. In its earlier phase, it is true, there had been a great deal of religious objection to the slave trade from individuals and particular sects. By 1823, however, slavery was uniformly denounced as unchristian and could, in consequence, anticipate the antipathy of all forms of organised religions. Time and again, in the 1820s and 1830s, slavery was dismissed as anti-Christian: 'a System full of Wickedness, hateful to God, and a Curse and disgrace to Britain'.[27]

Slavery, as anti-Christianity, was one of the major points made by Wilberforce in his influential 1823 tract, *An Appeal to the Religion, Justice, and Humanity of the Inhabitants of the British Empire on behalf of the Negro Slaves of the West Indies*. It was also a fundamental principle of the Abolition Society, which declared slavery 'opposed to the spirit and precepts of Christianity as well as repugnant to every dictate of natural humanity and justice'.[28] Indeed, between 1823 and 1838 anti-slavery was expressed most forcefully, more often, and more widely, in religious terms. At one level there is a simple explanation for this, since organised religions put the strength of their organisations and congregations behind the cause. The Quakers, the Churches of England, Ireland and Scotland, the Catholics and a plethora of dissenting churches, had all come out *en masse* against slavery by 1830. Not surprisingly, a great number of abolitionist petitions in the 1820s and 1830s came from the churches; no less surprising was the importance they attached to the unchristian nature of slavery which was 'highly offensive in the sight of God, disgraceful to us, as a free and a Christian people'.[29]

It is scarcely cynical to note that such a perception of slavery, however widespread it might be in the 1820s and 1830s, had been uncommon a mere 50 years before. On the eve of American Independence, for example, it was *not* axiomatic among people, even of the most refined Christian conscience, that slavery offended their religious feelings. This transformation in anti-slavery was not so much a function of the evangelical campaign, intent on winning the nation over to its own view of religious sensibility (though it would be wrong to diminish its effectiveness), but it was, primarily, a function of the major transformations in British society (discussed above), notably the demographic changes and the switches in institutional religions. To stress the importance of religion in this final phase of abolition is not, however, to return to a more traditional interpretation of anti-slavery as a triumph for all-conquering evangelicalism. What we need to recall is that religion itself had been tranformed most notably (and influentially) among working people. In this regard at least, popular religion, far from being a conservative force, was in fact an agent for radical change. Whatever the arguments about religion lulling the first generations of industrial labour into a mood of tranquil acceptance, those same churches provoked fierce and universal demands for a major radical change in the colonies; the ending of slavery. Both among the slaves themselves, and in plebeian communities in Britain, the new Nonconformist churches stimulated a radical response from among their plebeian worshippers. Clearly, the Christian churches were not the only element in the campaign for black freedom but they were, without question, one of the most important, most numerous, vocal and persuasive. Churches in Britain – as among the slaves in the Caribbean – did not set out consciously to pursue a radical programme, but their words, activities, and ambitions had very much that effect. The determination to dispatch missionaries – to bring light and salvation – to distressed communities had a major impact in the slave quarters and in the industrial and urban communities of Britain. The degree to which they won over unexpectedly large numbers of converts, and promoted (deliberately and incidentally) a commitment to black freedom proved to be one of the most decisive steps in the campaign to end black slavery. But to win – to emancipate the slaves – the abolitionists who renewed their agitation in 1823 felt the need to recruit popular backing. Ultimately, of course, black freedom would be granted by Parliament; like abolition in 1807, emancipation was to be the result of parliamentary and governmental deals and manoeuvres. But from the first, it was *assumed* that MPs and Ministers could only be persuaded of the need to end slavery by sustained and unrelenting public pressure.

The campaign to free the slaves repeated the tactics of a generation earlier. Lectures, tracts, petitions, all in conjunction with the varied activities of local organisations sought to drum up local (and hence national) feeling. Lectures were extremely important, to a degree which is hard to envisage in the modern world. Many of the anti-slavery speakers were, it is true, fine public orators. But oratorial skills cannot explain the extraordinary popularity (and influence) of the spoken word. Indeed, the lecture was a fundamental method of attracting crowds and disseminating information in all radical and reforming movements, from Wilkes to the Chartist movement. Many leaders of those agitations rose to prominence primarily *because* of their lecturing fame. What characterised the anti-slavery lectures was their size. When the campaign reached its crescendo, in 1830, reports of the lectures (given in their hundreds) invariably commented on the crowds. One in Edinburgh was thought to be 'one of the largest and most respectable meetings ever assembled in that intellectual city'.[30] Clearly, it was easier to attract crowds in the urban areas. But anti-slavery permeated rural life as well. In Roxburghshire (in 1833) a local lecturer 'had diffused correct information on the subject throughout the remotest dale of that pastoral district'.[31] The clearest indication of the importance of the spoken word to anti-slavery was the work of the Agency Committee, formed in 1832 as a radical ginger group by men anxious to hasten emancipation. The Committee was able to form 1300 local associations, dividing the nation into 'districts' and hiring paid lecturers, whose task was 'To prepare the way for a general expression of the public feeling when the time shall arrive, by widely disseminating an accurate knowledge of the nature and effect of Colonial Slavery.'[32] They, like all other abolitionists, *assumed* that merely to recite the 'facts' about slavery would be sufficient to lure outraged opinion into their fold.

Agency lecturers were given specific instruction how to advertise, organise and deliver their lectures; which evidence to use and which issues to avoid. Later, their lectures were published locally, thus reaching even larger audiences. As it was, their words were delivered to enormous crowds: the lecturers' own reports invariably spoke of the crowds pressed in to hear them. Throughout the county, such reports told much the same story. At St Albans, the local Weslyan Chapel 'was *crowded* with attentive hearers'. At Woburn, 'The Hall was literally packed.' In Newport Pagnall, 'we were compelled to seek more extensive accommodation for the second lectures'. At Hitchin, 'the chapel was crowded in every part, the aisles and doorways blocked up'. At Baldock, 'about 200 could not get in'. Bad weather failed to deter the audience and, in small communities, it seems clear that a substantial proportion of the local population turned out to listen.[33]

Nor was the audience daunted by the amazing duration of the lectures. Lecturers took great pride in reporting how long they took to harangue the throngs; two to three hours was not exceptional. From Dorking, one lecturer reported 'I kept my audience from seven until a quarter to ten o'clock, and so interested were they, that I verily believe they would have sat all night.' In places, many must have felt they had been there all night; one meeting in Barnstable lasted from 7 until 11 p.m.[34] Of course, such lectures provided an unusual occasion, a colourful and memorable event in what, for most people, were uneventful lives; a visit by a peripatetic lecturer provided one of the rare and anticipated breaks from the dull routines of local life.

The anti-slavery lectures were remarkable for other striking features. Perhaps most important of all, they appealed to (and were specifically designed for) audiences of all social classes. Indeed, many of the older abolitionists had doubts about whipping up such universal feeling about slavery.[35] A meeting in Hexham was badly arranged for 10 a.m.: 'The hour being very inconvenient to the shopkeepers and workmen of all kinds.' In Bedford, it was decided not to lecture on Saturday, which was 'an inconvenient day for families to attend public proceedings'.[36] Throughout this last phase of anti-slavery, women came to play an increasingly important role. Lectures naturally attracted numbers of local women ('Many of both sexes came from the neighbouring towns')[37] but women made their biggest impact in formal abolitionist politics. Leading abolitionists realised at an early stage that women could prove invaluable allies in presenting a case which was truly national; 'our powerful and unusually diffused allies'.[38] Specific steps were taken to form 'Ladies' Anti-Slavery Associations' with the hope that 'information may be prepared, printed and diffused; subscriptions may be raised; petitions to legislature, when necessary, may be promoted; the use of sugar; the growth of free labour, in preference to that grown by slaves, may be efficiently encouraged'.[39] There was, naturally enough, little hint that this new-found enthusiasm for female politics should have a wider application. None the less, anti-slavery provided an important political outlet for large numbers of women, traditionally denied even a cursory political role. The purpose (in the eyes of the male initiators of female anti-slavery) was to use female influence at its most seminal; within the family and broader community.[40] Members of the Colchester Ladies Anti-Slavery Association were urged, in 1825, 'to endeavour to awaken in the minds of their families, and all those over whom they have influence, a lively sense of the injustice, inhumanity and impiety of Negro Slavery'.[41] By the mid 1820s, the leaders of abolition were struck by the proliferation of female anti-slavery organisations.[42] Nor was it simply a matter of numbers, for the women's groups exercised a distinctive influence. First, their sheer weight of numbers added to the abolitionist push. Secondly, they brought to this area of British politics a unique quality, not previously felt on this scale before, of the female nation registering a political voice and demanding redress for grievances. They were, in addition, important in raising money for the cause, and in recruiting names to local petitions.[43] These may seem marginal, almost inconsequential, matters but they have a significance which surpasses their immediate results. Anti-slavery offered women – admittedly from the propertied orders – their first effective role in modern, formal British politics. It was limited to the attack on slavery and doubtless, to many, seemed but another opportunity to indulge in 'good works'; part of that charitable activity which provided one of the few public outlets to women of that class. But women's activities were more directly influential within the anti-slavery drive itself for they undertook much of the tedious, time-consuming (but ultimately vital) work without which the campaign could not have maintained its momentum. It would be easy to condescend towards their achievements. Instead, we ought to remember the praise which their menfolk heaped upon them.

Women were, then, clearly important in disseminating the ideas of anti-slavery throughout their immediate circle. But what fanned the call for black freedom far and wide was the printed word, often, as we have seen, a printed version of verbal abolitionism. Clarkson, writing of the initial campaign, noted that the pioneers 'formed themselves into a committee for procuring such information and evidence, and for publishing the same, as might tend to the abolition of it'.[44] It was, again, commonly assumed that the facts would speak for themselves, and that, when the British people read the evidence, they must inevitably side with black freedom. Of course, all hinged upon the existence of widespread literacy. There was, in fact, an important literary tradition which went far beyond the bounds of the propertied and the formally educated. There is abundant evidence of the remarkable extent of popular literacy from the mid eighteenth century onwards, always more striking in towns than rural life and normally more extensive among men. The radical movement, from Wilkes onwards, made great political capital from the existence of popular literacy. There was, in the words of a pamphleteer of 1765 'scarce a human creature so poor that it cannot afford to buy or hire a Paper or a Pamphlet, or so busy that it cannot find the leisure to read it'.[45] In the same period, newspapers sold in London surpassed 12 million in the year; a parallel explosion in provincial newspapers pointed to a similar, provincial readership. In addition, there was a plethora of tracts, broadsheets and ephemera which rolled from the presses in growing numbers, never more so than in the politically sensitive decade of the 1790s. Despite continuing attempts to stifle and control popular literacy, it was quite impossible to deny that Britain, by the turn of the century, was a highly literate society; one in which literature – of all sorts and conditions – played an instrumental role in most areas of economic and social life. It was perfectly natural that abolition should feed the public appetite for the printed word, and similarly benefit from the political support which was excited by abolitionist literature.

To a substantial degree, the *pros* and *cons* of abolition versus the slave trade and slavery were fought out in print. Long before formal abolition began to direct its attention towards Parliament, individual sympathisers had attacked slavery in print (and had, in their turn, been attacked by the West India lobby). But each successive wave of abolition was accompanied by some extraordinary literary outpourings. Indeed, the historian of anti-slavery is able to plot the course of that movement largely because of the surviving masses of printed sources. The figures involved are quite astonishing. Between 1823 and 1831, the Anti-Slavery Society published almost 3 million tracts, distributed, via their London headquarters, to friends and colleagues throughout the country.[46] In one year alone, 1831, almost half-a-million tracts were issued. Moreover, this tide of abolitionist literature (paralleled, though never matched by the opposing slave lobby's output) was compounded by local and private publications. Many local societies, and many individuals, sought to establish their abolitionist sentiments and credentials by publishing their views on slavery.[47] Indeed, so voluminous, national and inescapable was this abolitionist tide that it simply swamped its political opponents, burying their arguments beneath an advancing and irresistible tide of abolitionist print. With the exception of the West India lobby, so overwhelming was the propaganda of anti-slavery that few people were willing to stand up and declare themselves in favour of slavery. Speaking at a York parliamentary election in 1826, one candidate declared 'On the gradual abolition of Colonial Slavery, I am happy to believe that there are not two opinions in the Country.'[48] That slavery was able to survive until the mid 1830s was due to the political complexity of contemporary Britain; the difficulty of clinching emancipation in a political system troubled by other, more pressing, issues.

The initial pressure of the Abolition Society had forced the British Government, in 1823, to commit itself to gradual freedom. Wilberforce, still the figurehead of the movement, now handed over the parliamentary leadership to Thomas Fowell Buxton. This was an important move since the West Indians in Parliament were more powerful a group than on the eve of abolition in 1806/7. Paradoxically, at the time public opposition to slavery reached new heights, in the 1820s, parliamentary abolitionists had decreased; their support lay primarily among the Whigs who were out of office until 1830.[49] Thus, the parliamentary cause of black freedom languished, and faced stiff opposition, at a time of unparalleled public backing. Year after year passed with abolitionists despairing of the prospects for black freedom when they examined the records of successive

Ministers.[50] Moreover, there was a failure to link free trade effectively to the cause of emancipation, despite the fact that abolitionists themselves realised the political potential of illustrating the favoured economic position enjoyed by West Indian slave produce.[51] If it is true that the East Indians' economic interests lay in undermining slavery by removing the duties favourable to the Caribbean, they consistently failed to act, politically, in their own interests. It has been shown, for instance, that on only 19 occasions, between 1823 and 1830, did MPs with East Indian interests speak or vote for abolition. By 1830, the movement in Parliament had made little progress. There was a growing realisation (notably when confronted by Wellington's Government) that the campaign needed revitalisation. Black freedom seemed no nearer in 1830 than 1823.

Slavery was, of course, only one of the issues taxing successive governments. Most pressing of all was the gathering storm about the reform of Parliament. The arguments about 'The Bill', about the nature and details of reform, formed the major preoccupation of the period, and, while it is true that the fate of the slaves was, to a degree, tied up with any changes in representation, it would be wrong to suggest that slavery held the pride of political place. Faced by a Parliament and Government preoccupied with other issues, younger abolitionists, rapidly losing patience with the long-suffering stoicism of their elders, began to press for immediate emancipation. But all hinged on the outcome of the political crisis surrounding the Reform Bill. It was into this volatile political climate that the more radical and immediatist Agency Committee was launched, led by George Stephen and the two Quakers, Emmanuel and James Cropper. The Committee gave abolition a new impetus which was maintained until black freedom was secured.[52] Two unexpected elements now entered the political arena to heighten the general confusion and to accentuate the arguments about slavery. First – and most important – the first spasmodic cholera epidemic struck Britain with a deathly force not seen since the plague of the seventeenth century, killing almost 32,000 people and afflicting 83,000. The cholera created a major national panic; the populace, terrified and not knowing how to escape its ghastly ravages, men in government (in localities and capital) confused and apparently helpless to control or curtail its deathly march. The cholera seemed to accentuate the complex political and social difficulties of governing a volatile (and increasingly urban) British society; it certainly induced a panic and a terror not seen for centuries. Many, inevitably perhaps, saw it as the hand of God smiting a nation characterised by various sins and wickedness. And which sin was greater, in more people's eyes, than the continuance of slavery? Indeed, the Agency Committee had already declared that 'to uphold Slavery is a crime before God and the condition thereof must be immediately abolished'.[53] Then, in the midst of the cholera epidemic, news reached England of a massive slave revolt in Jamaica.

Abolitionists had been expecting trouble among the slaves, although it has to be mentioned that planters, for their part, lived in a permanent expectation of slave unrest; it was a sort of collective plantocratic psychosis. By 1830, however, it was clear that the slave quarters were alert to the fierce British arguments about their prospective freedom. Sympathisers wrote to abolitionists from the West Indies: 'The Slaves are wonderfully informed of late years – far more knowing and intelligent.' This particular informant was reported (in 1830) as saying that he 'considers an insurrection quite a matter of certainty and of right'.[54] In fact, the extent and savagery of the Jamaican revolt took most people – on the island and in Britain – by surprise.

The Jamaican slave revolt of 1831–2 was known, significantly, as 'The Baptist War'. Jamaica was the most important of Britain's sugar islands, its history punctuated by successive acts of slave resistance and rebellion, but nothing in its previous history could match the scale of this revolt. It involved upwards of 60,000 slaves, in an area of 750 square miles, resulting in the deaths of 540 slaves and 14 whites.[55] What surprised many, especially on the island, was the fact that revolt errupted in a society where Creoles were (inevitably) becoming more numerous, where black Christianity had emerged as a major force among large groups of slaves and where slaves clearly knew that their freedom was imminent and that their owners' political and economic power was in the wane. These factors were, at heart, key elements in the revolt itself. Obliged to revise their managerial policies after abolition in 1807, planters treated slaves more harshly, while many slaves (from decaying properties) were hired out as jobbing gangs 'or were left virtually to their own devices as proto-peasants'.[56] Throughout, the local planters fought a rearguard action, against metroplitan pressure for slave amelioration and against the encroachment of missionaries and slave reglion. Once more, the joker in the pack was the planters' behaviour and careless conversations; their bitter public and dinner-table denunciation of the impending freedom to be bestowed from London was often issued forth in the presence of slaves. Local slaves were left in no doubt that the greatest obstacle to their own freedom was the local whites. One slave owner openly told a slave 'freedom was to come from England but that he would shoot every d——d black rascal before they should get it'.[57] Not surprisingly, then, the revolt was preceded by island-wide rumours that freedom had been conceded. The Christmas of 1831 was, for local whites, more nerve-wracking and fearful than usual.

Led by the literate Baptist preacher, Sam Sharpe, the revolt swept through western Jamaica, with the firing of properties as beacons to the slaves' rebellion; less graphic was the slaves' commitment to the idea of their own freedom. Sam Sharpe preached that the blacks were free; all they needed to do was to strike to secure it. Sharpe 'asserted the natural equality of man with regard to freedom'.[58] But Sharpe's simple ideals and his simple political solutions were rapidly pushed aside by thousands of slaves who wanted quicker, more dramatic results. Fires were soon consuming local estates; 'in terrible vengeance which the patient drudges had at length taken on those sugar estates, the causes and scenes of their lifelong toils and degradations, tears and blood'.[59] When the revolt was stilled, and when the courts had completed the bloody revenge begun by the armed forces, it was possible to analyse the kind of slaves at the heart of the revolt. They were primarily rural male, Creole slaves enjoying privileged occupations; large numbers were also Baptists.

It had been a savage, bloody and destructive affair, its purpose all the more perplexing since black freedom was clearly but a matter of time. But how were slaves to know that, when their perceptions of the abolitionist debate in Britain had passed through the bitterly distorting minds and words of their owners? Symbolically, too, plantocratic violence culminated in the execution of the saintly Baptist, Sam Sharpe, who went nobly to his death secure in the religious beliefs he had acquired from the whites: 'He thought and learnt from the Bible, that the whites had no more right to hold black people in slavery than black people had to make the white people slaves.' His final words were 'I would rather die upon yonder gallows than live in slavery.'[60]

Sharpe – a national hero in modern-day Jamaica – personified the processes which served to undermine slavery from within; a bright, literate Christian with great powers of oratory and a fundamental egalitarianism nurtured by his chapels and Bible. To kill such a man seemed an outrage, more especially since his role in the revolt was less instrumental than was alleged. But, as with the death of the Reverend Smith nine years earlier, it may be felt that the loudest yelps of metropolitan outrage were reserved for the Christian leaders of the armies of dead slaves. In fact, news of the revolt – and of its repression – provoked an unprecedented nationwide howl of outrage in Britain. Missionaries, returning from their own persecutions in Jamaica, stomped the country, arousing audiences with graphic stories of the revolt.[61] They arrived when national politics were dominated by the fight for the Reform Bill. The Whig victory at the General Election of 1831 paved the way for the ultimate reform of Parliament. News of the revolt thus became one more emotive ingredient fed into the confusing mix of British politics in 1831–2. Britain was in a state of heightened political excitement – in which news of the Jamaican outrages served to inflame public sentiment. There was clearly a mood for change which transcended the mere reform of Parliament. If the nation was to reform its corrupt and rotten systems, what better place to look than to the slave colonies where plantocratic resistance to change had, or so it seemed, illustrated the dangers of failing to concede. Resisting what (to many) seemed the irresistible was to encourage a human disaster; accommodation of those demands – reform – would ease the transition (in metropolis and colony) from uncertainty and turbulence to social tranquillity. And, of course, this was without resorting to the broader political (or religious) arguments, themselves fiercely debated throughout Britain in 1831–2.

The bodies already recruited to anti-slavery, the dissenting churches, were uniformly outraged by the persecutions in Jamaica. Macaulay wrote to Brougham that the Nonconformists were aroused 'to a feeling of intense interest in the matter and they have not only caught fire themselves but have succeeded in igniting the whole country'.[62] When, in the August of 1832, Parliament was dissolved – the election to be based on the newly reformed franchise – the abolitionists saw their chance. The Agency Committee was instrumental in securing abolitionists' 'pledges' from parliamentary candidates. This tactic, used with effect since the mid 1820, proved remarkably influential and saw the return of a block of upwards of 200 abolitionist MPs, the great majority of whom were liberal. The reform of Parliament had, as abolitionists had predicted, made smooth the way of the parliamentary abolitionist cause.[63] And, of course, the whole affair was accompanied by extraordinary abolitionist pressure; massive gatherings throughout the nation, a sustained (and popular) lecture campaign, volumes of printed material spitting from the presses and a deluge of abolitionist petitions. Once more, there was no serious doubt that the people – of all conditions, classes and both sexes – had overwhelmingly demanded black freedom.

Earl Grey's new administration, and the powerful abolitionist pressure in the Commons, ought to have ensured a swift passage of emancipation. But the West India interests – reduced by the Reform Act but with powerful support in the Lords – were able to maintain a rearguard defence of slavery. Wellington and his party in the Lords were prepared to safeguard the planters in their objections to black freedom. Thus, the matter resolved itself into the *nature* of the emancipation conditions, and the level of compensation Parliament was prepared to offer planters for the loss of their black property.[64] In August 1833, the Abolition of Slavery Bill ordered the ending of slavery on 1 August 1834; children under six were freed at once, older ones were transmuted into 'Apprentices' for a period of up to six years, working three-quarters of their time for their owners. The slave owners, guaranteed at least the short-term continuation of their labour supplies, also had the added compensation of £20 million. Bermuda and Antigua instantly freed their slaves: the other colonies enacted apprenticeship. Thereafter, British abolitionists monitored the progress of apprenticeship, arguing amongst themselves about the need for complete and unqualified freedom.[65]

From first to last, the West Indians had proved remarkably adept at defending their corner. In 1832, they were in no doubt that the institution to which they were wedded, black slavery, was doomed. But the rapid decline in their fortunes encouraged the planters to think, not in terms of total and outright opposition to emancipation, but of a compromise, a scheme which would give them a short-term labour supply and financial compensation for the loss of their slaves.[66] Thus, the apprenticeship scheme suited them well, though many complained that it fell short of their expectations. Many abolitionists, on the other hand, asked: why not compensate the victims – the slaves? Over the next four years, the progress of apprenticeship became a parliamentary issue, with abolitionists using evidence from the Caribbean to advance their case for total black freedom. The abuses of the scheme, and the maltreatment of the ex-slaves, were convincingly documented, in Parliament and in public. The popular clamour for emancipation reached new heights, through careful use of the well-tried abolitionist tactics. Once more, constituency pressure exercised enormous influence over the attitudes – and votes – of MPs. Abolition was at its strongest in the urban constituencies, among representatives of industrial or shipping towns, and those with large dissenting communities. Opponents of emancipation were primarily from rural seats; small-town MPs and Scottish MPs.[67] Analysis of the voting figures confirmed that it was the people of the 'new Britain', the urbanising, industrialising nation who sided with abolition; unreformed, rural Anglican life remained wedded to slavery. Clearly, there were exceptions to this rule; but the pattern is clear and unmistakable. Moreover, the incessant abolitionist pressure inside Parliament finally forced the Government to enact complete emancipation, from 1 August 1838.[68] In this, the last act against British slavery, grass-roots pressure had, once more, proved decisive. Pressure from without had ensured a powerful abolitionist body in Parliament; that same pressure provided those MPs with a powerful handle to beat Ministers and Government into an emancipist position.

At midnight on 1 August 1838, thousands of blacks attended their churches, chapels, thanksgiving parades and public meetings throughout the islands. The peaceful celebrations contradicted the white's fear of massive violence and the settling of old scores. Indeed, the transition to full black freedom in August 1838 was a remarkable event. Black slavery, born of and characterised by persistent and unrelenting violence towards its victims, ended peacefully. Unlike slavery in Haiti and, later, the USA, slavery in the British colonies peacefully transformed itself into freedom. At first contemporaries hoped, and predicted, that freedom would transmute the slaves into a 'cheerful and industrious peasantry'. Certainly, they flocked to the chapels as never before, and influence passed perceptibly from the planters to the preachers.[69] But the high hopes swiftly evaporated. The transformed world economy swiftly relegated the former slave islands to a position of economic marginality, their produce no longer required or competitive in a freer world market, their labour force – free, black peasantry – no longer the pressing concern of metropolitan abolitionists. Indeed, the economic decline of the islands, with the associated demise of their labourers, was viewed, within a very short space of time, as vindication for the traditional, plantocratic racist arguments that only the constraints of slavery would compel the slaves to work. It is, of course, easy to be cynical about the results of black freedom. But few of the 750,000 beneficiaries would have exchanged it for the hated system which had been the lot of their forebears for centuries past. However materially meagre, the benefits of freedom were incomparably preferable to a life in bondage.

Few of the pioneering abolitionists of 1787 lived to see black freedom; few, in 1787, could have reasonably hoped to see it ushered in in their lifetime. Equally, none of them could have foreseen the fundamental changes in British (and British imperial) life which made possible the abolition of the slave trade and slavery. To claim that changes in public opinion – the development of a massive, national antipathy to slavery – was primarily responsible for the political demise of slavery is, to a degree, tautological. There is no doubt that this opinion did come into being and that it came to exercise increasing and, at times, irresistible influence over politicians who were ever more susceptible to grass-roots and constituency pressures. But it is also true that this public voice was itself a function of the transformations in British life; the development of an urban (to a degree, industrial) society which was articulate, increasingly socially aware, and thoroughly permeated by the institutions, words and influence of new religions. It was also a society, after 1789, deeply and unalterably influenced by the new secular philosophy of social and political rights. Moreover, the economic changes within Britain, by the 1820s, provided a multitude of converging economic criticisms of slavery as an economic system. But this is far from claiming a crude economic determinism; that slavery was undermined because of changes in Britain's economic self-interest. There were, after all, precious few capitalist interests, including the East India lobby, actively or openly supporting emancipation in the years between 1823 and 1838.[70] It is true that an economic critique of slavery was incorporated into the main abolitionist onslaught on slavery. But it failed to register itself as a major theme in the growing volume of criticism of slavery, even in its last days. Of course, it is also true that it was not necessary to denounce slavery as uneconomic because, by the mid 1820s, it was self-evidently out-of-kilter with contemporary British economic, values, though this did not prevent the British buying slave-grown sugar from other countries.

More importantly, however, slavery had been thoroughly undermined on other, more influential, grounds. And this had been possible primarily because of the human and demographic revolution which was actively transforming the face of British society. And as British life changed – became more 'modern' – it began to shed the skins of its former self. Slavery was widely viewed as an institution from a former age, offensive to changing contemporary values (notably religious feelings), contrary to newly discovered social rights and of dubious economic benefit.

Historians have tended, quite naturally, to give pride of place in abolition to the abolitionists themselves, notably to the leadership who persevered through incalculable obstructions and throughout a whole lifetime. But relatively little attention has been paid by historians of abolition to the slaves themselves. Yet it should now be clear that the slaves materially shaped the course of abolition. It would be wrong to claim that British slaves seized their freedom like their contemporaries in Haiti. None the less, blacks played a crucial role in undermining British slavery. First and foremost, of course, they endured – and resisted – slavery throughout these years. By turns their stoicism or rebelliousness was a force which impressed itself on successive colonial and British observers. The slave revolts, beginning most dramatically in Haiti, and progressing through Barbados, Demerara and Jamaica, were spectacular (and compounding) reminders of the endemic violence in the slave system; of black resistance, white revenge and the horrifying escalation of violence and deaths. There was little to be said in favour of a system which bequeathed such violence to the successive offspring of slaves; little, too, for the British to take pride in. The slaves, through their resistance, periodically reminded their colonial masters of their grievances, their aspirations and their humanity. Indeed, it was one of the great achievements, of slaves and abolitionists together, that they convinced the British, as a nation, of the aptness of the abolitionist motto, 'Am I not a man and a brother?'

There was, in addition, a black voice and a black presence in Britain which repeatedly underscored the activities of the slaves in the colonies. Whether articulate and educated (like Equiano) or poor and deprived (like Billy Waters) the British blacks provided a living refutation of the regular calumnies flung at black society by the West India lobby. For those with eyes to see, the falsehoods of the plantocracy – and its ideology rooted in the assumption that only plantation slavery could secure a human and labour discipline from the blacks – could be refuted by glancing at free black life in Britain.

For British people of a religious persuasion, perhaps the most striking black achievement in these years was the rapid conversion to Christianity, notably to the Nonconformist sects. It could be argued, it is true, that the acceptance of black equality only *after* conversion to Christianity is a good illustration of the cultural imperialism endemic in the abolitionist world view. None the less, for the purposes of this study, it is important to recall that in black Christianity, with its piousness, its autodidactism, its collective strength, its qualities of leadership and nobility, the British recognised individual and collective human qualities which, once more, flew in the face of traditional plantocratic and racist arguments. Just to personify the matter (a favourite trick of contemporary abolitionists), it would be hard to imagine a more impressive person than Sam Sharpe. Yet he was executed by a colonial system seeking to maintain the credibility of slave society. It may be true that, for their part, the abolitionists came to place unrealistic expectations on the shoulders of free blacks; expecting them to shed the *persona* of slaves and instantly flourish as free peasants. Subsequent economic events were rapidly to disabuse white supporters of such unreasonable expectations. None the less, the abolitionists had come to believe – and the bulk of the nation accepted their belief – that the blacks were human, like all others, and *ought* to be allowed the exercise of their various human rights.

To a very marked degree the acceptance of this central fact emerged from a scrutiny of slave society itself; blacks were thus instrumental (though often unwittingly so) in transforming the perceptions of their metropolitan masters and friends. True, it also emerged from a tradition, stretching back well into the eighteenth century, of rational and theological analysis. But in the process of transforming that obviously minority, intellectual current into the broadly based, indeed populist tradition of the years between 1787 and 1838, the blacks (in Britain and the West Indies) played an important role. It is scarcely surprising that the heroes of abolition, immortalised in print, pictures and stone on both sides of the Atlantic, have traditionally been the prominent leaders of the abolition cause in Britain. Only now, in a post-colonial world, are recently independent nations keen to locate their own 'heroes' and to award them the place in their nation's history previously denied them by formal historiography. We need not feel the urge to follow an older tradition, and to pinpoint heroes, black and white, in such a complex historical transformation. But at the very least we need to establish the fact that in the final confrontation with slavery, the slaves themselves must be accorded a crucial and honourable role.

8 Freedom in the Shadow of Slavery

In August 1838, few people could have accurately predicted the fate of the former slaves; the future seemed more impenetrable than usual. Moreover, much depended on conditions in the particular colony, and its social and topographical condition. In the smaller, more densely settled islands, the freed slaves often had little alternative but to continue to work on the properties of their former owners. With little spare land for them to settle, they were thrown back, as ill-paid and generally under-employed labourers, into the arms of the former slave owners. Elsewhere – notably in Trinidad and Guiana – where land was relatively plentiful, the flight of the blacks from the estates created a labour shortage which was solved, in the short term, by a new imperial labour scheme; the importation of 'coolie labour' from India.[1] Thus were laid the foundations for yet another infamous traffic in humanity which, if lacking the formality of slavery, was unquestionably characterised by lack of freedom. The numbers involved were enormous, and continued until 1919, helping to transform the demographic face of Caribbean society.[2] For their part, the former slaves often quit the plantations, trying to create a viable future in the new free villages which proliferated throughout the islands. But they often encountered a host of difficulties. Land for cultivation (and accommodation) was often marginal and was often Crown or private land. The new black peasantry thus entered freedom under immediate and dire financial and legal difficulties.

Most difficult of all were their economic problems. Many former slaves continued to work for the surviving properties, for part of the year, producing marketable foodstuffs on their own land for the rest of the year. But the old plantation system itself began to come apart, dramatically in some islands and rapidly so after the gradual equalisation of the Sugar Duties. Thereafter,

Caribbean produce found itself competing with superior sugars from other parts of the world. Within a decade of emancipation, Jamaican planters were complaining that the industry was in a ruinous condition.[3] The lot of the local peasantry often varied according to the fortunes of local estates. Overall, however, the peasants and labourers, by mid century, had settled into a condition which was to characterise the lives of their descendants thereafter; perched on land of marginal economic value and dubious legal status, denied any social (or educational) services worth speaking of, these former slaves had become, in effect, a depressed free peasantry. Their condition was not, of course, of their own making but the wretchedness which characterised the lives of many of them was viewed, by growing numbers of mid-Victorians, as evidence and proof of many of the traditional allegations about black inferiority. The victims of the system were, not for the last time, taking the blame for the system's shortcomings.

Prominent British visitors reported on the distressed condition of the West Indian peasantry, often in absurdly dark (and racist) terms confirming the nascent mid Victorian view that the humanitarian pressure for black freedom had been a case of misapplied zeal and energy.[4] Yet it would be wrong to think that the image of West Indian peasant poverty was merely a fiction of hostile imaginations. When, in the mid century, a young radical preacher, the Reverend Henry Clarke, began to keep a diary about life in rural Jamaica, his picture was bleaker than most. Denouncing British abolitionists, he wrote:

> The error of the abolitionists was in supposing their work was done when emancipation was secured. . . . They destroyed slavery but made no attempt to replace it with freedom. . . . If these 'self-denying soldiers of the Cross' could just behold the misery, the darkness, the suffering and destitution under the Devil's empire in Jamaica, they would not clap their hands so long.

Clarke's sympathies were uniquely for the local blacks; his animus directed against Jamaican landowners and colonial officials: 'What can be the crime of the poor black people, that the Lord thus leaves them for centuries in the hands of their oppressors?'[5] Although Henry Clarke repeated such views publicly (and often) and incurred social and political hostility for doing so, his private diary entries, bristling with outrage at the lot of the mid century black peasantry, provide a revealing commentary on the abject condition of the former slaves. Whatever their achievements (and they were considerable),[6] the former slaves had, within a generation, become an impoverished peasantry, whose material well-being could not always be secured in the teeth of social and economic circumstances not of their making. The equation of slavery versus freedom cannot, of course, be drawn up merely in economic terms. But the high expectation held by many British abolitionists, that a free black peasantry would blossom and thrive, was seriously checked. Indeed, it has been argued that this was the first British experience 'of other races failing to react in the expected manner to what both sides in the transaction saw as an act of benevolence'.[7]

Slavery did not, of course, disappear in 1838. It thrived in a number of societies, notably in the USA, Brazil and Cuba. North American slavery, revived and expanded by the early nineteenth-century cotton boom (the produce of which fed the burgeoning industries of Lancashire) became an object of bitter denunciation not only by American abolitionists but also by the British movement, which was able to direct its organisation and energies – both rendered somewhat aimless in 1838 – into new directions. In the campaign against US slavery, there developed an important international Anglo-American movement; abolitionists (black and white), correspondence and publications criss-crossed the Atlantic in a remarkable show of international co-operation.[8] In fact, the resurgence of nineteenth-century slavery, and the slave trade to Brazil and Cuba, confronted abolitionists with as big an obstacle as the ones they had so recently surmounted. There was, in effect, a variety of overlapping campaigns (and a proliferation of abolitionist societies) directing their various activities at the surviving (and thriving) institutions of slavery and the slave trade.[9]

These efforts were greatly assisted, after British emancipation, by the support and agencies of British government and foreign policy. Throughout the period of abolitionist attacks on British slavery (1787–1838), successive British Ministers and governments had proved themselves generally reluctant to commit themselves formally to various abolitionist measures, however much they might support them privately. In 1838, the British had established themselves as an abolitionist nation; thereafter it became a fundamental feature of British international and maritime policy to insist, wherever possible, that other nations follow and accord to the British lead. Here, again, is a perfect illustration of the cultural imperialism of abolition. Not surprisingly, there were many people who took a more cynical view of what, after all, was a remarkable volte-face by the British. After two centuries of being renowned as the pre-eminent slaving nation, from 1838 the British sought to impress their new-found abolitionist zeal on the rest of the (generally reluctant) world. Foreign Office treaties – many with subservient or client states in no position to refuse or resist – were backed up by the considerable power of the Royal Navy. But even such diplomatic and military might was of little avail against the even more powerful market forces which persuaded traders to run the risks of shipping Africans into bondage in the Americas. Despite the powerful abolitionist bodies in Britain, despite official British opposition registered through diplomatic and military channels, Africa continued to be blighted by the predatory incursions of European and American slave traders. And, as long as slavery and the slave trade survived, it provided the British not only with an object for their crusading sense of outrage, but, equally, it provided a ready-made illustration – to be hawked around at home and abroad – of British moral superiority. Black freedom and anti-slavery were, in effect, cultural talismen, distinguishing the good (the British) from the bad (the slavers).

There was, in fact, a pronounced culture of anti-slavery in the nineteenth century which permeated British life, and became one of the distinguishing peculiarities in which the British took such pride. Indeed, anti-slavery entered the pantheon of freedom which the British so regularly displayed, to themselves and to others, as the distinguishing hallmark of the British people. Moreover, the lessons were taught at all levels of British society. Churches (and their growing numbers of missionaries) continued to inform their congregations of the wickedness of slavery and the slave trade. More influential still, perhaps, was the impact of children's literature; books, magazines, comics and ephemeral literature which often deal with slavery, and – of course – rehearsed the British virtue in being the pioneering crusader against this manifest wickedness. A children's board game, for instance, culminated in the square where the King of England grants freedom to a kneeling slave.[10] Stories about the Royal Navy suppressing the slave trade regularly appeared in Victorian boys' comics and magazines,[11] in that genre of military adventure which so fascinated the young (and which proved so perversely influential in exciting a popular commitment to empire and military glory). Factual accounts, fictional stories, historical episodes and even lessons from geography were all dangled before the young as proof of their country's superiority. And among the elements which went to make up that superiority was the British (often described as the English) love of liberty and hatred of oppression: 'The English are a grave, sober people, fond of their houses and families; they are kind to each other and to people in distress; industrious and active; fond of liberty themselves and willing to allow it to others.'[12] Native peoples were less sympathetically described. A child's book, *The World and its Inhabitants*, described the West Indies thus:

> The ground is cultivated by poor people who have been stolen away from Africa against their wishes, and who, till very lately, were most cruelly kept in a state of slavery. We may rejoice that this horrid system is now put an end to; but the Negroes have been for many years past so badly treated, that it will be a very long time before they recover from the effects of it, and become a civilised and happy people.[13]

Such sentiments became even more potent among the young in the last quarter of the century when, in the new Board Schools, the virtues of empire (and of the British 'race') were incorporated into the curriculum for even the poorest of children. Thus, did poor, working-class children come to receive and accept the ideology of empire and social superiority which, though fashioned by and for their social superiors, permeated down the social scale via popular literature (and song) and through formal school instruction.[14]

Anti-slavery was, then, one facet of the developing nineteenth-century cult of British freedoms. The Acts of 1807, 1833 and 1838 seemed to be splendid examples of the altruistic British commitment to freedom on a broad front. Just as domestic British life was (so it was claimed) the continuing march of material progress and social freedom (the material progress itself substantially shaped by the benefits of commercial and economic freedom), so too were British dealings with the wider world characterised by a commitment to freedom. There were, obviously, certain striking objections to such a view, none more obvious than the history of the two centuries *before* emancipation when the British had led the world in perfecting the slaving system. But there was also the equally powerful objection that, for all the British pride in the ability to export or impose freedoms, the slow accumulation of formal empire (with its parallel ideological support) actually involved the *denial* of freedoms to ever more native peoples. In fact, proponents of imperialism argued that a major benefit of the British imperial presence was that it ultimately conveyed the material and social benefits of British life. Thus, once more, British self-interests (in acquiring empire) could readily accommodate themselves to altruism (in bestowing British virtues); both imperial master and colonial subject thus benefitted from the spread of imperial control. The reality, of course, was at once more prosaic, more brutal and, not infrequently, more squalid.

British imperialism was not a uniformly even phenomenon, but varied greatly between different parts of the imperial possessions. But it seems ironic that the nation which took such pride (then and since) in ending the inhumanities of slavery should embark on two related phenomena – indentured labour and imperial conquest – both of which stemmed from the ending of slavery and which were to produce their own disfiguring scars on world history. Nor is this merely a present-day perception; a judgement informed by modern, post-colonial sensibilities. There were, after all, regular and strident criticisms of the progress of British imperialism – and indentured service – although it is also true that such voices were rare; a minority sensibility generally unheeded in a pervasive–imperialistic climate.

In the uneven development of British imperialism, in the years after the granting of black freedom, there was precious little evidence of that commitment to black equality which had so pervaded the various abolitionist campaigns since 1787. British dealings with black humanity were scarcely characterised by that earlier zealous attachment to the idea that all men were brothers. Where the British had 'face-to-face' dealings with blacks, most notably as subject or colonial peoples, the relationship was, by and large, shaped by British dominance suffused with an undiluted sense of racial superiority. The experience of blacks in mid-Victorian Britain was too marginal to be of more general application. But wherever black met white in the years after the ending of British slavery, it is hard to see even a residual survival of that fund of egalitarian *rapport* so essential to the abolitionist cause. Where had it gone? Or had it been merely a matter of meaningless words and gestures; deceptive arguments and claims advanced during a passionate political campaign and promptly forgotten when the objective had been achieved? Was the abolitionist campaign, in essence, an early example of 'telescopic philanthropy'; becoming excited about distant injustices to the exclusion of more immediate and pressing difficulties at home?

It is difficult to sift through the welter of private abolitionist papers and not be impressed by the passionate commitment and feeling of the men involved; their public utterances, it may be felt, ought to be judged more critically. Nor is it possible to dismiss the fervour which infected the peak years of abolition. It was, after all, a campaign which attracted a larger public commitment than any other contemporary reforming movement. There is a sense, however, that abolition was a movement which offered a cause which was non-divisive; a cause around which people of all social stations and classes could unite with little material or political loss or danger. All other contemporary campaigns were invested with particular sectional, political, trade or religious interests, and, as such, were inevitably divisive. This was true, for instance, of parliamentary reform, religious toleration, factory reform, poor law reform and any other campaign we care to scrutinise. Only slavery provided the chance for the nation to *unite* behind a political issue, a moral crusade, the outcome of which would apparently be to everyone's economic advantage, would be a victory for Christian virtue and humanity. Moreover, it was a campaign which purified its supporters; anti-slavery had that (not inconsiderable) quality of making its followers feel better for their support. In the eyes of their contemporaries, in their own eyes and, perhaps most important of all, in the eyes of their God, supporters of anti-slavery were seen to be undertaking good, improving and laudably altruistic work. Only the West India lobby could take exception. And who, apart from those with a vested interest, seriously paid attention to men whose contribution had been merely to add to the sum of abject human misery?

Yet, it *is* difficult to avoid the point that such united and unalloyed commitment and excitement developed on behalf of slaves many thousands of miles away. Would the fervour have been so unanimous had slavery survived as a major institution in Britain itself? In the USA, for instance, where abolition was an equally important crusade, black freedom proved to be a fatally divisive issue. Where Americans divided on the question of black freedom, the British united. But British slaves lived, 5000 miles away from the metropolis, in the Caribbean colonies. Hypothetical questions may seem out of place in historical analysis, but can we seriously imagine abolition provoking such a show of unity had slavery in Britain persisted in any other than a vestigal form? As sincere as abolitionists were in their demands for black freedom, it cost them little to bestow on West Indian blacks the equality which Americans denied to their fellow countrymen. All that Britain lost in granting black freedom was the end of the once-proud West Indian sugar kingdoms. And, in any case, the British could now buy tropical produce more cheaply elsewhere. It is of supreme irony that many of these products were cultivated by slaves – Brazilian or Cuban – or by indentured workers tied to the land no less effectively (and oppressively) than the former slaves.

It was as if the British had come full circle. It was in the sixteenth and seventeenth centuries that the British began to acquire the taste for tropical produce, created by the slaves of other European powers and by their indentured settlers in the Americas. By the mid nineteenth century, the British (and European) addiction to tropical produce – luxuries and essentials – was even more pronounced. Indeed, a major part of contemporary diet consisted of those products, notably sugar, while a substantial slice of the British economy was directly or indirectly dependent upon slave-grown cotton. However proud the British might feel in having shed their slaving past, the nature of early and mid nineteenth-century life and economy dictated a continuing involvement – albeit indirectly – with slave-grown produce. Again, it is scarcely cynical to note that the emancipation of British slaves was paralleled by an unqualified (and in some respects, a growing) indirect dependence upon the fruits of slave labour. It is true, of course, that a good deal of British effort and emotion was expended in denouncing slavery throughout the world and in trying to curtail Britain's economic links with slave economies. But these indirect slaving links and the controversy over the equalisation of sugar duties in 1846 failed to arouse that passionate and irresistible chorus of denunciation which had been the hallmark of the campaign up to 1838.

When placed in the longer perspective, slavery had clearly been a 'problem' in a great variety of ways. From its intrusion in English affairs, in the late sixteenth century, it was an alien institution, borrowed from other European (primarily Iberian) experiences and adapted in suitably modified form in the development of British colonies throughout the Americas. Even on the far side of the Atlantic, black slavery was an institution which, from the first, ran counter to contemporary English practice and law and was contrary to the economic and social development in England which had seen the slow but effective erosion of bondage (notably serfdom). There was, to put the matter simply, little in the recent English historical experience to prepare the way for the development of black chattel slavery. Yet, within a generation, mid seventeenth-century Englishmen (the same men so conscious of their own social and political rights confirmed by the Revolution) had established a form of black slavery which was to characterise many of the colonies for two centuries and which yielded such material wealth to colonial (and metropolitan) society while transforming the human face of the Americas. At one level, the adoption of slavery by a nation committed to confirming and extending the liberties of its own people provides an illustration of how wonderfully adaptable was a legal and social system when pressured by a major shift in economic self-interest. English doubts about the morality, legality or unchristian nature of slavery were relegated, for more than a century, to a subsidiary and generally unheeded role; overwhelmed by an irresistible and all-consuming rush to tap the dazzling slave-produced wealth of the Indies. The zeal to profit through slave-based labour was an overriding passion, shared by politicians in Westminster and institutional wealth in Britain as much as by the settlers and slave traders. All became key elements in a combined 'team' effort to advance the national interest through the slave empires.

There were, it is true, critics of black slavery voicing their complaints throughout its long and painful history. Indeed, the power and stridency of anti-slavery sentiment by the late eighteenth century has tended to obscure the longevity of this critical tradition. None the less, it is true that criticisms of slavery began to make an effective and influential impression only from the mid eighteenth century onwards. The success of anti-slavery and its power as a popular phenomenon, has been the substance of the second half of this book. It needs, however, to be said that anti-slavery sentiment broke out of its marginal, intellectual enclave in the very years when the British black society – itself a by-product of the slave system – reached its apogee. Indeed, the transition in anti-slavery, from intellectual (secular and theological) to popular concern was itself substantially due to the problems of British blacks and the attempts, notably by Granville Sharp, to throw back the advance of slavery and to establish the point, in England, that slavery was illegal. That legal battle, though never won in its entirety, confirmed the developing social practice of blacks securing their own freedoms. Slavery was effectively eroded in England; black self-help and humanitarian agitation ensured that the practice of slavery in England became progressively more difficult and not worth the slave-owners' efforts. In the process a great deal of publicity drew attention to the wider phenomenon of slavery. Thus, the problems and conditions of blacks in England offered the first effective glimpse, for an interested English public, of the problems of slavery in its broader setting. Clearly, abolitionism was not made possible by the recent history of blacks in England, but it seems perfectly clear that the rehearsal of arguments about slavery in England and about the consequent social wretchedness of ex-slaves determined the initial stages and direction of early abolition. Thus, as a practical issue, the perception of English slavery as a problem was a function, initially, of black society in England itself. Thereafter, it was but a short step towards confronting the broader (and more difficult problems of the slave trade and colonial slavery. Henceforth, as the political attention of abolition focussed on the slave trade and, later, on the West

Indies, less regard was paid to local black society (which, in any case, was in a state of relative numerical decline). By the time of emancipation, black life in England was more marginal than ever; a small and contracting reminder (though one which never disappeared) of the slave empire which had brought local black society into being in the first place. When English black life was thus marginal, the abolitionist cause successfully focussed the national attention and enthusiasm on the distant (though none the less more momentous) problems of colonial slavery.

It was only a half a century between the political furore about blacks in London (in 1787) and the ending of slavery in the colonies. The transformation in national sensibilities in that relatively brief period was quite remarkable (and encompassed of course far more than mere outrage against slavery). To a marked degree, the changes in sensibilities need to be located in the broader economic and social changes in English life, more especially the emergence of a populous and urban nation, whose patterns of industrial life were rapidly being transformed. In those years, a vital economic system – slavery – found itself eroded both by the economic changes at the heart of British life and by the waves of antipathy generated by the abolitionist cause. It is also true that the development of the concept of universal rights, more directly a result of the French revolution, infused another corrosive element into the general decay of slavery. But the most elusive element was the slaves themselves, for it was their resistance – in all its forms – and changes in their collective organisations (produced most crucially by the impact of abolition in 1807 and the coming of the churches) which gnawed away at slavery from within.

Black freedom, when it came, was hailed as a victory for light over darkness, for right over wrong, for traditional liberties over despotism. Few modern observers would care to challenge such views, but they do not provide a complete and sufficient explanation. Moreover, the triumph of 1838 has tended so often to deflect attention from the condition and problems of those millions of people living in the shadow and aftermath of slavery. The subsequent British recitation of their collective virtue in ending slavery (and continuing throughout the nineteenth century to secure its termination worldwide) often served to obscure post-slavery conditions. The British forgot or deliberately ignored the fate of the heirs of slavery (the black West Indian peasants), deflected their gaze from the tens of thousands of Indians and Chinese shipped to the colonial peripheries, and all this in addition to the untold millions who subsequently fell beneath British imperial sway and who were offered no access to that brotherly equality so beloved of the abolitionists. To minimise the achievement of black freedom would be to belittle an extraordinary phenomenon and to perpetuate a historical falsehood. Conversely, not to consider emancipation in the context of subsequent post-slave and imperial history would be no less distorting. One purpose of this book has been to illustrate that the campaign for black freedom, fought between 1787 and 1838, was, after all, only one episode – albeit a remarkable and unique one – in a long-established international history of relations between black and white. It is, moreover, a continuing story.

Notes

NOTES TO THE INTRODUCTION

1. Ian Law and Linda Loy, 'A History of Racism and Resistance in Liverpool', paper given at 'Blacks in Britain' Conference, London, September 1981.
2. Fiona Spiers, 'Blacks in Britain and the Struggle for Emancipation in the US', paper given at 'Blacks in Britain' Conference, London, September 1981.
3. Nigel File and Chris Power, *Black Settlers in Britain, 1555–1958* (London, 1981) pp. 55–63.
4. *The Black Man in Britain, 1550–1950*, BBC 2, November 1974.
5. *Passage to Britain*, Channel 4, April–May 1984.
6. See, for example, *The Fight Against Slavery*, BBC 2, 1975.
7. James Walvin, *Passage to Britain: Immigration in British History and Politics* (London, 1984) ch. 12.
8. Ibid., p. 203.
9. Ibid., ch. 9.
10. I. Crewe (ed.), *British Political Sociology Year Book* (London, 1975) vol. 2: *The Politics of Race*.
11. *The Brixton Disorders, 10–12 April 1981, Report of an Inquiry by the Rt Hon. The Lord Scarman*, Cmnd 8427 (London, 1981).
12. The following are among the more important books in the field: Anthony J. Barker, *The African Link: British Attitudes to the Negro in the 17th and 18th Centuries* (London, 1978); M. W. Debrunner, *Presence and Prestige: Africans in Europe, A History of Africans in Europe before 1918* (Basel, 1979); Paul Edwards and James Walvin, *Black Personalities in the Era of the Slave Trade* (London, 1983); Douglas A. Lorimer, *Colour, Class and the Victorians* (Leicester, 1978); Edward Scobie, *Black Britannia: A History of Blacks in Britain* (Chicago, 1972); Follarin Shyllon, *Black Slaves in Britain* (London, 1974); *Black People in Britain, 1555–1833* (London, 1977); James Walvin, *Black and White: The Negro and English Society 1555–1945* (London, 1973).
13. David Dabydeen (ed.), *The Black Presence in English Literature* (Wolverhampton, 1983).
14. This analysis was effectively begun by Eric Williams, *Capitalism and Slavery* (London, 1944). For recent discussions on the economics of abolition, see Seymour Drescher, *Econocide: British Slavery in the Era of Abolition* (Pittsburgh, Penn, 1977); Seymour Drescher and Selwyn H. H. Carrington, 'Debate: Econocide and West Indian Decline, 1783–1806',

183

Boletin de Estudios Latinoamericanos y de Caribe, no. 36 (June 1984) pp. 13–67; W. A. Green, *British Slave Emancipation: The Slave Colonies and the Great Experiment, 1830–1865* (Oxford, 1976).

15. See David Brion Davis, *The Problem of Slavery in Western Culture* (Ithaca, NY, 1966), and his *The Problem of Slavery in the Age of Revolution, 1770–1823* (Ithaca, NY, 1975); Roger Anstey, *The Atlantic Slave Trade and British Abolition, 1760–1810* (London, 1975). See also Roger Anstey, 'The Historical Debate on the Abolition of the British Slave Trade', in Roger Anstey and P. E. H. Hair (eds), *Liverpool, the African Slave Trade and Abolition* (Liverpool, 1976).

16. C. L. R. James, *The Black Jacobins: Toussaint l'Ouverture and the San Domingo Revolution* (1938; repr. New York, 1963). Michael Craton, *Testing the Chains: Resistance to Slavery in the British West Indies* (Ithaca, NY, 1982); David Geggus, *Slavery, War and Revolution* (Oxford, 1981).

NOTES TO CHAPTER 1: SLAVERY AND A FREE LAND

1. For the most recent analysis, see Orlando Patterson, *Slavery and Social Death* (Cambridge, Mass., 1983).

2. James Walvin, 'The Propaganda of Anti-Slavery', James Walvin (ed.), *Slavery and British Society, 1776–1846* (London, 1982).

3. *The School Reader* (London, 1875) p. 61.

4. G. E. Aylmer (ed.), *The Levellers* (London, 1975); Christopher Hill, *The World Turned Upside Down* (London, 1975).

5. Christopher Hill, 'The Norman Yoke', in J. Saville (ed.), *Democracy and the Labour Movement* (London, 1954).

6. Abolitionist Petitions (1830) in *Journal of the House of Lords*, vol. LXIII (1830) p. 101.

7. Davis, *Problem of Slavery in Western Culture*.

NOTES TO CHAPTER 2: SLAVES IN ENGLAND

1. Quoted in Rodney Hilton, *The Decline of Serfdom in Medieval England* (London, 1970) p. 56.

2. Christopher Hampton (ed.), *A Radical Reader* (London, 1984) p. 190.

3. Ibid., p. 192.

4. Ibid., p. 207.

5. Ibid., pp. 252–3.

6. R. Hakluyt, *The Principal Navigations, Voyages, Traffiques and Discoveries of the English Nation* (London, 1926) vol. IV, p. 65.

7. Ibid., vol. VII, pp. 5–6.

8. M. Craton, *Sinews of Empire: A Short History of British Slavery* (London, 1974) p. 446; H. Klein, *The Middle Passage: Comparative Studies in the Atlantic Slave Trade* (Princeton, NJ, 1978) p. 12.

9. Bernard Bailyn, *et al.*, *The Great Republic* (Boston, Mass., and New York, 1977) p. 45.

10. George Downing to John Winthrop, Aug 26 1645, in Elizabeth Donnan (ed.), *Documents Illustrative of the History of the Slave Trade to America*, 4 vols (Washington, DC, 1930–5) vol. III, p. 8.

11. 'The Guinea Company to James Pope', 17 September 1651, ibid., vol. I, p. 128.

12. J. Latimer, *The Annals of Bristol in the Eighteenth Century* (Frome, 1893) p. 146.

13. H. T. Catterall, *Judicial Cases Concerning American Slavery and the Negro*, 5 vols (Washington, DC, 1926–37) vol. I.

14. J. Abraham, *Lettsum* (London, 1933) p. 53; J. J. Hecht, *Continental and Colonial Servants in 18th Century England* (Northampton, Mass., 1954) p. 34.

15. *Acts of the Privy Council, 1596–97*, vol. XXVI, p. 16; P. L. Hughes and J. F. Larkin (eds), *Tudor Royal Proclamation, 1588–1603* (New Haven, Conn., 1969) pp. 20–1.

16. Syhllon, *Black Slaves*, pp. 6–7.

17. See, for example, the portrait of *Second Duke of Perth* in the National Portrait Gallery of Scotland.

18. *Calendar of State Papers, Colonial America and the West Indies, 1669–1674* (London, n.d.) p. 412; Royal Proclamation (1674) in Donnan, *Documents*, vol. I, pp. 195–6.

19. 'Butts v. Penny' (1677), in Catterall, *Judicial Cases*, vol. I, p. 9.

20. Will of Thomas Papillon, 1700 (Kent Archives), V.1015, T.44.

21. 'Butts v. Penny' (1677), in Catterall, *Judicial Cases*, vol. I, p. 9.

22. 'Chamberline v. Harvey' (1696/7), ibid., p. 11.

23. 'Smith v. Gould' (1706), ibid., pp. 11–12.

24. 'The Yorke–Talbot Opinion' (1729), ibid., p. 12.

25. 'Pearne v. Lisle' (1749), ibid., pp. 12–13.

26. 'Shanley v. Harvey' (1762), ibid., p. 13.

27. Granville Sharp, 'An Account of the Occasion which First Impelled Granville Sharp to Study Law and Undertake the Defence of Negro Slaves', *The Sharp Papers*, Box 54, Hardwick Court, Gloucestershire.

28. William Blackstone, *Commentaries on the Laws of England*, 3rd edn, vol. I (Oxford, 1773) p. 317; P. Hoare, *Memoirs of Granville Sharp* (London, 1820) p. 91 n.; F. T. M. Fletcher, 'Montesquieu's Influence on Anti-Slavery Opinion in England', *Journal of Negro History*, vol. XVIII (1933) p. 417.

29. Shyllon, *Black Slaves*, pp. 76–9.

30. 'The Case of James Somerset, 1772', *Howell's State Trials*, vol. XX (London, 1814).

31. Long, *Candid Reflections* . . . (London, 1772) p. 46; 'Minutes for the the Relief of the Black Poor', PRO, T.630–47.

32. *Felix Farley's Bristol Journal*, 12 March 1757.

33. *Gentleman's Magazine* (1764) p. 493; Sir John Fielding, *Penal Laws* (London, 1768) pp. 144–5.

34. Long, *Candid Reflections*, p. 51.

35. *Tenth Report of the African Institution 1816* (London, 1816) p. 38.

36. *Felix Farley's Bristol Journal*, 15 November 1746.

37. *Cal. S.P., Col. Am. W.I., 1677–1680*, p. 611.
38. See chapter 7 below.
39. Walvin, *Black and White*, ch. 5.
40. 'The Yorke–Talbot Opinion' (1729), in Catterall, *Judicial Cases*, vol. I, p. 3.
41. B. Dobrée, *The Letters of Philip Dormer Stanhope, 4th Earl of Chesterfield*, vol. II (London, 1932) p. 54.
42. Walvin, *Black and White*, pp. 65–6.
43. *Felix Farley's Bristol Journal*, 5 November 1746 and 5 March 1757; *Public Advertiser*, 28 November 1769; *Daily Courant*, 29 March 1712.
44. T. Rowlandson, 'L'école des Armes', in C. Paston, *Social Caricature in the 18th Century* (London, 1905).
45. O. Equiano, *Interesting Narrative of the Life of Olaudah Equiano . . .*, 2 vols (London, 1787).
46. The best analysis of this case is in Shyllon, *Black Slaves*, chs 6–10.
47. J. Bigelow (ed.), *The Works of Benjamin Franklin*, vol. IV (New York, 1887) p. 507.
48. Quoted in *A Letter to Philo-Africanus . . .* (London, 1789) p. 39; see also Shyllon, *Black Slaves*, pp. 168–9.
49. *Scot's Magazine*, vol. 36 (1774) p. 53; *Bristol Gazette and Public Advertiser*, 4 November 1773; Shyllon, *Black Slaves*, ch. 10.
50. 'Knight v. Wedderburn' (1778), in Catterall, *Judicial Cases*, vol. I, p. 18.
51. Shyllon, *Black Slaves*, ch. 12; Hoare, *Memoirs*, pp. 237–44; Granville Sharp, 'Diary 1783–1798, 19 March 1783', *Sharp Papers*, Box 56, Book H.
52. 'Keane v. Boycott' (1795), in Catterall, *Judicial Cases*, vol. I, p. 21.
53. 'Africa v. Marquis of Fitzjames' (1799), ibid., p. 22.
54. 'The Slave Grace' (1827), ibid., vol. II, p. 34.
55. *The History of Mary Prince* (London, 1831) p. 20.

NOTES TO CHAPTER 3: BLACK SOCIETY IN ENGLAND

1. *Gentleman's Magazine* (1764) p. 443.
2. Quoted in Barker, *The African Link*, p. 25. There may have been between 15,000 and 20,000 blacks in late eighteenth-century London alone. For the evidence see Peter Fryer, *Staying Power: The History of Black People in Britain* (London, 1984) p. 64.
3. Quoted in W. Cohen, *The French Encounter with Africans* (Bloomington, Ind., 1980) p. 111.
4. Granville Sharp, *Letter Book*, p. 19 (York Minster Library).
5. *St James Post*, 19–22 March 1726.
6. Quoted in Edwards and Walvin, *Black Personalities*, p. 20.
7. Walvin, *Black and White*, p. 52.
8. Winthrop Jordan, *White over Black: American Attitudes towards the Negro, 1550–1812* (Baltimore, Md, 1969) pp. 32–40.
9. James Tobin, *Cursory Remarks upon the Rev Mr Ramsay's Essay . . .* (London, 1785) p. 118.

10. Long, *Candid Reflections*, pp. 48–9.
11. N. Pearson, *Society Sketches of the 18th Century* (London, 1911) p. 139.
12. Jordan, *White over Black*, p. 141.
13. Samuel Estwick, *Considerations on the Negro Cause . . .* (London, 1773) pp. 94–5.
14. *London Chronicle*, vol. xxxiii, 13–16 March 1773, p. 250.
15. Long, *Candid Reflections*, pp. 48–9.
16. *Cal. of S.P., Col. Am. W.I., 1677–1680*, p. 611.
17. Evidence of Mr Braithwaite in *British Sessional Papers, Commons Accounts and Papers* (1789) Part iii.
18. Mary Turner, *Slaves and Missionaries: The Disintegration of Jamaican Slave Society, 1787–1834* (Urbana, Ill., 1982) ch. 1.
19. E. B. Underhill (ed.), *Records of a Church of Christ Meeting in Broadmead, Bristol, 1640–1687*, The Hanserd Knollys Society (London, 1847) p. 35.
20. M5P/1717/Sept 17, Oct/91, Middlesex Sessions Papers, Greater London Record Office.
21. East Hampstead Parish Register, 31 January 1769, D/P49 1/2, Berkshire Record Office.
22. Sir John Fielding, *Extracts from such of the Penal Laws as Particularly Relate to the Peace and Good Order of the Metropolis* (London, 1768) p. 145.
23. Earls Colne Parish Register, 24 June 1739, 24 November 1744, 14 April 1749, Essex Record Office.
24. Sunninghill Parish Register 1755, Berkshire Record Office; *Notes and Queries*, vol. 10 (1878) p. 338; Boxgrove (par. 27/1/1); Baptism, 21 August 1772, Carlisle Record Office.
25. Thursby Register, 24 February 1772, Carlisle Record Office; Shelve Parish Register, 18 June 1704, Shropshire Record Office; John Kennedy, *A History of the Parish of Leyton* (Leyton, 1894) p. 18.
26. *Equiano's Autobiography*, vol. i, p. 134; Warfield Parish Register, January 1760, Berkshire Record Office.
27. Stoke Damerd Bishop's Transcripts, 1 April 1786, Devon Record Office; Kennedy, *Leyton*, p. 118; Cobham, 20 September 1792 (P/96/1/2) Kent Archives.
28. *Notes and Queries*, vol. clx (1931) p. 80.
29. Bishops' Returns, 30 October 1762 (R.Bp) 20/B/98; 20 July 1768, (R.Bp) 20/F/10, Borthwick Institute, York; *Yorkshire Record Office Series*, vol. lxxi (1743) p. 105.
30. *Gentleman's Magazine* (1765) p. 145.
31. *The Works of John Wesley*, vol. iii (Grand Rapids, Mich., n.d.) pp. 433, 466.
32. C. F. Pascoe, *Two Hundred Years of the SPG* (London, 1901) p. 256; C. Fyfe, *History of Sierra Leone* (Oxford, 1962) p. 11.
33. M. Banton, *The Coloured Quarter* (London, 1955) p. 23.
34. Hoare, *Memoirs*, p. 369.
35. M. Priestley, 'Philip Quaque of Cape Coast' in P. D. Curtin (ed.,), *Africa Remembered* (Madison, Wis., 1967) pp. 99–139.
36. Walvin, *Black and White*, pp. 66–7.
37. *Letters of Ignatius Sancho* (London, 1782) p. 173.
38. *Equiano's Autobiography*, i, pp. 105, 133–4; vol. ii, pp. 12–19.
39. Ibid., vol. ii, p. 150.

40. Ottobah Cugoano, *Thoughts and Sentiments . . .*, ed. P. Edwards (London, 1787; 1969) pp. v–vii.
41. Turner, *Slaves and Missionaries*.
42. *Equiano's Autobiography*, vol. I, p. 178.
43. Ibid., p. 182.
44. Edmund Burke, 'Sketch of a Negro Code' (1792), in *The Works of the Rt Hon. Edmund Burke*, 16 vols (London, 1826) vol. IX.
45. William Knox, *Three Tracts respecting the Conversion and Instruction of the free Indian and Negro Slaves in the Colonies* (London, 1768) p. 35.
46. *Christian Directions and Instructions for Negroes* (London, 1807) p. iii.
47. Ibid., pp. 12, 84, 124.
48. Ibid., p. 137.
49. Knox, *Three Tracts*, p. 37.
50. *Works of John Wesley*, vol. II, p. 338.
51. *Equiano's Autobiography*, vol. I, p. 10.
52. E. Bellasis (ed.), *Westmorland Church Notes*, vol. II (Kendal, 1889) p. 296.
53. G. Francklyn, *Observations on the Slave Trade* (London, 1789) pp. xi–xii.
54. *The Times*, 11–12 February 1794.
55. Shyllon, *Black Slaves*, ch. 12.
56. Shyllon, *Black People*, p. 128.
57. Cugoano, *Thoughts and Sentiments*, pp. 139–42.
58. Walvin, *Black and White*, ch. 9.
59. Edwards and Walvin, *Black Personalities*, pp. 6, 147–8, 163–70.
60. Ibid., p. 172.

NOTES TO CHAPTER 4: RECURRING THEMES. BLACK IMAGES IN WHITE CULTURE

1. Quoted in Cohen, *French Encounter*, pp. 1–2.
2. See P. J. Marshall and G. Williams, *The Great Map of Mankind* (London, 1982).
3. Cohen, *French Encounter*, pp. 1–2; Edwards and Walvin, *Black Personalities*, p. 5.
4. Eldred Jones, *Othello's Countrymen* (Oxford, 1965).
5. Jordan, *White over Black*, pp. 32–43.
6. Jones, *Othello's Countrymen*, p. 11.
7. Jordan, *White over Black*, pp. 6–8.
8. Donnan, *Documents*, vol. I, p. 88.
9. *Cal. of S.P., Col. Am. W.I., 1677–1780*, p. 120.
10. *Considerations on the Emancipation of Negroes* (London, 1788) p. 3.
11. 'A Statement of the Laws that at present subsist in the West Indian Islands . . .', *British Sessional Papers, Commons, A.P.*, vol. XXXVI (London, 1789) p. 646a.
12. Anstey, *Atlantic Slave Trade*, ch. 9.
13. Ibid., ch. 10; D. B. Davis, 'New Sidelights on Early Anti-slavery Radicalism', *William & Mary Quarterly*, 3rd series, vol. XXVI (1971) no. 4.

14. Marshall and Williams, *Great Map of Mankind*, pp. 228–9.
15. Ibid., pp. 232–3.
16. Quoted in ibid., pp. 236–9.
17. See Fryer, *Staying Power*, pp. 148–50.
18. David Hume, in *Essays, Moral, Political and Literary*, ed. T. H. Green and T. M. Goose (Darmstadt, 1964) p. 252n.
19. Quoted in Fryer, *Staying Power*, p. 153.
20. Quoted in ibid., p. 154.
21. Walvin, *Black and White*, ch. 6–8; Shyllon, *Black Slaves*.
22. Quoted in Fryer, *Staying Power*, p. 156.
23. Long, *Candid Reflections*, pp. 48–9.
24. Edward Long, *History of Jamaica*, 3 vols (London, 1774) vol. II, pp. 356–75.
25. The italics are mine.
26. Ignatius Sancho, *The Letters of the Late Ignatius Sancho*, ed. P. Edwards (London, 1968) pp. 101, 143, 209–10, 218, 252.
27. Ibid., p. 214.
28. See William Beckford, *A Descriptive Account of the Island of Jamaica* (London, 1790).
29. Alexander McDonnell, *A Letter to Thomas Fowell Buxton* (1833).
30. T. Carlyle, 'Discourse on the Nigger Question' (1849) in *Critical and Miscellaneous Essays* (London, 1872) vol. II.
31. T. Carlyle, 'Shooting Niagara and After?', *Macmillan's Magazine*, vol. XVI (1867) p. 321.
32. Quoted in Fryer, *Staying Power*, p. 173.
33. Quoted in Walvin, *Passage to Britain*, p. 41.
34. Christine Bolt, *Victorian Attitudes to Race* (London, 1971) chs III and v.
35. V. G. Kiernan, *The Lords of Human Kind* (London, 1972) p. 49.
36. Quoted in Lorimer, *Colour, Class*, p. 184.
37. Quoted in Bolt, *Victorian Attitudes*, p. 210.
38. R. Knox, *The Races of Man: A Fragment* (London, 1850) p. v.
39. Quoted in Walvin, *Passage to Britain*, pp. 40–1, 42.
40. Bolt, *Victorian Attitudes*, ch. 2.
41. Ibid., p. 1.
42. Quoted in Walvin, *Passage to Britain*, p. 42.
43. David Newsome, *Godliness and Good Learning* (London, 1961) p. 222.
44. J. and A. Taylor, *Hymns for Infant Minds* (London, 1812) p. 1.
45. C. Merton, *Funny Foreigners* (London, 1878).
46. V. E. Chancellor, *History for their Masters* (London, 1970) pp. 118, 122.
47. Ibid., p. 124.
48. Ibid., p. 115.
49. Stephen Jay Gould, *The Mismeasurement of Man* (London, 1981) pp. 32–5.
50. Lorimer, *Colour, Class*, p. 101.
51. Bernard Semmel, *The Governor Eyre Controversy* (London, 1962) pp. 134–5.
52. Quoted in Walvin, *Passage to Britain*, p. 52.
53. Melanie Tebbutt, 'The Evolution of Ethnic Stereotypes', MA thesis Manchester University, 1982, p. 13.

NOTES TO CHAPTER 5: ABOLISHING THE TRADE. PUBLIC SENTIMENT
AND ABOLITION, 1776–1807

1. *Annual Register* (1788) p. 133.
2. Minute book of the Society for the Abolition of the Slave Trade (1790–1819) vol. III, 20 July 1790, Add.Ms.21,256.
3. Anstey, *Atlantic Slave Trade*, p. 102.
4. Ibid., pp. 102–6.
5. Davis, *Problem of Slavery in Western Culture*, p. 395.
6. R. T. & S. Wilberforce, *The Life of William Wilberforce*, 5 vols (London, 1838) vol. I, pp. 152–3.
7. Burke, 'Sketch of a Negro Code' in *Works of the Rt Hon. Edmund Burke*, vol. IX.
8. Anstey, *Atlantic Slave Trade*, pp. 119–23; Davis, *Problem of Slavery in Western Culture*, pp. 415–17.
9. Anstey, ibid., p. 133; D. B. Davis, 'Slavery and "Progress"', in C. Bolt and S. Drescher (eds), *Anti-Slavery, Religion and Reform* (Folkestone, 1980).
10. Anstey, *Atlantic Slave Trade*, ch. 9.
11. *John Wesley's Journal*, abridged by P. L. Parker (London, 1902) p. 370.
12. Quoted in R. Davies and G. Rupp (eds), *A History of the Methodist Church* (London, 1965) vol. I, p. 66.
13. A. D. Gilbert, *Religion and Society in Industrial England* (London, 1976) pp. 31–40.
14. Anstey, *Atlantic Slave Trade*, p. 235.
15. Granville Sharp, *Letter Book* (York Minster Library).
16. Follarin Shyllon, *James Ramsay: The Unknown Abolitionist* (Edinburgh, 1977) ch. 2.
17. Douglas Hall, *A Brief History of the West India Committee* (Barbados, 1971); L. Ragatz, *Fall of the Planter Class* (London, 1928).
18. James Tobin, *Cursary Remarks upon the Reverend Mr Ramsay's Essay . . .* (London, 1785) pp. 117–18.
19. Quoted in Shyllon, *Ramsay*, p. 84.
20. Thomas Clarkson, *History of the Abolition of the Slave Trade . . .*, 2 vols (London, 1808) vol. I, p. 241.
21. Wilberforce, *Life of Wilberforce*, vol. I, p. 53.
22. Clarkson, *History*, vol. I, pp. 283–9.
23. Minute book, Add.Ms.21,255, f. 50.
24. Anstey, *Atlantic Slave Trade*, p. 257.
25. W. Sypher, *Guinea's Captive Kings* (Chapel Hill, NC, 1942).
26. Anstey, *Atlantic Slave Trade*, p. 261–5.
27. Clarkson, *History*, vol. I, pp. 415–16.
28. *The Manchester Directory*, 2 vols (1788) vol. II, pp. 152, 171–3 (Manchester Central Library); L. Ragatz, *Guide for the Study of British Caribbean History* (Washington, DC, 1930) p. 466; *Annual Register* (1788) p. 134; *Gentleman's Magazine* (1788) p. 1079; 'Diaries of William Dyer, 1744–1801', 30 January 1788, vol. II, p. 244 (Bristol Central Library).
29. *Hansard's Debates, 1066–1918*, vol. XXVII (1788–9) cols 495, 501.
30. Anstey, *Atlantic Slave Trade*, pp. 271–3.
31. Clarkson, *History*, vol. I, chs xiv–xv.

32. Ibid., pp. 442–3.
33. G. S. Veitch, *The Genesis of Parliamentary Reform* (London, 1965) p. 44; *Wyvill's Papers*, vol. I, pp. 135–7; letters to SCI, T.S.960.3506(1) (PRO).
34. Hannah More, *Strictures on the Modern System of Female Education* (London, 1799) vol. I, pp. 172–3.
35. Minute book, Add.Ms.27, 811 f. 9.
36. London Corresponding Society Minute book (1791–3) Add.Ms.27,811 ff. 4, 9.
37. *Proceedings of the Public Meeting held at Sheffield, April 7th 1794*, pp. 22–5.
38. Anstey, *Atlantic Slave Trade*, p. 275; *The Times*, 12 March 1793.
39. Wilberforce, *Life of Wilberforce*, vol. I, p. 349.
40. Fiona Spiers, 'Wilberforce', in Jack Hayward (ed.), *Out of Slavery* (London, 1985).
41. Anon., 18 November 1791, in CO 137/89.
42. George Cruickshank, *The Comic Almanack, 1834–43* (London, n.d.) p. 185.
43. *Annual Register* (1793) p. 90; *Hansard's Debates*, vol. xxx (1792–4) cols 632–59.
44. *Annual Register* (1793) p. 157.
45. Ibid., p. 148; *Gentleman's Magazine* (1789) p. 1167.
46. *Annual Register* (1793) pp. 148–50; M. Thale (ed.), *Selections from the Papers of the London Corresponding Society* (Cambridge, 1983) p. 64, n.93.
47. *Pitt Papers*, November–December 1792, William L. Clements Library, University of Michigan, Ann Arbor.
48. Wilberforce, *Life of Wilberforce*, vol. II, p. 18.
49. *A very new PAMPHLET indeed . . .* (London, 1792) pp. 3–4.
50. Quoted in E. M. Howse, *Saints in Politics* (London, 1971) p. 44.
51. *A very new PAMPHLET indeed*, pp. 3–5.
52. Geggus, *Slavery, War and Revolution*.
53. John Thelwall, *Speech to the LCS*, 26 October 1795, p. 10; *The Rights of Nature* (London, 1796), p. 20; letter, 13 February 1794, in T. S. 11.959.3505(1), (PRO); see also Mrs Thelwall, *The Life of John Thelwall* (London, 1837) pp. 115ff.
54. Fryer, *Staying Power*, pp. 106–7.
55. Melbourne Corresponding Society, Privy Council Papers, 1/3514.
56. Quoted in A. Cobban (ed.), *Debate on the French Revolution* (London, 1950) p. 289.
57. Anstey, *Atlantic Slave Trade*, pp. 321–2.
58. Ibid., pp. 326–31.
59. Dale Porter, *The Abolition of the Slave Trade in England, 1784–1807* (Hamden, Conn., 1970) pp. 103–7.
60. Drescher, *Econocide*, ch. 5.
61. Ibid., pp. 122–3.
62. Anstey, *Atlantic Slave Trade*, p. 275.
63. Ibid., p. 388.
64. Ibid., pp. 397–8, 399.
65. *The Edinburgh Review*, vol. x (1807) pp. 205–6.

NOTES TO CHAPTER 6: OUTRAGING OPINION. SLAVERY IN THE
AFTERMATH OF ABOLITION

1. P. D. Curtin, *The Slave Trade: A Census* (Madison, Wis., 1969) ch. 8; David
   Eltis, 'The Impact of Abolition on the Atlantic Slave Trade', in D. Eltis
   and J. Walvin (eds), *The Abolition of the Atlantic Slave Trade* (Madison,
   Wis., 1981) ch. 9.
2. William Wilberforce, *A Letter on the Abolition of the Slave Trade* (London,
   1807).
3. D. B. Davis, 'The Emergence of Immediatism in British and American
   Anti-Slavery Thought', *Journal of American History*, vol. xlix, no. 2.
4. Thomas Clarkson, 'The Account of Efforts, 1807–1824', *Thomas Clarkson
   Papers*, p. 1, Huntington Library (hereafter *Clarkson Papers*), C.N.33.
5. Ibid., pp. 12, 16–17.
6. Letter, 8 October 1814, *Clarkson Papers*, C.N.84.
7. See 'Account of Efforts', p. 20. See also Betty Fladeland, 'Abolitionist
   Pressure on the Concert of Europe, 1814–22', in *Journal of Modern History*,
   vol. 38 (1966) pp. 355–73; and letters in British Library, September 1814,
   Add.Ms.41,267,A, f. 58–60.
8. Thomas Clarkson to R. W. Fox, 13 August 1813, *Clarkson Papers*, HM
   35527.
9. Prospectus, 30 June 1814, *Clarkson papers*, HM 35528.
10. *The Times*, 24 June 1814.
11. Lord Cockburn, *Memorials of his Time* (London/Edinburgh, 1909) p. 271.
12. Samuel Romilly, *Memoirs of the Life of Sir Samuel Romilly, Written by Himself*,
    2nd edn, 3 vols (London, 1840) vol. iii, p. 141.
13. Ibid., pp. 139–40; *Index to the Journal of the House of Lords, 1780–1819*
    (London, n.d.) pp. 49, 846—51.
14. F. D. Cartwright (ed.), *The Life and Correspondence of Major Cartwright*, 2
    vols (London, 1826) vol. ii, p. 84.
15. *The Times*, 12, 15, 20, 28, 31 March, 24, 28, 30 June 1814; *Gentleman's
    Magazine* (1816) pp. 26–7.
16. Quoted in Chester New, *The Life of Henry Brougham* (London, 1961)
    p. 138.
17. Thomas Clarkson, 14 September 1819, Add.Ms.41, 267A, f. 60.
18. Thomas Clarkson, 30 June, 1 July 1814, *Clarkson Papers* C.N.43, 44.
19. Quoted in J. Reich, 'The Slave Trade and the Congress of Vienna',
    Journal of Negro History, vol. 53 (1968).
20. Thomas G. Babington, 30 December 1822, *Clarkson Papers*, M.Y. 52.
21. Sir Alan Burns, *History of the British West Indies* (London, 1954) p. 590.
22. Ibid., p. 611; James Stephen, *Reasons for Establishing a Registration of
    Slaves . . .* (London, 1815).
23. Letter, 16 September 1854, quoted in Sir George Stephen, *Anti-Slavery
    Recollections* (London, 1859).
24. Paper [1815], *Clarkson Papers*, C.N. 56.
25. See B. Higman, *Slave Population and Economy in Jamaica 1807–34* (Cambridge,
    1976) ch. 5.
26. Zachary Macaulay, 31 May 1822, *Clarkson Papers*, M.Y.553.
27. Quoted in Craton, *Testing the Chains*, p. 256.

28. Ibid., p. 259.
29. Ibid., pp. 259–60, 264, 265.
30. Quoted in ibid., p. 266.
31. 'Buckra' means white man, quoted in ibid., p. 241.
32. J. T. Gilmour, 'Episcopacy, Emancipation and Evangelisation', PhD thesis, Cambridge University, 1984.
33. Turner, *Slaves and Missionaries*, ch. 1.
34. Quoted in ibid., p. 9.
35. Quoted in ibid., p. 16.
36. Macaulay, 20 May 1796, *Clarkson Papers*, M.Y.46.
37. R. Furneaux, *William Wilberforce* (London, 1974) p. 41.
38. Burke, 'Sketch of a Negro Code'.
39. Stephen, *Recollections*, 16 September 1854.
40. Gilbert, *Religion and Society*, p. 31.
41. Ibid., pp. 34–5.
42. Craton, *Testing*, p. 163.
43. Higman, *Slave Population*, pp. 2–3.
44. Ibid., p. 187.
45. For a good account of these rules see Thomas Roughley, *The Jamaica Planter's Guide* . . . (London, 1823) pp. 97–119.
46. Higman, *Slave Population*, pp. 188–201.
47. Ibid., ch. 6.
48. Ibid., pp. 201–11.
49. Craton, *Testing*.
50. Quoted in ibid., p. 269.
51. Ibid., ch. 21; S. Thompson (ed.), *The Journal of G. Stedman* (London, 1962).
52. Craton, *Testing*, ch. 21.
53. Turner, *Slaves and Missionaries*, p. 109.
54. Furneaux, *Wilberforce*, p. 416.
55. Quoted in ibid., p. 419.
56. Quoted in ibid., p. 421.

NOTES TO CHAPTER 7: CONFRONTING SLAVERY. PRESSING FOR BLACK FREEDOM

1. Clarkson, 'The Account of Efforts', p. 110.
2. James Cropper, 5 March 1822, letter, Add.Ms.41,267A f. 106.
3. Quoted in W. L. Burn, *Emancipation and Apprenticeship* (London, 1937) p. 86.
4. Cropper, letter, Add.Ms.41,267A, f. 108, 110.
5. James Cropper, ibid., f. 112.
6. Ibid., f. 113.
7. Ibid., f. 122, 125.
8. Printed pamphlet, 12 October 1822, ibid., f. 126.
9. Clarkson, 'The Account of Efforts', p. 11.

10. Ibid., pp. 112–14.
11. *Substance of a Speech delivered by John Joseph Gurney* . . . (Norwich, 1824).
12. Clarkson, 'The Account of Efforts', p. 12, the first italics are mine, the second Clarkson's.
13. Clarkson, *History*, vol. I, p. 86.
14. Quoted in Howard Temperley, 'Anti-Slavery as Cultural Imperialism', in Bolt and Drescher (eds), *Anti-Slavery, Religion and Reform*, p. 344.
15. Clarkson, 'The Account of Efforts', p. 115.
16. Circular from Lord Bathurst, 9 July 1823, in V. Harlow and F. Madden, *British Colonial Developments 1774–1834* (Oxford, 1953) pp. 562–4.
17. Clarkson, 'The Account of Efforts', p. 115.
18. 1823, undated, Add.Ms.41,267A, f. 126.
19. Clarkson, 30 March 1823, *Clarkson Papers*, M.Y.139.
20. Clarkson, 13 April 1823, ibid., M.Y.140.
21. Clarkson, 19 May 1823, ibid., M.Y. 142.
22. Clarkson, 8 June 1823, ibid., M.Y.143.
23. 'Notes on supporters . . .' [1823], ibid., C.N.71.
24. 'List of supporters', ibid., C.N. 72.
25. Thomas Clarkson, 'Speech Used at Forming of Committees, 1823–24', ibid., C.N.73.
26. Ibid.
27. Petition from Brook St, Derby, *Journal of the House of Lords*, vol. LXII (Sep. 1830–Nov. 1831) p. 32.
28. See Stiv Jakobsson, *Am I Not a Man and a Brother?* (Uppsala, Sweden, 1972) p. 235.
29. *Anti-Slavery Monthly Reporter*, no. 62, July 1830, p. 300.
30. Ibid., no. 74, 5 January 1831, p. 31.
31. *Anti-Slavery Record*, 18 April 1833, p. 169.
32. *Report of the Agency Committee of the Anti-Slavery Committee* (London, 1831) pp. 3–4.
33. Ibid., pp. 8, 12–13, 16.
34. Ibid., pp. 12, 16.
35. Furneaux, *Wilberforce*, p. 445.
36. *Agency Committee*, p. 11; E. Losh (ed.), *The Diaries and Correspondence of James Losh*, 2 vols (publication of the Surtees Society, London, 1962–3) nos 171–2, vol. II, pp. 97–102.
37. *Agency Committee*, p. 10.
38. Lord Brougham, 1825, no date, *Clarkson Papers*, M.Y. 95; see also Wilberforce, 28 August 1829, ibid., M.Y.926.
39. *Ladies' Anti-Slavery Association* (n.d.) p. 5.
40. Ibid.
41. *Anti-Slavery Monthly Reporter*, 30 September 1825, p. 32.
42. Ibid., no. 1, 31 July 1826, p. 212.
43. Walvin, 'The Propaganda of Anti-Slavery', in Walvin (ed.), *Slavery and British Society*, pp. 61–3.
44. Clarkson, *History*, vol. I, pp. 276–7.
45. John Brewer, *Party Ideology and Popular Politics at the Accession of George III* (Cambridge, 1976) pp. 140–7.

46. *Accounts of the Receipts and Disboursements of the Anti-Slavery Society* (no date but covers the years 1823–31).

47. *First Annual Report of the Swansea and Neath Auxiliary Anti-Slavery Association* (Swansea, 1826); *First Report of the Suffolk Auxiliary Society* (Ipswich, 1825).

48. *Speeches and Addresses of the Candidates for the Representation of the County of York in the Year 1826* (Leeds, 1826) pp. 26, 52, 55, 99.

49. Roger Anstey, 'The Pattern of British Abolitionism in the Eighteenth and Nineteenth Centuries', in Bolt and Drescher (eds), *Anti-Slavery, Religion and Reform*, pp. 24–5.

50. Brougham, 1829, *Clarkson Papers*, M.Y.101.

51. Thomas Clarkson, Speech, n.d., ibid., C.N.74; Anstey, 'Pattern of British Abolitionism', in Bolt and Drescher (eds), *Anti-Slavery, Religion and Reform*, p. 25.

52. Burn, *Emancipation and Apprenticeship*, pp. 88–90.

53. Quoted in ibid., p. 90.

54. Brougham, autumn 1830, n.d., *Clarkson Papers*, M.Y.109.

55. Craton, *Testing the Chains*, p. 291.

56. Ibid., p. 294.

57. Quoted in ibid., p. 295.

58. Ibid., p. 300.

59. Quoted in ibid., p. 303.

60. Quoted in ibid., p. 321.

61. Burn, *Emancipation and Apprenticeship*, pp. 96–7.

62. Quoted in Anstey, 'Pattern of British Abolitionism', in Bolt and Drescher (eds), *Anti-Slavery, Religion and Reform*, p. 28, n.36.

63. Ibid., p. 28.

64. Ibid., pp. 28–9; Burn, *Emancipation and Apprenticeship*, pp. 97–120.

65. I. Gross, 'Parliament and the Abolition of Negro Apprenticeship, 1835–38', *English Historical Review*, July 1981, pp. 560–1.

66. Anstey, 'Pattern of British Abolitionism', in Bolt and Drescher (eds), *Anti-Slavery, Religion and Reform*, pp. 30–1.

67. Gross, 'Parliament and Abolition', pp. 569–70.

68. Ibid., pp. 574–5.

69. Alex Tyrrell, 'The "Moral Radical Party" and Anglo-Jamaican Campaign . . .', *English Historical Review*, July 1984, p. 500: Jakobsson, *Am I not a Man?*, pp. 574–5.

70. Anstey, 'Pattern of British Abolitionism', in Bolt and Drescher (eds), *Anti-Slavery, Religion and Reform*.

NOTES TO CHAPTER 8: FREEDOM IN THE SHADOW OF SLAVERY

1. Alan H. Adamson, *Sugar without Slaves* (New Haven, Conn., 1972) ch. 2.

2. Hugh Tinker, *A New System of Slavery* (London, 1974).

3. D. G. Hall, *Free Jamaica* (New Haven, Conn., 1959) p. 86.

4. Eric Williams, *British Historians and the West Indies* (London, 1966).

5. Letter, 1861, 1861/11/24 in *Letters of Henry Clarke, 1855–66*, in possession of Mr George Clarke of Silver Sands, Jamaica.
6. Hall, *Free Jamaica*, pp. 263–4; but see, William G. Sewell, *The Ordeal of Free Labour in the British West Indies* (New York, 1861).
7. David Eltis, 'Abolitionists' Perceptions of Society after Slavery', in Walvin (ed.), *Slavery and British Society*, p. 212.
8. Clare Taylor, *British and American Abolitionists* (Edinburgh, 1974).
9. Howard Temperley, *British Anti-Slavery, 1833–70* (London, 1972).
10. *British Sovereigns: A Game* (a children's board game) (London, 1836?) Osborne Collection, Toronto Public Library.
11. *Beeton's Annual: A Book for the Young* (London, 1866) p. 113.
12. T. Bowring, *The First Book of Geography* (London, 1838) p. 25.
13. 'West Indies', in *The World and its Inhabitants* (London, *c.* 1845).
14. V. E. Chancellor, *History for their Masters* (London, 1970).

Index